AMERICA'S SECRET

ESTABLISHMENT

AN INTRODUCTION TO
THE ORDER of SKULL & BONES

ANTONY C. SUTTON

Updated Reprir

AMERICA'S SECRET ESTABLISHMENT: AN INTRODUCTION TO THE ORDER OF
SKULL & BONES
© 1983, 1986, 2002 BY ANTONY SUTTON
ADDITION MATERIALS & PRESENTATION © 2002, 2009 TRINEDAY, LLC

Published by:
TrineDay LLC
PO Box 577
Walterville, OR 97489
1-800-556-2012
www.TrineDay.com
publisher@TrineDay.net

Sutton, Antony C
America's Secret Establishment: An Introduction to the Order of Skull
& Bones
  p. cm. (acid-free paper)
Includes bibliographical references and index.
(ISBN-13) 978-0-9720207-4-9 (ISBN-10) 0-9720207-0-5
1. Order of Skull and Bones—Political Activity 2. Secret Societies—
United States 3. Russell Trust Association—Connecticut 4. RTA
Inc.— Connecticut 5. Yale University—Senior Societies 1. Title
366 20

FIRST EDITION
10 9 8 7 6 5 4

Printed in the USA
Distribution to the Trade by:
Independent Publishers Group (IPG)
814 North Franklin Street
Chicago, Illinois 60610
312.337.0747
www.ipgbook.com

Publisher's Foreword

Antony Sutton was a giant among men. His integrity cost him dearly: his vocation, his income, his family … maybe even his life.

After coming across this book in 1988, I searched out and read all that I could find of Professor Sutton's works. One reason: his books helped me to understand what my father had told me in 1969, ten years after he had quit a high-level job at the CIA — because he wouldn't go along with their corrupt practices. Dad had mentioned "secret societies," drug trafficking, and that the fight-to-the-death struggle between Communism and Capitalism was a "managed" conflict. Almost twenty, I was newly married with a baby, and had no idea what my father was talking about. *America's Secret Establishment* contributed greatly to my garnering a different thesis of how the world actually works, versus what was presented to me by the media and schooling.

I had tried to contact Antony while researching secret societies, and a subject I call CIA-Drugs, but to no avail. After some years of study, I started to put my findings into an article, and began to shop it around. Nobody would touch it. Then came the bulletin boards, and newsgroups of the emerging Internet. I posted my article, it spread to many websites, and one day came an email from Antony Sutton. Whoa, was I taken aback and absolutely flabbergasted to be in contact. We began emailing and talking over the telephone, becoming fast friends, but it was still some time before he would agree to meet me in person.

He had become reclusive, interacting with the world through a p.o. box. He had gone back to producing a newsletter, this one focusing on his early interest in technology: *Future Technology Intelligence Review*. He told me the only folks who showed up at his door were people from "three-letter" agencies of the Federal government. After several years, he agreed to meet, and I drove over to Reno. We enjoyed each other's company, and our friendship deepened. Later, he told me his publisher, Liberty House, was pulling up stakes, and *America's Secret Establishment* would be going out of print. Not wanting to see that happen, TrineDay was born.

Tony was excited about a new printing, but also very cautious. When I presented him with a new typesetting, he said, "No, let's simply make a copy of the old book, I don't want them to think I am even thinking much about them these days." I went about arranging distribution and interviews. Then, in June 2002, less than three weeks after the books were printed, Tony was dead.

Little, Brown moved up the release date of *Secrets of the Tomb*, and a young initiate of Scroll & Key, another of the senior secret societies at Yale University, suddenly became the talking-head expert on the Order of Skull & Bones. She said stories about the Order's power were just empty boasts, Bones was like the Wizard of Oz, and "Oz needed its Wizard." She dismissed the ties of Bones, specifically of Prescott Bush, to Nazi finances with one trite spurious sentence.

Tony had collapsed to his kitchen floor early one morning. All the coroner would tell me was "natural causes." I asked his partner of many years what happened; she said she didn't know, she was sleeping. The only thing strange was that some folks had moved into the apartment upstairs a few weeks before, and then moved out right after Tony's passing.

I sent out an obituary, it went 'round the Web, but nary a newspaper ran it. Your books resonant with truth and scholarship. Blessings on you Tony, and thanks. R.I.P.

Kris Millegan
March 3, 2009

The "Tomb" (circa 1900)

By ABRAHAM DE SILVA.

YALE.

New Haven, Conn.

On High Street — New Haven, CT

Introduction for 2002 Edition

AMERICA'S SECRET ESTABLISHMENT has had an unusual publishing history.

The book began with an anonymous donation to the author of an 8-inch package of documents in the early 1980s. Nothing less than the membership list and supporting documents for a truly secret society—the Yale Skull and Bones.

The late Johnny Johnson, of Phoenix Arizona was the spark that moved me to write first a four-part series and later, a jumbo volume based on this material. This volume went to several editions with several publishers, even a Russian edition of 12,000 copies. Probably in the past few years, as many copies have been sold in Russia as in the United States.

America's Secret Establishment has had little publicity, few reviews—ignored by mainline distributors yet, has sold steadily for the past 16 years at a rate of several hundred copies a month.

This activity, in turn, has generated other articles and books by other authors. But my real intent, to generate an exploration of Hegelian influence in modern America, has not been fulfilled. In great part, this can be attributed to an educational system based on a statist-Hegelian philosophy, and which has already achieved the "dumbing down" of America.

This disastrous, destructive philosophy, the source of both Naziism and Marxism, has infected and corrupted our constitutional republic. Much of the blame for this corruption is with an elitist group of Yalie "Bonesmen." Their symbol of Skull and Bones, and their Hegelian philosophy, says it all, although with typical duplicity, they would have you believe otherwise.

Hegelianism glorifies the State, the vehicle for the dissemination of statist and materialist ideas and policies in education, science, politics and economics.

Wonder why we have a "dumbed-down" society? Look no further than the Bonesman troika who imported the Prussian education system into the U.S. in the 19th Century. A political philosophy in direct opposition to the classical liberalism nurtured in 19th Century British and American history. In classical liberalism, the State is always subordinate to the individual. In Hegelian Statism, as we see in Naziism and Marxism, the State is supreme, and the individual exists only to serve the State.

Our two-party Republican-Democrat (= one Hegelian party, no one else welcome or allowed) system is a reflection of this Hegelianism. A small group — a very small group — by using Hegel, can manipulate, and to some extent, control society for its own purposes.

More than that, reflect on their pirate flag. An emblem found on poison bottles, the symbol of the Nazi Death Head Division in World War Two. Not only did Skull and Bones become a major force in drug smuggling (the Bush and Prescott families in the 1860s), but in true Hegelian fashion, generated the antithesis, the so-called "war on drugs." This hypocritical policy maintains the price of drugs, controls supply, and puts millions in jail while the gainers, in great part, are none other than the same "Bonesmen" who pass the laws to prohibit (Bonesman Taft, 1904).

Right and Left — A Control Device

For Hegelians, the State is almighty, and seen as "the march of God on earth." Indeed, a State religion.

Progress in the Hegelian State is through contrived conflict: the clash of opposites makes for progress. If you can control the opposites, you dominate the nature of the outcome.

We trace the extraordinary Skull and Bones influence in a major Hegelian conflict: Naziism vs. Communism. Skull and Bones members were in the dominant decision-making positions — Bush, Harriman, Stimson, Lovett, and so on — all Bonesmen, and instrumental in guiding the conflict through use of "right" and "left." They financed and encouraged the growths of both philosophies and controlled the outcome to a significant extent. This was aided by the "reductionist" division in science, the opposite of historical "wholeness." By dividing science and learning into narrower and narrower segments, it became easier to control the whole through the parts.

In education, the Dewey system was initiated and promoted by Skull and Bones members. Dewey was an ardent statist, and a believer in the Hegelian idea that the child exists to be trained to serve the State. This requires suppression of individualist tendencies and a careful spoon-feeding of approved knowledge. This "dumbing down" of American education is not easily apparent unless you have studied in both foreign and domestic U.S. universities — then the contrast becomes crystal clear.

This dumbing down is now receiving attention. Two excellent books are The Deliberate Dumbing Down of America, by Charlotte Thomson

Iserbyt (Conscience Press, Revenna Ohio, 2001), and The Dumbing Down of America, by John Taylor Gotta. Both books trace this process to the impact of education, and both give remarkable detail of the process. We go further, in that we trace the import of the system to three Yalies — members of Skull & Bones.

For Iserbyt, in The Deliberate Dumbing Down of America, the American education system begins with Rockefeller and Gates. But in fact, this statist system is a reflection of the Hegelian ideas brought to the United States by the Skull and Bones "troika" of Gilman, White and Dwight, and then financed by Rockefeller.

People Control

Today in California, one can see in real time the use of controlled conflict to achieve a desired outcome. The debate over the energy crisis is carefully contained to a debate over price caps and price control. Republicans want no caps and no controls. Most Democrats want price controls through caps.

But look at what is NOT discussed anywhere. The entire spectrum of almost free energy, based on a decade of research is carefully kept out of the discussion. Isn't this highly relevant to an energy crisis?

In fact, the existence of free energy systems just down the road is the reason for the controlled debate. Mills Blacklight Power now has its patents and some utilities have already bought in. Bearden's MEG energy from space, is under discussion. Working models exist. The maligned cold fusion has hundreds of successful experiments, but so far as we know, cannot be repeated with sufficient assurance. Other systems have come into the view of government agencies, and then disappear from sight.

A knowing public would ask, Why are these not included in the discussion?" — Simple. Because the utilities know they are for real, and only a few years down the road. The problem for utilities is not the price of energy today, but how to dump their fixed assets (hydro plants, transmission lines, etc.) onto the public. These "valuable" assets will have zero value down the road, because all new systems are stand-alone units which don't need fixed plant and transmission lines. If the public is aware of the dilemma of the utilities, the ability to dump assets onto the State is heavily reduced.

The Republican-Democrat debate over "caps" is a diversion. The relevant question carefully avoided is, how long will it take to get these new systems into production?

Another example is Monsanto Corporation development of genetic engineering and predator seed, a barely-concealed effort for world domination of agriculture.

President George Bush, Jr. , a Bonesman, appoints a Monsanto vice president, Dr. Virginia Weldon, as Director of Food and Drug Administration, which has the power to block labeling of genetically-engineered foods, and pass on other corporate control efforts.

Just before this, in New Technology, we had the 1989 dramatic announcement of "cold fusion." When this announcement was made public, President George Bush (also a Bonesman) called establishment scientist the late physicist Seagrum into his office and gave instructions.

We don't know what was said, but we know what happened. Cold fusion, a valid process for free energy, as was subsequently revealed, was slandered and harassed by the establishment, no doubt fearful of what free energy would do to the oil industry.

What is to be Done?
If the voting public was even vaguely aware of this rampant and concealed scenario, it could, and possibly would force change. However, this is not a likely possibility. Most people are "go-along" types, with limited personal objectives and a high threshold for official misdeeds.

What has taken over a century to establish cannot be changed in a few years. The initial question is education. To eliminate the Hegelian system that stifles individual initiative and trains children to become mindless zombies, serving the State.

We need a lot less propaganda for "education" and a more individual creative search for learning. Instead of more money for education, we need to allocate a lot less. The existing system of education is little more than a conditioning mechanism. It has little to do with education in the true sense, and a lot to do with control of the individual.

It is more likely that time, rather than the voting booth, will erode the secret power of this Yale group, Nothing this outrageous can survive forever.

Antony Sutton

Introduction to
THE ORDER

322

historians. Although an historian who will stick out his neck and buck the trend is rare, some who do are victims of an even deeper game.

Conspiracy then is an accepted explanation for many events at the intelligent grass roots level, that level furthest removed from the influence of The Order. We can cite at random the Kennedy assassination where the official "lone gunman" theory was never accepted by Americans in the street; Watergate, where a "deep throat" informer and erased tapes reek of conspiracy, and Pearl Harbor, where Rear Admiral Husband E. Kimmel and Major General Walter C. Short took the rap for General George C. Marshall and President Franklin D. Roosevelt.

The revisionist historian has a double burden as well as a double task. The double burden is that research likely to question the official historical line will not get financed. The double task is that research must be more than usually careful and precise.

A non-official work is not going to be judged on its merits. The work will be judged on the basis of its acceptability to a predetermined historical standard. What this standard is we shall explore later.

Hypotheses and Method

Which brings us to methodology. In this volume we will present three hypotheses. What is a hypothesis? A hypothesis is a theory, a working theory, a start point, which has to be supported by evidence. We arrived at these three hypotheses by examining certain documents which will also be described. The official history hatchet mongers will scream that our hypotheses are now being presented as proven assertions — and whatever we write here will not stop the screams. But again, these are only hypotheses at this point, they have to be supported with evidence. They are a first step in a logical research process.

Now in scientific methodology a hypothesis can be proven. It cannot be disproven. It is up to the reader to decide whether the evidence presented later supports, or does not support, the hypotheses. Obviously no one author, critic, or reader can decide either way until all the evidence has been presented.

We also intend to use two other principles of scientific research ignored by official establishment historians.

Firstly, in science the simplest explanation to a problem is always the most acceptable solution. By contrast, in establishment history, a simple answer is usually criticized as "simplistic." What the critic implies is "The poor writer hasn't used all the facts," In other words, it's a cheap "put-down" without the necessity of providing an alternate answer, or additional facts.

Secondly, again in science, an answer that fits the most cases, i.e., the most general answer, is also the most acceptable answer. For example, you have 12 events to explain and a theory that fits 11 of these events. That theory is more acceptable than a theory that fits only 4 or 5 of the events.

The Devil Theory of History

Using this methodology we are going to argue and present detailed precise evidence (including names, dates and places) that the only reasonable explanation for recent history in the United States is that there exists a conspiracy to use political power for ends which are inconsistent with the Constitution.

This is known by the official historians as the "devil theory of history," which again is a quick, cheap device for brushing facts under the rug. However, these critics ignore, for example, the Sherman Act, i.e., the anti-trust laws where conspiracy is the basic accepted theory. If there can be a conspiracy in the market place, then why not in the political arena? Are politicians any purer than businessmen? Following the anti-trust laws we know that conspiracy can only be proven in a specific manner. A similar pattern of market actions is not proof of conspiracy. Just because something looks like a duck, walks like a duck, and all the ducks act similarly, does not make it a duck — or a conspiracy. Under the Sherman Act a similar pattern of prices, where all prices are the same, is **not** proof of conspiracy. Similarity of prices can occur in a purely competitive market. Neither is similar political action necessarily a conspiracy.

Proof of conspiracy requires specific types of evidence, i.e.,:

(a) there must be **secret** meetings of the participants and efforts made to conceal joint actions,

(b) those meetings must jointly agree to take a **course of action,**

(c) and this action must be **illegal.**

The Council on Foreign Relations

Widely accepted explanations of recent history based on a conspiracy theory do not present evidence that fits the above criteria. For example, the Council on Foreign Relations cannot be claimed as a conspiracy even for the period since its founding in 1921. Membership in the CFR is not a secret. Membership lists are freely available for the cost of a postage stamp. There is no proof that the entire membership conspires to commit illegal acts.

What has to be **proven** in any conspiracy explanation of history is that the participants have secret groupings, and meet to plan illegal actions.

Members of the CFR, when accused of being involved in a conspiracy, have protested to the contrary. And by and large they are right. Most CFR members are not involved in a conspiracy and have no knowledge of any conspiracy. And some personally known to the

— 3 —

author are about the last people on earth to get involved in an illegal conspiracy.

HOWEVER, there is a group WITHIN the Council of Foreign Relations which belongs to a secret society, sworn to secrecy, and which more or less controls the CFR. CFR meetings are used for their own purposes, i.e., to push out ideas, to weigh up people who might be useful, to use meetings as a forum for discussion.

These members are in The Order. Their membership in The Order can be proven. Their meetings can be proven. Their objectives are plainly unconstitutional. And this ORDER has existed for 150 years in the United States.

Memorandum Number Two: The Order — What It Is And How It Began

Those on the inside know it as The Order. Others have known it for more than 150 years as Chapter 322 of a German secret society. More formally, for legal purposes, The Order was incorporated as The Russell Trust in 1856. It was also once known as the "Brotherhood of Death." Those who make light of it, or want to make fun of it, call it "Skull & Bones," or just plain "Bones."

The American chapter of this German order was founded in 1833 at Yale University by General William Huntington Russell and Alphonso Taft who, in 1876, became Secretary of War in the Grant Administration. Alphonso Taft was the father of William Howard Taft, the only man to be both President **and** Chief Justice of the United States.

What Is The Order?

The Order is not just another campus Greek letter fraternal society with passwords and handgrips, common to most campuses. Chapter 322 is a **secret** society whose members are sworn to silence. It only exists on the Yale campus (that we know about). It has rules. It has ceremonial rites. It is not at all happy with prying, probing citizens — known among initiates as "outsiders" or "vandals." Its members always deny membership (or are supposed to deny membership) and in checking hundreds of autobiographical listings for members we found only half a dozen who cited an affiliation with Skull & Bones. The rest were silent. An interesting point is whether the many members in various Administrations or who hold government positions have declared their members in the biographical data supplied for FBI "background checks".

Above all, The Order is powerful, unbelievably powerful. If the reader will persist and examine the evidence to be presented — which is overwhelming — there is no doubt his view of the world will suddenly come sharply into focus, with almost frightening clarity.[1]

Before we go further we need to add a couple of important observations about The Order:

• It is a Senior year society which exists only at Yale. Members are chosen in their Junior year and spend only one year on campus, the Senior year, with Skull & Bones. In other words, the organization is oriented to the post graduate outside world. The Order meets annually — patriarchs only — on Deer Island in the St. Lawrence River.

• Senior societies are unique to Yale. There are two other senior societies at Yale, but none elsewhere. Scroll & Key and Wolf's Head are supposedly competitive societies founded in the mid-19th century. We believe these to be part of the same network. Rosenbaum commented

— 5 —

in his *Esquire* article, very accurately, that anyone in the Eastern Liberal Establishment who is not a member of Skull & Bones is almost certainly a member of either Scroll & Key or Wolf's Head.

What is the significance of the "322" in Chapter 322? William Russell imported the society from Germany and so it has been argued the 322 stands for '32 (from 1832), the second chapter, of this German organization. Possibly a chapter 320 and a chapter 321 may exist somewhere and 323 is the designation of a room within the Skull & Bones temple at Yale.

Another interpretation is that The Order is descended from a Greek fraternal society dating back to Demosthenes in 322 B.C. This has perhaps some credibility because Bones records are dated by adding 322 to the current year, i.e., records originating in 1950 are dated Anno - Demostheni 2272.

How A Member Is Chosen By The Order

The selection procedure for new members of The Order has not changed since 1832. Each year 15, and only 15, never more, never fewer, are selected. In the past 150 years about 2500 Yale graduates have been initiated into The Order. At any one time about 500-600 are alive and active. Roughly about one-quarter of these take an active role in furthering the objectives of The Order. The others either lose interest or change their minds. They are silent drop-outs.

A Yale Junior cannot ask to join. There is no electioneering. Juniors are **invited** to join and are given two options: accept or reject. Apparently some amount of personal information is gathered on potential members. The following is the kind of evaluation made in the last century; we doubt it has changed too much down to the present time:

- "Frank Moore is an ideal Bones man, he is a hard worker and a man whose efforts have been more for Yale than himself. He is manager of the Musical clubs and has been active in Dwight Hall. His election will be well deserved and popular."
- "Don Thompson is a sure man whom the class wishes well for and will be glad to see go. He comes from a Bones family."

In selection emphasis is placed on athletic ability — the ability to play on a team. The most unlikely potential member of The Order is a loner, an iconoclast, an individualist, the man who goes his own way in the world.

The most likely potential member is from a Bones family, who is

---

[1]Readers who want more on the cermonial and initiation aspects should read the September, 1977 *Esquire* article by Ron Rosenbaum, "The Last Secrets of Skull and Bones". Unfortunately, the article completely misses the historical significance of Skull & Bones, although it is an excellent source of lurid details and the mumbo-jumbo rites.

energetic, resourceful, political and probably an amoral team player. A man who understands that to get along you have to go along. A man who will sacrifice himself for the good of the team. A moment's reflection illustrates why this is so. In real life the thrust of The Order is to bring about certain objectives. Honors and financial rewards are guaranteed by the power of The Order. But the price of these honors and rewards is sacrifice to the common goal, the goal of The Order. Some, perhaps many, have not been willing to pay this price.

Inside The Order

Entry into The Order is accompanied by an elaborate ritual and no doubt by psychological conditioning. For example:

"Immediately on entering Bones the neophyte's name is changed. He is no longer known by his name as it appears in the college catalogue but like a monk or Knight of Malta or St. John, becomes Knight so and so. The old Knights are then known as Patriarch so and so. The outside world are known as Gentiles and vandals."

The Catalogue (or membership list — it became "Addresses" sometime in this century) of Chapter 322, however, is made with the usual "outside" names and is unique and impressive. Each member has a copy bound in black leather with peculiar symbols on the outside and inside. The symbols presumably have some meaning.

The owner's name and the single letter "D" is gilt-stamped on the outer cover of earlier issues, at least up to the mid-19th century. It then appears to have been omitted, at least on copies we have seen. Each right-hand page, printed one side only, about 6 x 4 inches, has the members listed for one year and surrounded by a heavy black border, thick in the early years, not so thick in recent decades. This symbolizes the death of the person named as he adopts his new name and new life upon entering The Order.

Most interesting is an entry between the decade lists of members. On the 1833 list, before the 15 founders' names, are the words "Period 2 Decade 3." Similarly, before names on the 1843 list are the words "Period 2 Decade 4." In brief, "Period" stays the same throughout the years, but the "Decade" number increases by one in each ten years. No doubt this means something to The Order, else it wouldn't be there. Another mystical group of letters and numbers is at the top of the first list of names in 1833, "P.231-D.31." The numbers increase by one in each succeeding class. In 1834, for example, the entry reads "P.232-D 32."

Furthermore, the first class list of 1833 has two blank lines in place of the eleventh name on the list. This supports the argument that the society has German origins and this is the listing of the anonymous German connection.

The Members of 1833

We estimate that at any one time only about one-quarter of the membership is active. Even the active quarter is not always effective or successful. It's instructive to compare 1833 with 1983 and how, over the century and a half span, a group of 20-30 families has emerged to dominate The Order.

The very first name on the very first membership list, Samuel Henshaw Bates, was a private in the Union Army, went west to farm in Santa Rosa, California, at that time very much in the boondocks, and died in 1879. A life not different to millions of other Americans.

In fact, out of the first 15 members (actually 14 plus the anonymous member), achievements were not much greater than we would expect from the cream of a Yale "class". Rufus Hart spent several years in the Ohio Senate, Asahel Hooker Lewis was in the Ohio Legislature for a couple of years, Samuel Marshall was an Illinois State Legislator for a while, and Frederick Mather was in the New York Legislature. Other members, apart from the two founders of The Order, did nothing much with their lives or for The Order.

By contrast, the two founding members, William Huntington Russell and Alphonso Taft, went far. William Russell was a member of the Connecticut State Legislature in 1846-47, a General in the Connecticut National Guard from 1862-70, and founded the Collegiate and Commercial Institute in New Haven, Connecticut. Alphonso Taft went further: he was Secretary of War in 1876 — the first of several members of The Order to hold this post down into the 1950s. Taft became U.S. Attorney General in 1876-7, then U.S. Minister to Austria in 1882-4, and finally U.S. Ambassador to Russia in 1884-5.

During the 150-year interval since 1833, active membership has evolved into a core group of perhaps 20-30 families; it seems that active members have enough influence to push their sons and relatives into The Order, and there is significant inter-marriage among the families. These families fall into two major groups.

First we find old line American families who arrived on the East coast in the 1600s, e.g., Whitney, Lord, Phelps, Wadsworth, Allen, Bundy, Adams and so on.

Second, we find families who acquired wealth in the last 100 years, sent their sons to Yale and in time became almost old line families, e.g., Harriman, Rockefeller, Payne, Davison.

Some families, like the Whitneys, were Connecticut Yankees **and** acquired wealth in the nineteenth century.

In the last 150 years a few families in The Order have gained enormous influence in society and the world.

One example is the Lord family. Two branches of this family date from the 1630s: Those descended from Nathan Lord and those from Thomas Lord. Other Lords arrived in the U.S. over the years but do not enter our discussion. Of these two main branches, only the Thomas Lord group appears to have contributed members to The Order. Their ancestry traces to Thomas Lord, who left Essex, England in 1635 in a company led by Rev. Thomas Hooker, and settled in what is now Hartford, Connecticut. In fact, part of Hartford is still known as Lord's Hill. The line of descent for this Lord family is full of DeForest and Lockwood names because intermarriage is more than common among these elite families.

The first Lord to be initiated into The Order was George DeForest Lord (1854), a New York lawyer. Together with his father, Daniel Lord (another Yale graduate), George DeForest Lord established the New York law firm of Lord, Day and Lord. Among its present day clients are *The New York Times* and the Rubin Foundation. The Rubin Foundation is one of the financial angels for the Institute for Policy Studies in Washington, D.C.

In the next hundred years five more Lords were initiated into The Order:

Franklin Atkins Lord	('98)
William Galey Lord	('22)
Oswald Bates Lord	('26)
Charles Edwin Lord, II	('49)
Winston Lord	('59)

When we ask the question, what have these members achieved? and what are they doing today? a dramatic picture emerges . . . as demonstrated in the chart . . .

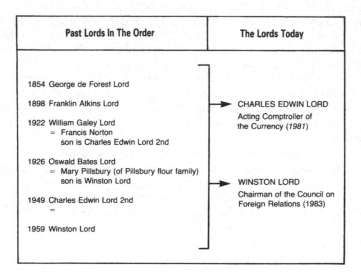

Past Lords In The Order	The Lords Today
1854 George de Forest Lord	
1898 Franklin Atkins Lord	CHARLES EDWIN LORD
1922 William Galey Lord = Francis Norton son is Charles Edwin Lord 2nd	Acting Comptroller of the Currency (1981)
1926 Oswald Bates Lord = Mary Pillsbury (of Pillsbury flour family) son is Winston Lord	
	WINSTON LORD
1949 Charles Edwin Lord 2nd =	Chairman of the Council on Foreign Relations (1983)
1959 Winston Lord	

Memorandum Number Three: How Much Is Known About The Order?

The openly published literature on The Order amounts to merely two articles over a span of one hundred years: *The Iconoclast* (Volume One, Number One only) published October 13, 1873 and an already-cited article in *Esquire* by Ron Rosenbaum, published in 1977. This book and its successors are based on unpublished archival material originating with The Order.

The Iconoclast (October 1873)

Back in October 1873 an enterprising Yale student, stung to action because The Order had taken over Yale finances and left the University near poverty, took it upon himself to publish an expose. Unfortunately, some of the anonymous student's acutest observations were buried in not-so-good verse. We will reprint some of the verse below as in the original *Iconoclast* because it's impossible to summarize.

The Yale college newspapers, *Courant* and *Record*, had a blackout policy on The Order. As *Iconoclast* puts it,

"We speak through a new publication, because the college press is closed to those who dare to openly mention 'Bones'."

The College Press was controlled by The Order. From time to time Yale newspapers were run by Editors in The Order. For example, one noteworthy editor of the Yale *Record* also in The Order was Thomas Cochran ('94), who went on to make a career as an influential partner in the influential banking firm of J.P. Morgan.

Three paragraphs in this anonymous publication summarize the *Iconoclast* accusation.

First, there is a Yale secret society open only to a select few:

"For more than forty years a secret society called Skull and Bones has existed in Yale College. It receives a certain number of men from each class. These are chosen nominally by the members of the class . . ., although it is understood that a prominent man's influence avails for his friends and relatives through several years after his graduation. By observing the men elected from year to year, we find that they are chosen with a distinct end in view, namely, that of obtaining for the society the most honors. Some of these honors are given to literary, some to wealthy men. This, then, is the case. Men receive marks of distinction from Yale College or from their entire class, because of which they are taken into this secret society. Since Yale honors men, this fraternity professes to honor them also."

Secondly, the *Iconoclast* states that The Order has obtained control of Yale, and its members care more for their society than for Yale:

To Whom It May Concern

We come before the college now on Justice's side arrayed;
To claim redress for open wrongs that Vandal hands have made,
To give a college sentiment expression bold and free,
Asserting each man's native right, if such a thing there be.

We represent no clique or clan, but honest men and true,
Who never will submit to that which **fifteen** men may do,
Who feel the shameful yoke that long has on the college lain,
And who propose to do their best to break that yoke in twain.

We are not "soreheads." God forbid that we should cherish strong
Desires to be identified with principles that long
Have been a blight upon the life and politics of Yale,
Before whose unjust aims the glow of "Boss Tweed's" brass
  would pale.

We represent the neutral men, whose voices must be heard,
And never can be silenced by a haughty look or word.
Of those whose influence here at Yale would be but void and null
Did they not wear upon their breasts **two crossed bones and a
  skull.**

We hold no grudge 'gainst any man, but wish that all may be
United by the common bond of peace and harmony;
Yet, when a **few** do to themselves most proudly arrogate
The running of affairs, there can be no such happy state.

What right, forsooth, have **fifteen** men to lord it over all?
What right to say the college world shall on their faces fall
When they approach? Have they, indeed, to "sickly greatness
  grown,"
And must each one with servile speech them his "superiors" own?

If they have grounds on which they base their claim as just and
   true,
We challenge them to set them forth exposed to public view,
That all may know the reasons why this oligarchy proud
Elect themselves as lords supreme o'er us, the "vulgar crowd."

We offer no objections to their existing clan, —
No one disputes with them this right, we question but the plan
On which they act, — **That only he who wears upon his
   breast
Their emblem, he for every post shall be considered best.**

We wish this understood by all. Let none who read this say
That we are moved by petty wrongs or private spite obey;
It is for principles of right that we with them contend,
For principles which they've ignored, but which we here defend.

O fellow students, who with us revere these classic halls,
O ye across whose pathway bright their sacred glory falls, —
Ye men of every class who feel our Alma Mater's care,
Shall college life beneath these elms this loathsome aspect wear?

Shall none assert the right to act as to each seemeth best,
But cringe and fawn to him who wears a **death's head** on his
   breast?
Nay, let all rise and break the spell whose sickly glamour falls
About all that originates within those brown stone walls.

And if they will not hear our claims, or grant the justice due,
But still persist in tarnishing the glory of the blue,
Ruling this little college world with proud, imperious tones,
Be then the watchword of our ranks — Down, Down With Skull
   and Bones!

"Out of every class Skull and Bones takes its men. They have gone out into the world and have become, in many instances, leaders in society. They have obtained control of Yale. Its business is performed by them. Money paid to the college must pass into their hands, and be subject to their will. No doubt they are worthy men in themselves, but the many whom they looked down upon while in college, cannot so far forget as to give money freely into their hands. Men in Wall Street complain that the college comes straight to them for help, instead of asking each graduate for his share. The reason is found in a remark made by one of Yale's and America's first men: Few will give but Bones men, and they care far more for their society than they do for the college.' "

Finally, the *Iconoclast* calls The Order a "deadly evil" growing year by year:

"Year by year the deadly evil is growing. The society was never as obnoxious to the college as it is today, and it is just this ill-feeling that shuts the pockets of non-members. Never before has it shown such arrogance and self-fancied superiority. It grasps the College Press and endeavors to rule it all. It does not deign to show its credentials, but clutches at power with the silence of conscious guilt.

To tell the good which Yale College has done would be well nigh impossible. To tell the good she might do would be yet more difficult. The question, then, is reduced to this — on the one hand lies a source of incalculable good, — on the other a society guilty of serious and far-reaching crimes. **It is Yale College against Skull and Bones!!** We ask all men, as a question of right, which should be allowed to live?"

The power of The Order is put to use on behalf of its members even before they leave Yale. Here's a case from the late 19th century which predates the cases we will present later and suggests how long immoral use of power has prevailed within The Order:

"The Favoritism Shown To Bones Men"

"Are not we coming to a sad state when open injustice can be done by the Faculty, and when the fact that a man is a member of Skull and Bones can prejudice them in his favor? Briefly, the case which calls forth this question is this: Two members of the Senior class, the one being a neutral, the other a Bones man, returned at the beginning of the college year laden with several conditions, some of which, upon examination, they failed to pass. Up to this point the cases were parallel, and the leniency, if there was to be leniency, should have been shown to the neutral, who has done all that lay in his power to further the interests of the college, rather than to the Bones man, who has, during his three years at Yale, accomplished nothing that we wot of. But, strange to say, the former has been suspended until the end of the term and obliged to leave town, not being permitted to pass another examination until he returns. The Bones man, on the contrary, is allowed to remain in New Haven, attends recitation daily, is called upon to recite, and will have a second examination in less than six weeks. Why is this distinction made? 'O, Mr. So-and-so's is a **special** case,' said a professor (a Bones man), — the specialty, we presume, being the fact that Mr. So-and-so wears a death's head and cross bones upon his bosom. We understand that Mr. So-and-so claims to have been ill during vacation and offers the illness as an excuse for not passing the examination; but the neutral gentleman was also ill, as the Faculty were expressly informed in a letter from his father."

"The circumstance has caused a very lively indignation throughout the Senior class. It is certainly time for a radical reform when the gentlemen who superintend our destinies, and who should be just if nothing else, can allow themselves to be influenced by so petty a thing as society connections."

Esquire (September 1977)

Only one article is known to have been published within the last 100 years on The Order. Unfortunately, it is a superficial, almost mocking, review and provides some enlightenment but little contribution to historical knowledge. The article is the "Last Secrets of Skull and Bones" by Ron Rosenbaum (*Esquire*, September 1977).

Rosenbaum is a Yale graduate attracted by the fictional possibilities of a secret society out to control the world; he is apparently not aware of the political implications. The contribution is a blend of known authentic documents and outright hearsay. On the other hand, Rosenbaum does make some notable observations. Among these are: ". . . the people who have shaped America's national character since it ceased being an undergraduate power had **their** undergraduate character shaped in that crypt over there" (i.e., the "temple" on the Yale campus).

Another comment: when a new member is initiated into The Order, "tonight he will die to the world and be born again into The Order as he will thenceforth refer to it. The Order is a world unto itself in which he will have a new name and fourteen new blood brothers, also with new names."

And when Rosenbaum starts to inquire about The Order, he is told: "They don't like people tampering and prying. The power of Bones is incredible. They've got their hands on every lever of power in the country. You'll see — it's like trying to look into the Mafia. Remember they're a secret society too."

The *Esquire* piece is well worth reading, it gives a side of The Order that doesn't concern us too much.

The "Addreses" Books

As The Order is a secret society it does not publish minutes or journals. As Rosenbaum suggests, "they don't like people tampering and prying."

This author does, however, possess copies of the "Addresses" books, which used to be called "Catalogues." These are the membership lists all the way back to 1832, the founding date in the United States. How did this material make its way into outside hands? It is possible that one or more members, although bound by oath, would not be dismayed if the story became public knowledge. That's all we will say.

Other material exists, Skull & Bones is always a lively topic for Yale conversation. Some time back a few practical minded students made their own investigation; they did a break-in job, a "Yalegate." A small hoard of Bones momentos, a layout diagram and considerable embarrassment resulted.

The core of the research for this book is the "Addresses" books. With these we can reconstruct a picture of motives, objectives and operations. The actions of individual members are already recorded in open history and archives.

By determining when members enter a scene, what they did, what they argued, who they appointed and when they faded out, we can assemble patterns and deduce objectives.

Memorandum Number Four:
Who Is In This Secret Society?

The membership list of about 2500 initiates into The Order has very obvious features:

- Most members are from the Eastern seaboard United States. As late as 1950 only three members resided in Los Angeles, California, but 28 members resided in New Haven, Connecticut.
- Members are **all** males and almost all WASPS (**W**hite **A**nglo **S**axon **P**rotestant). In great part they descended from English Puritan families, their ancestors arrived in North America in the 1630-1660 period.
- These Puritan families either intermarried with financial power or invited in sons of money moguls, e.g., Rockefellers, Davisons, and Harrimans, whose sons became members of The Order.

From this preliminary information we can derive Hypothesis One:

THERE EXISTS IN THE UNITED STATES TODAY, AND HAS EXISTED SINCE 1833, A SECRET SOCIETY COMPRISING MEMBERS OF OLD LINE AMERICAN FAMILIES AND REPRESENTATIVES OF FINANCIAL POWER.

The chart on page 19 presents a simplified layout of this hypothesis. Full information remains for a later book — for now we'll give details of just two key families, the Whitneys and the Harrimans.

The Whitney Family

A key family is the Whitneys, descended from English Puritans who came to the U.S. about 1635 and settled in Watertown, Mass. Eight Whitneys have been members of The Order. Of these, three had brief lives; Emerson Cogswell Whitney died a few months after initiation and Edward Payson Whitney "disappeared in 1858" according to his biographer. However, three Whitneys, William Collins Whitney and his two sons, are the core of Whitney influence in The Order which survives today through the Harriman family and intermarriage with Paynes and Vanderbilts.

Whitneys In The Order:

Initiation	Name	Field
1851	Emerson Cogswell Whitney	Education: "Died December 1, 1851."
1854	Edward Payson Whitney	Medicine: "Disappeared in 1858"
1856	James Lyman Whitney	Library work: Boston Public Library
1863	William Collins Whitney	Secretary of Navy (1885-9) Promoter and Financier
1878	Edward Baldwin Whitney	Law: Justice, New York Supreme Court
1882	Joseph Ernest Whitney	Education: "Died Feb. 25, 1893"
1894	Payne Whitney (son of W.C. Whitney)	Finance: Knickerbocker Trust Co.
1898	Harry Payne Whitney (son of W.C. Whitney)	Finance: Guaranty Trust and Guggenheim Exploration Co.

Hypothesis Number One: A Secret Society Dominated By Old Line American Families And New Wealth Has Existed From 1833 To The Present Day.

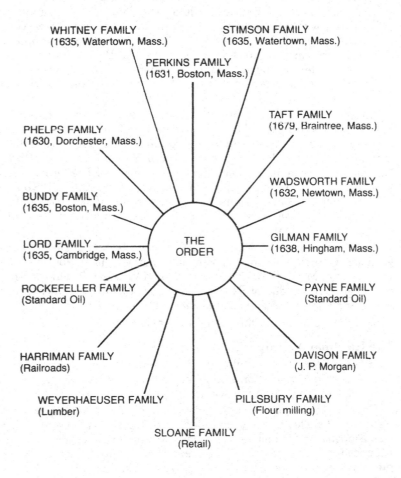

WHITNEY FAMILY
(1635, Watertown, Mass.)

STIMSON FAMILY
(1635, Watertown, Mass.)

PERKINS FAMILY
(1631, Boston, Mass.)

TAFT FAMILY
(1679, Braintree, Mass.)

PHELPS FAMILY
(1630, Dorchester, Mass.)

WADSWORTH FAMILY
(1632, Newtown, Mass.)

BUNDY FAMILY
(1635, Boston, Mass.)

LORD FAMILY
(1635, Cambridge, Mass.)

THE ORDER

GILMAN FAMILY
(1638, Hingham, Mass.)

ROCKEFELLER FAMILY
(Standard Oil)

PAYNE FAMILY
(Standard Oil)

HARRIMAN FAMILY
(Railroads)

DAVISON FAMILY
(J. P. Morgan)

WEYERHAEUSER FAMILY
(Lumber)

PILLSBURY FAMILY
(Flour milling)

SLOANE FAMILY
(Retail)

William Collins Whitney (1841-1904) is a fine example of how members of The Order rise to fame and fortune. W.C. Whitney was initiated in 1863 and by 1872 had only advanced his career to Inspector of Schools for New York. However, in the last three decades of the century, he rolled up a massive fortune, became a power behind the throne in the Cleveland Administration, and directed the often unscrupulous activities of a cluster of capitalists known as "the Whitney Group". A brief quotation suggests the power that Whitney amassed in a brief 30 years. This is a list of Whitney estates at the turn of the century:

". . . a city residence in New York, a Venetian palace and 5,000 acres in Wheatley Hills, near Jamaica, L.I.; a Sheepshead Bay house, with a private track covering 300 acres; a mansion at Berkshire Hills, Mass., with 700 acres of land; October Mountain house, with a large tract of land; Stony Ford Farm, New York, used as an auxiliary to his Kentucky Stock Farm; an Adirondack game preserve of 16,000 acres; a lodge at Blue Mountain Lake with a fine golf course, a Blue Grass farm of 3,000 acres in Kentucky; and an estate at Aiken, S.C., comprising a mansion, race course, and 2,000 acres of hunting land."

William C. Whitney married Flora Payne, daughter of Standard Oil Treasurer Oliver Payne. The Paynes are not in The Order, but adding the Payne piece of the Standard Oil fortune made Whitney's fortune that much larger. Their two sons, Harry Payne ('94) and Payne Whitney ('98), went to Yale and became members of The Order. After Yale Harry Payne promptly married Gertrude Vanderbilt in 1896 and so the Whitney-Payne fortune now joined some Vanderbilt money. This financial power was channeled into Guaranty Trust, the J.P. Morgan and Guggenheim outfits.

And it gets more complicated. For example, the son of Harry Payne Whitney, Cornelius Vanderbilt Whitney, married Marie Norton. After their divorce, Marie Norton Whitney married W. Averell Harriman (his first wife) who is today at 91 a key member. It is these tightly woven family and financial interlocks that make up the core of The Order.

So let's take a look at the Harriman family.

The Harriman Family

In the first few days of June 1983 a prominent American, a private citizen, flew to Moscow for a confidential chat with Yuri Andropov. A State Department interpreter went along.

This American was not the President, nor the Vice-President, nor the Secretary of State, nor any member of the Reagan Administration. It was a private individual — W. Averell Harriman. The first time any American had talked with Yuri Andropov since the death of his predecessor, Brezhnev. So who is W. Averell Harriman?

The elder Harriman, a prominent and not too scrupulous railroad magnate, sent both his sons to Yale. William Averell Harriman ('13) and Edward Roland Noel Harriman ('17) joined The Order. A good example of how old line families in The Order absorbed new wealth families, although as history has unfolded it may be that Harriman and his fellow investment bankers have dominated the direction of The Order in the past few decades.

THE WALL STREET JOURNAL, Tuesday, July 11, 1972   21

Business Established 1818

BROWN BROTHERS HARRIMAN & CO.
PRIVATE BANKERS

NEW YORK • BOSTON • PHILADELPHIA • CHICAGO • ST. LOUIS

STATEMENT OF CONDITION, JUNE 30, 1972

ASSETS

Cash on Hand and Due from Banks	$125,311,119
U.S. Government Securities, Direct and Guaranteed	45,083,406
State, Municipal and Other Public Securities	59,169,090
Other Marketable Securities	1,408,308
Loans and Discounts	178,690,568
Customers' Liability on Acceptances	11,940,935
Other Assets	21,879,118
	$443,482,545

LIABILITIES

Deposits	$398,446,959
Acceptances: Less Amount in Portfolio	12,389,930
Other Liabilities	5,860,372
Capital	8,000,000
Surplus	19,785,284
	$443,482,545

PARTNERS

J. Eugene Banks	John C. Hanson	Thomas McCance
Moreau D. Brown	E. R. Harriman	L. J. Newquist
Walter H. Brown	Frank W. Hoch	William F. Ray
Prescott Bush	Stephen Y. Hord	Robert V. Roosa
Granger Costikyan	R. L. Ireland III	I. Robie Glidden, Jr.
William R. Denten Jr.	F. R. Kingsbury, Jr.	Maarten van Hengel
Terrence M. Farley	Robert A. Lovett	John C. West
Elbridge T. Gerry	John B. Madden	Knight Woolley

LIMITED PARTNERS

Louis Curtis   Gerry Brothers & Co.   W. Averell Harriman

COMPLETE BANKING FACILITIES

Deposit Accounts • Commercial Loans and Discounts
Commercial Letters of Credit and Acceptances • Foreign Exchange
Custody of Securities • Corporate Financial Counseling
Investment Advisory Service
Brokers for Purchase and Sale of Securities
Members of Principal Stock Exchanges

BROWN HARRIMAN INTERNATIONAL LTD.   LONDON

Licensed as Private Bankers and subject to examination and regulation by the Superintendent of Banks of the State of New York and by the Department of Banking of the Commonwealth of Pennsylvania. Subject to examination and regulation by the Commissioner of Banks of the Commonwealth of Massachusetts. The facilities of the Chicago and St. Louis offices are limited to Investment Advisory and Brokerage Services.

Brown Brothers Harriman, advertisement from Wall Street Journal listing partners.

In the 1930s W.A. Harriman & Company merged with Brown Brothers. This was an older financial house whose partners were also members of The Order. Alexander Brown was founded 1800 in New York and Philadelphia.

By the 1970s the relatively unknown private international banking firm of Brown Brothers, Harriman, with assets of about one-half billion dollars, had taken in so many of "the Brotherhood" that out of 26 individual partners, **no fewer than 9 were members of The Order.** We don't know of any greater concentration of members.

And to make it more interesting, Prescott Bush, father of President George H.W. Bush (both in The Order), was a partner in Brown Brothers, Harriman for over 40 years.

Finally, because Brown Brothers, Harriman is a private banking firm it has relatively no government supervision and does not publish an annual report. In other words, we know NOTHING about its operations — at least we know nothing from Brown Brothers, Harriman sources.

Here's a line-up of Brown Brothers, Harriman partners who were also members of The Order in the mid 1970s:

Name of Partner	Date Initiated
Walter H. Brown	1945
Prescott Sheldon Bush	1917
Granger Kent Costikyan	1929
Edward Roland Noel Harriman	1917
W. Averell Harriman	1913
Stephen Young Hord	1921
Robert Abercrombie Lovett	1918
John Beckwith Madden	1941
Knight Woolley	1917

It's worth thinking about this concentration of names and the power it represents in the light of outside comments on The Order over the years.

After the title page of this volume we reprint the verse of an anonymous Yale student of the 1870s. He commented on the requirement to put The Order ahead of all else.

The Editor of *The Iconoclast* (also in the 1870s) wrote:

And on their breasts they wear a sign
That tells their race and name
It is the ghastly badge of death
And from his kingdom came
The son of Satan, son of sin
The enemy of man.

Another writer in the 1870s called The Order the "Brotherhood of Death":

Outside already, in the doubtful dawn,
Thither, from this side and from that, slow sweep,
And settle down in silence solidly,
Crow-wise, the frightful Brotherhood of Death.
Black-hatted and black-hooded huddle they,
With black cravats a-dangling from each neck;
So take they their grim station at the door,
Torches lit, skull-and-cross-bones-banner spread.

Ron Rosenbaum in his 1977 *Esquire* article a century later, was no less caustic. Rosenbaum called it a Mafia.

From evidence to be presented later this author would term The Order "an international Mafia" . . . unregulated and all but unknown.

To the outside world, however, it's merely Brown Brothers, Harriman, 59 Wall Street, New York. But obviously Yuri Andropov over in Moscow knows who holds the cards.

The British Connection

Some well read readers may raise a question — how does The Order the its families relate to Cecil Rhodes secret society, Milners Round Table, the Illuminati and the Jewish secret society equivalents? How do these fit into the picture?

We are concerned here only with the core of a purely American phenomenon with German origin. It is undoubtedly linked to overseas groups. The links between The Order and Britain go through Lazard Freres and the private merchant bankers. Notably the British establishment was also founded at a University — Oxford University, and especially All Souls College at Oxford. The British element is called "The Group."

The Group links to the Jewish equivalent through the Rothschilds in Britain (Lord Rothschild was an original member of Rhodes "inner circle"). The Order in the U.S. links to the Guggenheim, Schiff and Warburg families. There were no Jews at all in The Order until very recently. In fact, The Order has, as Rosenbaum suggests, some definite anti-semetic tendencies. Token Jews (and token blacks) have been admitted in recent years.

There is an Illuminati connection. Some details are in the *Esquire* article, more details will be in our future volumes.

All these groups have cooperative and competitive features. But to argue that all the world's ills can be ascribed to any **one** of these groups is false. The core of The Order, like the core of "The Group" in England, comprises about 20 families. In the U.S. case they are mostly descendents from the original settlers in Massachusetts. New wealth did not enter The Order until the mid-19th century and until recently, has never dominated The Order. On the other hand, key families, the Whitneys and the Harrimans, are linked to their own banking interests.

In many ways these old line Yankee families have outsmarted the bankers. The Puritans diverted bankers' wealth to their own objectives without always absorbing the banker families. The Order controls the substantial wealth of Andrew Carnegie, but no Carnegie has ever been a member of The Order. The Order used the Ford wealth so flagrantly against the wishes of the Ford family that two Fords resigned from the board of the Ford Foundation. No Ford has been a member of The Order. The name Morgan has never appeared on the membership lists, although some Morgan partners are with the inner core, for example, Davison and Perkins. Interestingly, the Astor name is prominent in "The Group" in England, but not in The Order in the U.S.

Memorandum Number Five:
What Organizations Has It Penetrated?

The Order has either set up or penetrated just about every significant research, policy, and opinion-making organization in the United States, in addition to the Church, business, law, government and politics. Not all at the same time, but persistently and consistently enough to dominate the direction of American society. The evolution of American society is not, and has not been for a century, a voluntary development reflecting individual opinion, ideas and decisions at the grass roots. On the contrary, the broad direction has been **created artificially** and stimulated by The Order.

Not all organizations know they have been penetrated or used for another purpose. It's a situation very much as Quigley (see page 30) found in "The Group":

> "there is . . . an inner core of intimate associates who unquestionably knew that they were members of a group devoted to a common purpose and an outer circle of a larger number on whom the inner circle acted by personal persuasion, patronage distribution and social pressure. It is probable that most members of the outer circle were not conscious that they were being used by a secret society."

Therefore our Hypothesis Number Two is:

THE ORDER HAS PENETRATED OR BEEN THE DOMINANT INFLUENCE IN SUFFICIENT POLICY, RESEARCH AND OPINION MAKING ORGANIZATIONS THAT IT DETERMINES THE BASIC DIRECTION OF AMERICAN SOCIETY.

Hypothesis Number Two:
The Order Has Penetrated Every Segment
Of American Society

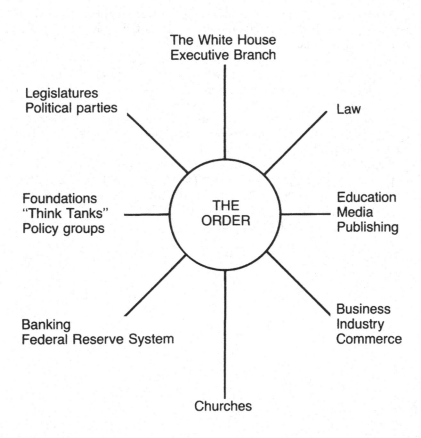

The Order Is The Original Impulse

One observation is that The Order gets the ball rolling in new organizations, i.e., puts in the FIRST President or Chairman and the ideas and then, when operations are rolling along, often just fades out of the picture.

Among universities we can cite Cornell University, where Andrew Dickson White ('53) was its FIRST President, and Johns Hopkins University, based on the German educational system, where Daniel Coit Gilman ('52) was the FIRST President (1875-1901).

Among academic associations the American Historical Association, the American Economic Association, the American Chemical Society, and the American Psychological Association were all started by members of The Order or persons close to The Order. These are key associations for the conditioning of society.

This phenomenon of The Order as the FIRST on the scene is found especially among foundations, although it appears that The Order keeps a continuing presence among Foundation Trustees. It does more than just be FIRST where money is concerned. It stays around to keep an eye on expenditures. The FIRST President of the Carnegie Institution (1902-5) was Daniel Coit Gilman, but other members of The Order have been on Carnegie boards since the turn of the century. Gilman was on the scene for the founding of the Peabody, Slater, and Russell Sage Foundations. McGeorge Bundy was President of the Ford Foundation from 1966-1979.

The FIRST Chairman of an influential but almost unknown organization established in 1910 was also a member of The Order. In 1920 Theodore Marburg founded the American Society for the Judicial Settlement of International Disputes, but Marburg was only President. The FIRST Chairman was member William Howard Taft ('78). The Society was the forerunner of the League to Enforce the Peace, which developed into the League of Nations concept and ultimately into the United Nations.

In United Nations we find, for example, that Archibald McLeash ('15) was the brains behind the constitution of the UNESCO organization.

We find the same FIRST on the scene phenomenon in "think tanks." In 1960, James Jeremiah Wadsworth ('27) set up the Peace Research Institute. In 1963 this was merged to become the Institute for Policy Studies, along with Marcus Rashkin, who had been National Security Council Aide (1961-3) to McGeorge Bundy ('40), a very active member of The Order.

The Church

About 2 percent of The Order is in the Church (all Protestant denominations), although this percentage has declined in recent years.

A key penetration is the Union Theological Seminary, affiliated with Columbia University in New York. This Seminary, a past subject of investigation for Communist infiltration, has close links to The Order. Henry Sloane Coffin ('97) was Professor of Practical Theology at Union from 1904 to 1926 and President of Union Theological Seminary, also known as the "Red Seminary," from 1926 to 1945. Union has such a wide interpretation of religious activity that has, or used to have, an Atheists Club for its students.

Henry Sloane Coffin, Jr. ('49) was one of the Boston Five indicted on federal conspiracy charges.

And this is only **part** of The Order's penetration into the Church.

The Law

The major establishment law firms in New York are saturated with The Order.

In particular, Lord, Day and Lord, dominated by the Lord family already discussed; also Simpson, Thacher and Bartlett, especially the Thacher family; David, Polk, Wardwell and Debevoise, Plimpton, the Rockefeller family law firm.

Communications

There has been a significant penetration into communications. Some examples:

- Henry Luce of *Time-Life* is in The Order.
- so is William Buckley ('50) of *National Review*
- and *Alfred Cowles ('13), President of Cowles Communications, Des Moines Register, Minneapolis Star*
- and *Emmert Bates ('32) of Litton Educational Systems, plus*
- *Richard Ely Danielson ('07) of Atlantic Monthly*
- Russell Wheeler Davenport ('23), *Fortune*
- John Chipman Farrar ('18), of Farrar, Straus, the publishers.

The most prestigious award in journalism is a Nieman Fellowship at Harvard University. Over 300 were granted from 1937-68. The FIRST Director of the Nieman Fund was member Archibald McLeash.

Industry

The oil companies have their links to The Order. Members Percy Rockefeller, the Paynes, the Pratts, all link to Standard Oil. Shell Oil, Creole Petroleum, and Socony Vacuum also link. A wide variety of manufacturing firms have members in The Order from the Donnelley family in Chicago (printers of the Official Airline Guide and other references); lumber companies like Weyerhaeuser, who is also a Trilateralist; Dresser Industries, and so on.

The Federal Reserve System

A dozen members can be linked to the Federal Reserve, but one appointment is noteworthy, Pierre Jay ('92), whose only claim to fame in 1913 was to run a private school and be an obscure Vice President of Manhattan Bank yet he became FIRST Chairman of the New York Federal Reserve, the really significant Reserve Bank.

The White House, Politics and Government

This is the area where The Order has made headway: with names like Taft, Bush, Stimson, Chafee, Lovett, Whitney, Bundy and so on. It will take a separate volume to cover this story and in Memorandum Nine we describe just one example, THE BUNDY OPERATION.

Memorandum Number Six:
Operations Of The Order

In 1981 *The Anglo American Establishment*, by Carroll Quigley, was published in New York by a small anti-Establishment publisher. Quigley was formerly instructor at Princeton and Harvard and then Professor at the School of Foreign Service, Georgetown University. The publisher notes in his introduction that Quigley had been unable to find a major publisher for the manuscript. This is not surprising. The book blows the lid off the British equivalent of The Order.

The *Anglo American Establishment* has nothing at all to do with the American establishment, which is hardly mentioned, but it has a lot to do with the British establishment. The publisher probably inserted the word "AMERICAN" into the title to enhance marketability in the States. Quigley describes in minute detail the historical operations of the British establishment controlled by a secret society and operating very much as The Order operates in the U.S. This is the real significance of Quigley's explosive book.

The Group

The British secret society, known as "The Group" or just plain "US", was founded at Oxford University, much as The Order was founded at Yale, but without the Masonic mumbo jumbo. As we noted in Memorandum Five, the Group operates in a series of concentric circles and like The Order consists of old line families allied with private merchant bankers, known in the U.S. as investment bankers.

Bearing in mind, the proven existence of The Group, the operations of The Order and the kind of penetration it has achieved cannot be explained by mere chance. By examining The Order's operations we can generate a picture of its objectives without access to any internal constitution or statement of objectives even if such exists. It may only be word of mouth.

By contrast, The Group's objective is recorded in Cecil Rhodes' will. It was:

"The extension of British rule throughout the world, the perfecting of a system of emigration from the United Kingdom and of colonization by British subjects of all lands wherein the means of livelihood are attainable by energy, labour and enterprise . . . and the ultimate recovery of the United States of America as an integral part of the British Empire."

This objective is, of course, ridiculous and somewhat immature, but no less ridiculous and immature than the New World order objective of The Order. Yet The Group has controlled British policy for a hundred years and still does.

Both The Group and The Order have been created by Anglophiles who want to pattern the world on a Hegelian-Anglo hybrid culture. Where the Latins, the Slavs and the Sino races fit is not considered, but clearly these cultures will be disinclined to become pawns of either the British Empire or New England Yankees. Even within the Commonwealth, a voluntary association of nations, it is unlikely that Canada, Australia and New Zealand would accept the constitutional bondage envisaged by Cecil Rhodes. Both secret organizations overlook, and there is a philosophic basis for this neglect, the natural right of any ethnic group, be it white, black or yellow, English, Slavic or Latin, to develop its own culture without coercion.

Unlike this author, Quigley sympathizes with the ends of The Group, although he terms their methods despicable. Both The Group and The Order are unwilling or unable to bring about a global society by voluntary means, so they opted for coercion. To do this they have created wars and revolutions, they have ransacked public treasuries, they have oppressed, they have pillaged, they have lied — even to their own countrymen.

How have they done this?

Modus Operandi Of The Order

The activities of The Order are directed towards changing our society, changing the world, to bring about a New World Order. This will be a planned order with heavily restricted individual freedom, without Constitutional protection, without national boundaries or cultural distinction.

We deduce this objective by examining and then summing up the actions of individual members: there has been a consistent pattern of activity over one hundred years. Part of this activity has been in cooperation with The Group, with its parallel and recorded objectives.

Now if, for example, we found that the dominant interest of members was raising ducks, that they wrote articles about ducks, bred ducks, sold ducks, formed duck-studying councils, developed a philosophy of ducks, then it would be reasonable to conclude that they had an objective concerning ducks, that this is not mere random activity.

Historically, operations of The Order have concentrated **on society,** how to change society in a specific manner towards a specific goal: a New World Order. We know the elements in society that will have to be changed in order to bring about this New World order, we can then examine The Order's actions in this context.

More or less these elements would have to be:

Education — how the population of the future will behave,

Money — the means of holding wealth and exchanging goods,

Law — the authority to enforce the will of the state, a world law and a world court is needed for a world state,

Politics — the direction of the State,

Economy — the creation of wealth,

History — what people believe happened in the past,

Psychology — the means of controlling how people think,

Philanthropy — so that people think well of the controllers,

Medicine — the power over health, life and death,

Religion — people's spiritual beliefs, the spur to action for many,

Media — what people know and learn about current events,

Continuity — the power to appoint who follows in your footsteps.

Operations in each of these areas will be detailed in subsequent volumes. For example, in the next volume, *The Order Controls Education*, we will describe how Daniel Coit Gilman, President of Johns Hopkins University, imported Wundt psychological methods from Germany, then welded education and psychology in the U.S., established laboratories, brought these educational laboratories into major Universities and generated 100s of PhDs to teach the new educational conditioning system. One of the first of these Johns Hopkins doctorates was John Dewey. The result we well know. The educational morass of the '80s where most kids — not all — can't spell, read or write, yet can be programmed into mass behaviour channels.

The Order's next move was to control the Foundations. They got all the big ones — Carnegie, Ford, Peabody, Slater, Russell Sage and so on. That's the topic of another volume. As in education, the modus operandi of The Order was to get in FIRST and set the stage for the future. The initial objective was to establish a direction in an organization. Selection of managers, intuitive or amoral enough to catch on to the direction, kept the momentum going. In the case of Foundations, The Order has usually maintained a continuing presence over decades.

When it comes to activities by individual members, at first sight the pattern is confusing and superficially inconsistent. Let's give some examples:

- Andrew Carnegie profited from war through his vast steel holdings, but under the guidance of member Daniel Coit Gilman, Carnegie was also an enthusiastic president and financial backer of the American Peace Society. This is seemingly inconsistent. Could Carnegie be for war *and* peace at the same time?

- The League to Enforce the Peace, founded by members William H. Taft and Theodore Marburg, was promoting peace, yet active in urging U.S. participation in World War One. How could the League be for war **and** peace at the same time?

- In the 1920s, W. Averell Harriman was a prime supporter of the Soviets with finance and diplomatic assistance, at a time when such aid was against State Department regulations. Harriman participated in RUSKOMBANK, the first Soviet commercial bank. Vice-President Max May of Guaranty Trust, dominated by the Harriman-Morgan interests, became the FIRST Vice-President of RUSKOMBANK in charge of its foreign operations. In brief, an American banker under guidance of a member of The Order had a key post in a Soviet bank! But we also find that Averell Harriman, his brother Roland Harriman, and members E.S. James and Knight Woolley, through the Union Bank (in which they held a major interest) were prime financial backers of Hitler.

Now our textbooks tell us that Nazis and Soviets were bitter enemies and their systems are opposites. How could a rational man support Soviets and Nazis at the same time? Is Harriman irrational or is the inconsistency explainable?

- The Bundy family (we have a Memorandum on them later) gives us another example of seeming inconsistency. William Bundy was with the Central Intelligence Agency for a decade. McGeorge Bundy was National Security Assistant to Presidents Kennedy and Johnson. So the Bundys presumably support U.S.-European policy which is pro-NATO. Yet the Bundys have been linked to activities and organizations which are anti-NATO and, indeed, pro-Marxist — for example, the Institute for Policy Studies. Are the Bundys inconsistent?
- Among individual members of The Order we find a wide variety of publically proclaimed beliefs, ideologies and politics. William Buckely periodically chews out the Soviets. On the other hand, member John Burtt has been a member of a dozen communist front groups. Member William S. Coffin, Jr. spent three years with CIA and then became a leader of anti-Vietnam war activity through the National Conference for a New Politics and Clergy and Laymen Concerned about Vietnam. In fact, Coffin was one of the Boston Five charged and indicted for conspiracy to violate Federal laws. And, of course, W. Averell Harriman is elder statesman of the Democratic Party.

Quite a mixture of beliefs and activities. Do they reflect inconsistent philosophies? How can The Order have a consistent objective with this potpourri of individual actions?

The answer is, they are not at all inconsistent: **because the objective of The Order is above and beyond these actions and in fact needs these seeming contradictions.**

The State is Absolute

How can there exist a common objective when members are apparently acting in opposition to one another?

Probably the most difficult task in this work will be to get across to the reader what is really an elementary observation: that the objective of The Order is **neither** "left" **nor** "right." "Left" and "right" are artificial devices to bring about change, and the extremes of political left and political right are vital elements in a process of controlled change.

The answer to this seeming political puzzle lies in Hegelian logic. Remember that both Marx and Hitler, the extremes of "left" and "right" presented as textbook enemies, evolved out of the same philosophical system: Hegelianism. That brings screams of intellectual anguish from Marxists and Nazis, but is well known to any student of political systems.

The dialectical process did not originate with Marx as Marxists claim, but with Fichte and Hegel in late 18th and early 19th century Germany. In the dialectical process a clash of opposites brings about a synthesis. For example, a clash of political left and political right brings about another political system, a synthesis of the two, neither left nor right. **This conflict of opposites is essential to bring about change.** Today this process can be identified in the literature of the Trilateral Commission where "change" is promoted and "conflict management" is termed the means to bring about this change.

In the Hegelian system conflict is essential. Furthermore, for Hegel and systems based on Hegel, the State is absolute. The State requires complete obedience from the individual citizen. An individual does not exist for himself in these so-called organic systems but only to perform a role in the operation of the State. He finds freedom only in obedience to the State. There was no freedom in Hitler's Germany, there is no freedom for the individual under Marxism, neither will there be in the New World Order. And if it sounds like George Orwell's *1984* — it is.

In brief, the State is supreme and conflict is used to bring about the ideal society. Individuals find freedom in obedience to the rulers.

So who or what is the State? Obviously it's a self-appointed elite. It is interesting that Fichte, who developed these ideas before Hegel, was a freemason, almost certainly Illuminati, and certainly was promoted by the Illuminati. For example, Johann Wolfgang Goethe (Abaris in the Illuminati code) pushed Fichte for an appointment at Jena University.

Furthermore, the Illuminati principle that the end justifies the means, a principle that Quigley scores as immoral and used by both The Group and The Order, is rooted in Hegel. Even the anonymous Yale student who wrote the verse in Memorandum Three observed this principle at work on the Yale campus.

This, then, is a vital part of our explanation of The Order. When its co-founder, William Russell, was in Germany in 1831-2, there was no way he could have avoided Hegelian theory and discussion. It was the talk of the campus. It swept intellectual Germany like a Pac Man craze. Most Americans haven't heard of it. And those who have don't want to hear any more about it. Why? Because its assumptions are completely at variance with our sense of individual freedom and Constitutional guarantees. Most of us believe the State exists to serve the individual, not vice versa.

The Order believes the opposite to most of us. That is crucial to understanding what they are about. So any dicsussion between left and right, while essential to promote change, is **never** allowed to develop into a discussion along the lines of Jeffersonian democracy, i.e., the best government is least government. The discussion and the funding is **always** towards more state power, use of state power and away from individual rights. So it doesn't matter from the viewpoint of The Order whether it is termed left, right, Democratic, Republican, secular or religious — so long as the discussion is kept within the framework of the State and the power of the State.

This is the common feature between the seemingly dissimilar positions taken by members — **they have a higher common objective in which clash of ideas is essential.** So long as rights of the individual are not introduced into the discussion the clash of ideas generates the conflict necessary for change.

As the objective is also global control an emphasis is placed on global thinking, i.e., internationalism. This is done through world organizations and world law. The great contribution of the Tafts to The Order was on the world court system and world law — to the internationalist aspect of the New World Order.

Memorandum Number Seven: How The Order Relates To The Council On Foreign Relations, Trilateral Commission And Similar Organizations

Organizations like the Council on Foreign Relations (CFR) do not fit the requirements for a conspiracy. They are simply too large and their membership is not secret. The membership list for The Order has never surfaced until now. Anyone can obtain a list of members for the CFR and the Trilateral Commission. Also, too many people are included as members in these organizations who are just not given to membership in conspiratorial groups.

Certainly there is off-the-record discussion and certainly the general direction of U.S. policy reflects majority thinking in these organizations — but they are not conspiracies.

Moreover, the CFR and its sister organizations are not geared to action and implementation of policy. Compare, for example, the Brown Brothers, Harriman firm with nine members of The Order and the CFR. Obviously the first is more cohesive, yet more low profile, more able to conceal its actions, yet more action oriented.

The larger open organizations are a forum for discussion, a place where ideas can be kicked around, "a rich man's club", as someone commented, where people can be assessed, where discrete comment and criticism can be made away from a nosy press and a possibly unsympathetic public. They may not be elected bodies, but neither are they conspiracies; they fall in the shadow of a conspiracy. They are neither democratic or dictatorial.

The Role Of The Order

The Order is represented in these organizations but does not always dominate. David Rockefeller, a former chairman of the CFR, is not a member of The Order (only Percy Rockefeller has represented the family), but the present CFR chairman, Winston Lord, is.

We can represent the relationship between The Order and the larger groups as a series of concentric circles. The CFR, etc. form an outer circle, i.e., a penumbra. They exist in a shadow cast by an inner organization. It is this inner organization that needs to be surfaced. The Order is the inner circle and Chapter 322 is a **part** of this inner circle because it is unlikely Chapter 322 is the only chapter in the U.S. We suspect, but cannot yet prove, at least one other.

How Chapter 322 Of The Order Relates To Other Organizations

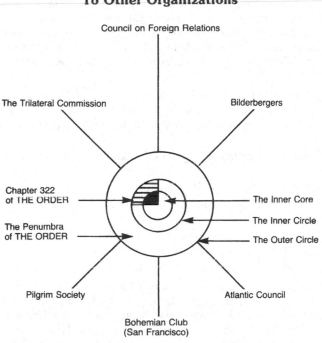

In brief, it looks like three segments:

(1) **The outer circle,** made up of large, open organizations with some membership coming from The Order.

(2) **The inner circle,** made up of one or more secret societies

In brief, it looks like three segments:

(1) **The outer circle,** made up of large, open organizations with some membership coming from The Order.

(2) **The inner circle,** made up of one or more secret societies like Chapter 322. We can only prove one chapter at this time.

(3) **The inner core,** a secret society within a secret society. This is the inner decision-making core. We cannot prove it exists, but logic suggests that some members of the inner circle will form an executive committee, an action group, an inner core. While we cannot prove the existence of an inner core, there are some obvious candidates for memberhsip and we could hazard a guess as to the identity of the Chairman.

The Outer Circle

The Council on Foreign Relations is the largest organizaiton in the outer circle. It has about 2500 members at any one time, as many as The Order in its entire history. The Trilateral Commission has 200 members world wide, but only 70 in the United States. These are younger organizations. The CFR dates from 1922, The Pilgrims from 1900, The Trilateral Commission from 1973, and the Bilderbergers from the 1950s.

How many members of The Order are in the CFR?

This is not the place for an exhaustive analysis, but a general idea can be gained from looking at names in The Order beginning with the letter "B":

The following are members of The Order **and** the Council on Foreign Relations:

Jonathan Bingham (Congressman)

William F. Buckley (Editor, *National Review* and The Order's house conservative)

McGeorge Bundy (Foundation executive)

William Bundy (Central Intelligence Agency)

George Herbert Walker Bush (President of the United States)

The make-up of the Council on Foreign Relations reflects its purpose as a meeting ground, a discussion forum. The CFR mainly consists of government officials, industrialists and academics. The Order has a distinctly different make-up, i.e., many more lawyers, for example, and a wider variety of declared occupations with far fewer industrialists.

The Trilateral Commission

The Trilateral Commission was founded in 1973 by David Rockefeller and comprises 200 members world wide, of whom about 77 are American. There is no overlap among memberships; for example, lumber industrialist Frederick Weyerhaeuser was in The Order, but his son is in the Trilateral Commission and not The Order. Similarly, Robert Taft, Jr., is in the Trilateral Commission but not The Order, even though The Order was co-founded by his great grandfather and eight Tafts have been members. The link is elusive, conceivably there may not be a link.

The Trilateral Commission is not a conspiracy. Its membership list is completely public — it costs a postage stamp to get one. The Commission publishes dozens of booklets. The organization is completely above ground. In fact, this author has openly debated with George Franklin, Jr., Coordinator of the Trilateral Commission on the radio. Mr. Franklin did show a rather ill-concealed dislike for the assault on his pet global New World Order — and made the mistake of attempting to disguise this objective, but evasion and hostility do not constitute conspiracy. Conspirators just don't appear on radio talk shows to debate their objectives.

Temporarily the following facts should be held in mind:
- J. Richardson Dilworth, at Room 3600 Rockefeller Plaza, and the Rockefeller Family Associates' chief financial and administrative officer, **is** a member of The Order.
- Percy Rockefeller (1900) was a member of The Order, but no other Rockefeller name is on the list.

It may be that the Trilateral Commission will prove to be a purely David Rockefeller personal endeavor rather than a broader establishment vehicle. However, Trilateral purposes, as portrayed in the literature, are almost identical to those of The Order. It may be a vehicle to attain an interim goal, i.e., three regional groupings. In this case J. Richardson Dilworth is the conduit and liaison.

Bilderbergers

So far as we can trace, only William F. Buckley is a member of the Bilderbergers and The Order.

Pilgrim Society

The Order does not show up directly on the Executive Committee of the Pilgrim Society, but only through family names, i.e., Aldrich and Pratt. The Pilgrim Society is probably a rather harmless social club using its annual dinners to cement ties between the British and American establishment.

The Inner Circle

Chapter 322 of The Order differs from the CFR, the Trilateral Commission and similar ogranizations in that it is truly a secret society. Its purposes and membership are not disclosed It is paranoid about secrecy and in covering its trail.

The circumstances that surround the founding of Scroll & Key in the 1850s suggest this secret society may in fact be Chapter 323. But this is pure speculation. So we have two secret societies that differ extensively from the CFR, Trilaterals and others and which can be seen as making up an inner circle.

Even this inner circle is too large for decision making. No doubt it includes many active or just plain bored members, even many who have forgotten they were ever initiated and who might be shocked to read in this book that they belong to a subversive organization. So logically there is a secret society within the secret society. Again, we cannot prove it, but it's a logical deduction. This would be an executive committee that controls finances and makes basic decisions.

Another important distinction between the outer core and the inner circle is in funding. This is important because funding controls everything. The families in The Order are closer to more foundations and more sources of funding than the Rockefeller family. To be sure, the Rockefeller family has 1 percent of Chase Manhattan stock, enough for control, and it has influence in the Rockefeller Foundation, but this doesn't compare to the centuries long pervasive influence of The Order. Remember, it was The Order that got John D. Rockefeller off the ground with his General Education Board, not the other way round.

It's an open question quite how the Trilaterals fit with The Order. It may be the international aspect of The Order, it may be a Rockefeller dominated group.

Many of these old line families see the Rockefellers as upstarts, as nouveau riche, not quite on the outside looking in, but definitely not socially acceptable without some reservations — except for their money, of course. Anyone who heard Nelson Rockefeller speak and compared his syntax to the polished charm of a Boston Brahmin will understand. There's a New England saying that "the Lowells only talk to the Cabots and the Cabots only talk to God." The Rockefellers just are not in this league.

And if we may be excused a little gossip: we have been told by several establishment people that David Rockefeller is just "not too bright," and Nelson Rockefeller was the only man in America who could torture the English language to the extent of placing **two** "non sequiters" in **one** sentence.

If we were to look back to 1983 from the year 2083, it could be that the Rockefellers will have followed in the footsteps of the Carnegies and the Morgans. Names in dusty files but no longer represented in the power group.

Memorandum Number Eight:
The Chain Of Influence

Initiates into The Order are assured of career advancement and success, even wealth, providing they follow the rule "to get along you must go along."

Intermarriage consolidates the power of the families and expands their span of influence.

Finally, a chain of influence spread over many years guarantees continuity and must be extraordinarily impressive to any new initiate who doubts the power of The Order.

We can identify two types of influence chains: a horizontal chain and a vertical chain. Both types are duplicated many times, for the moment we'll give a single example.

Horizontal Chains of Influence

Members of The Order are to be found in every segment of society: in education, in foundations, in politics, in government, industry, law and finance. Consequently, at any time The Order can tap influence in any area of society. The occupational breakdown of The Order demonstrates the great breadth of this horizontal chain of influence. The major occupations of members are law, education, business, finance and industry.

Approximately, the breakdown is as follows:

Occupation	Percent of members involved (approximately)
Law	18 percent
Education	16 percent
Business	16 percent
Finance	15 percent
Industry	12 percent
	77 percent

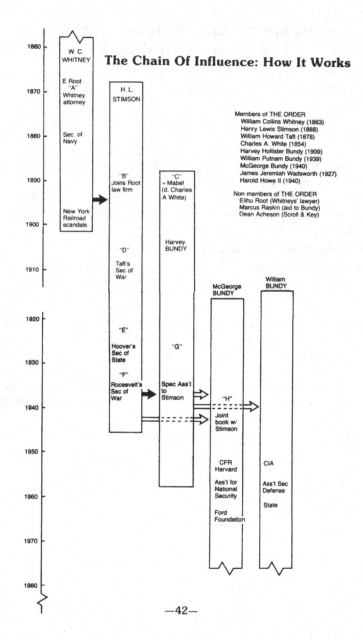

The Chain Of Influence: How It Works

Members of THE ORDER
William Collins Whitney (1863)
Henry Lewis Stimson (1888)
William Howard Taft (1878)
Charles A. White (1854)
Harvey Hollister Bundy (1909)
William Putnam Bundy (1939)
McGeorge Bundy (1940)
James Jeremiah Wadsworth (1927)
Harold Howe II (1940)

Non members of THE ORDER
Elihu Root (Whitneys' lawyer)
Marcus Raskin (aid to Bundy)
Dean Acheson (Scroll & Key)

—42—

In other words, these five occupations account for over three quarters of the membership, and these are the key fields for control of society.

Government and politics account for only about 3 percent at any one time. This is misleading, as any member in the above five fields can find himself temporarily in and out of government through the "revolving door" phenomenon.

The Church accounts for only 2 percent of members. These are concentrated in the Union Theological Seminary (the so-called "Red Seminary") and the Yale School of Divinity.

Notably the areas of society **least** represented are those with the **least** ability to influence the structural direction of society. They may give depth and richness to society, but are not essential to its control and direction. For example, very, very few engineers have ever been members of The Order — we only identified five engineers in the 150 year span. Yet engineering and technology are key elements to the success of the material aspects of American society. Art, architecture, and music are under represented. We can only identify 16 members in these three occupations over 150 years. Again, these occupations are not influential in determining the structure of society. Farmers are under-represented; only 16 in 150 years, but we suspect some took up farming to get away from The Order.

In brief: at any one time The Order can call on members in any area of American society to do what has to be done.

Vertical Chains of Influence

A tribute to the success of The Order has been an ability to implement one of its principles. This principle is:

"That only he who wears upon his breast, Their emblem, he for every post shall be considered best."

The practice of absolute preferment for members of The Order has worked to perpetuate its influence over time in a remarkable manner. Before we look at this chain of influence we need to look at some basic statistics. The Order has only initiated about 2500 members in its history in the United States. Each year 15 new members are initiated, no more, no less. On the other hand, between 800,000 and 1 million persons receive college degrees **each year** from an institute of higher learning, including about 30,000 doctorates.

When you follow the chain of influence below, hold in mind that out of 30-40 million degree holders, a few hundred men (never women) or in this case less than a dozen men, are presumed to be the only ones fit to occupy top posts in government. No one else is even seriously considered. We are asked to believe that only a few hundred members of The Order are capable of guiding the United States.

If we assume a random distribution of ability throughout the United States, then our evidence cannot be accounted for by chance. It must reflect, just on the basis of mathematical laws of average, a conscious series of choices. Unless you want to assume that all wisdom and all ability in the United States is generated solely by 15 Yale graduates each year. And that gets you back to the argument of this book.

ON
ACTIVE SERVICE
IN PEACE AND WAR

BY

HENRY L. STIMSON

Secretary of War 1911-13, Secretary of State 1929-33
Secretary of War 1940-45

AND

McGEORGE BUNDY

Junior Fellow, Society of Fellows
Harvard University

HARPER & BROTHERS, NEW YORK

**On Active Service In Peace And War
authored by two members of The Order**

— 44 —

Furthermore, there are approximately 2500 institutions of higher learning in the United States. Are we to believe that only **one** of these institutions can generate the talent to lead the country?

The Whitney-Stimson-Bundy-Acheson Chain of Influence

Four families provide an example of one such chain of influence. Multiply this chain by a few dozen and you readily see how control is perpetuated by a small group. The families in this chain are Whitney, Stimson, Acheson and Bundy. The Acheson family is only partly in The Order. Dean Acheson was a member of Scroll & Key at Yale. This is an offshoot of The Order and at least influenced by it. Dean Acheson's daughter, Mary Acheson, married William Bundy (The Order). Dean Acheson's son, David, is a member of The Order.

(1) We start with the Whitneys in the late 19th century. Whitney (The Order), along with Ryan and a handful of other capitalists, have been heavily criticized in several books on grounds of massive corruption and fraud. New York street railway franchises generated enormous profits for the Whitney group. When Whitney was Secretary of the Navy he promoted a giant naval ship building program — which didn't hurt his friends who owned shipyards and steel mills.

Whitney's attorney and close associate was Elihu Root. Although not a member of The Order, Root has been called "Whitney's artful attorney" (Point "A" on our chart). Root, one of the sharpest legal minds in American history and a power in his own right, worked along with the purposes of The Order.

(2) In 1890 along comes young Henry Stimson, fresh out of Yale, The Order, and Harvard Law School. Stimson joins Root's law firm ("B"), then called Root & Clark. After a while, in 1897, it became known as Root, Howard, Winthrop & Stimson and by 1901 it became Winthrop and Stimson. In the meantime ("C"), Stimson married Mabel White, daughter of Charles A. White (The Order).

Stimson proved he was capable in the law and when Taft (The Order) was looking for a Secretary of War in 1911, he appointed Stimson (The Order), which brings us to Point "D."

Then Stimson's career went like this:

• As Secretary of War Stimson completed a reorganization begun by his predecessor none other than Elihu Root.

• From 1917 to 1922 Stimson was in the Army, with ranks up to Brigadier General.

• In 1927 Coolidge appointed Stimson Governor-General of the Philippine Islands.

• In 1929 Herbert Hoover appointed Stimson Secretary of State (Point "E" on the chart).

• In 1940 Franklin D. Roosevelt appointed Stimson Secretary of War (Point "F" on the chart).

• In 1945, as Truman's Secretary of War, Stimson recommended the atomic bomb drops on Japan.

(3) During World War II Stimson had a special assistant — Harvey Hollister Bundy (The Order), (Point "G"). Special Assistant Harvey Bundy was the key Pentagon man on the Manhattan Project and was Stimson's constant companion to conferences in North Africa, Italy and Germany.

(4) While Stimson was still Secretary of War he brought Harvey Hollister's son, McGeorge Bundy (The Order), into the Pentagon to work on a book manuscript ("H" on the chart). This was published in 1948, entitled *On Active Service In Peace And War*. The joint authorship (see illustration) gave McGeorge Bundy a quick start in his career, as we shall describe in the next Memorandum when we pick up the career of the two younger Bundys, both members of The Order.

In a nutshell:

• Stimson was appointed to government offices by every President, except Harding, from 1911 to 1946, i.e., Taft, Wilson, Coolidge, Hoover, Roosevelt, and Truman.

• Stimson used his office to advance the career of fellow members of The Order, in particular Harvey Hollister Bundy and his son, McGeorge Bundy.

Memorandum Number Nine:
The Bundy Operation

If The Order had a reasonably "normal" life style, there would be no necessity for, and no substance in, this book. Unfortunately for us they do not have a normal life style.

The Order does not just go to college, look for a secure post with an establishment law firm, intermarry with the sisters and daughters of other members, get noisily drunk at the country club and go to church on Sunday. These may be reasonably "normal" patterns, but certainly not topics for research and analysis.

A proportion of The Order follows a life style which can best be described as: AMBITIOUS ACTIVISM TOWARDS A NEW WORLD ORDER GOAL.

Let's select one family — the Bundy family — fairly typical of another 20 or so families in The Order, and take a closer look.

The Bundy family came to the United States from England before 1635 and settled first in Boston, then in Taunton, Massachusetts. The family is one of lawyers and politicians with four members in The Order.

Date Initiated	Name	Key Activities
1909	Harvey Hollister Bundy	Special assistant to Secretary of War Stimson.
1921	Frederick McGeorge Bundy	Selling fish fillets
1939	William Putnam Bundy	CIA, Editor *Foreign Affairs*.
1940	McGeorge Bundy	Government and foundation official.

Frederick McGeorge Bundy is an example of a member who is initiated and then, apparently, is disinclined to do more. We can safely ignore Fred: his great achievement in life was Chairman of the North Atlantic Fillet Council which sounds vaguely like a government policy organization, but is concerned merely with marketing fish fillets. If the other Bundys had followed in Fred's honest, industrious footsteps and confined their activism to fish fillets, the world would be a lot safer, saner place.

Unfortunately, they didn't. The other three Bundys — Harvey Hollister and two of his three sons, William Putnam and McGeorge — are key activists and the activism has a Hegelian pattern, i.e., creation of conflict to bring about change.

Let's take a look at each of the activist Bundys:

Harvey Hollister Bundy

Born Grand Rapids, Michigan 1888, died 1963. His grandfather was a lawyer and Congressman, and **his** father was a lawyer too. Harvey Hollister described himself as lawyer and government official. Bundy was initiated into The Order in 1909. After a Harvard law degree and some world travel he became law clerk to Supreme Court Associate Justice Wendell Holmes (1914-1915). By coincidence, Alger Hiss, later convicted of perjury in the celebrated Chambers-Hiss trials involving Soviet espionage, was also a law clerk to Justice Holmes (1929-1930).

Harvey Hollister Bundy senior had five children, of whom three linked themselves to The Order.

The eldest son, Harvey Hollister, graduated Yale 1938, but was not initiated into Skull & Bones. He's a banker who, like Fred, keeps away from activism.

The next eldest is William Putnam Bundy, initiated in 1939. The next son is McGeorge Bundy, initiated in 1940. The eldest daughter, Harriet Lowell Bundy, married Gasper d'Andelot Belin, a partner in Covington and Burling and initiated with William Bundy in 1939. The youngest daughter, Katherine Lawrence Bundy, married Hugh Auchincloss, Jr.

The two Bundy boys have been the **real** activists.

William P. Bundy

Here's William Bundy's career in brief:

- 1947-1951   Law firm Covington & Burling in Washington, D.C.
- 1951-1961   Central Intelligence Agency
- 1960   Staff Director of Presidential Commission on National Goals
- 1961-3   Deputy Assistant Secretary of Defense for International Security Affairs
- 1964-9   Assistant Secretary of State for East Asian and Pacific Affairs in the Vietnam War period.
- 1969-71   Visiting Professor at Center for International Studies, MIT
- 1972   Editor of *Foreign Affairs*, the Council on Foreign Relations (CFR) quarterly and the most prestigious foreign affairs journal in the U.S. A guide for all policy makers. Winston Lord (The Order) is Chairman of CFR.

Bundy is a member of the American Assembly and the Council on Foreign Relations.

Clearly, Mr. Bundy has been appointed to some very influential positions in the last 30 years. As the Washington law firm of Covington &

Burling is intimately linked to Government regulatory affairs, it's reasonable to presume that Bundy probably had CIA dealings in the 1947-51 period and then moved to CIA to expand on these projects. The firm of Covington & Burling represents more than 100 top U.S. firms in Washington. Former partners have included William Bundy's father-in-law, Dean Acheson, and brother-in-law, Gasper Belin, (The Order).

An interesting aspect of this law firm, where the Bundy family consists of the single most influential element in the past few decades, is its creation of "left wing" political activity. This creative activity brings to mind the McCarthy Senate hearings on subversion of the 1953 era when Senator Joseph McCarthy wanted to call William Bundy as a witness before the Committee and found the establishment strongly arrayed against this idea (Bundy had given $400 to the Alger Hiss Defense Fund). In retrospect it may have been more than McCarthy's harsh treatment of witnesses — which is on the record — that prompted establishment horror. There may indeed have been some skeletons in the closet (and perhaps some bones) that the Senator could have unwittingly unearthed, and these skeletons had nothing to do with domestic communism.

In any event, as Quigley pointed out in *Tragedy and Hope*, the J.P. Morgan firm had financed the non-communist left in the United States for political control. It seems that Covington & Burling may well be another conduit. Some preliminary evidence:

- Covington & Burling partner John Douglas is the son of Paul H. Douglas — who was one of the most prominent radicals of the 30s and 40s and an outspoken member of the non-communist left. John Douglas was a key coordinator in the 1972 George McGovern campaign: McGovern, of course, being on the left end of the political spectrum.

- Another former partner is Senator Charles Mathias, whose political stance is more or less at the left end of the Republican Party and along the lines of George Bush's (The Order) internationalist line.

- Yet another partner is Michael Boudin, son of Leonard Boudin and brother of Kathy Boudin. This should raise some eyebrows as Kathy was on the FBI "Most Wanted" list. Leonard Boudin is the long time communist front lawyer and member of the National Lawyers Guild ("The foremost legal bulwark of the Communist Party"), *New Masses* ("a communist periodical") and a dozen other Communist fronts. Kathy was a founder of Students for a Democratic Society and a leader in its terrorist Weathermen faction. A bomb manufacturing enterprise got the group into trouble with the law and Kathy onto the FBI list.

In brief, we have the elements of a hypothesis that left wing activity in the U.S., down to bomb making and outright terrorism, may link to Covington and Burling — and the CIA. This is not a new assertion. Statements have been made before that the CIA has funded the left in the U.S. This claim hasn't received too much publicity for two reasons: (a) it offends the establishment media, which prefers to pose the CIA as a "right" organization and (b) it doesn't make much sense.

It certainly doesn't make any sense unless you throw your mind back to Memorandum Number Six and the Hegelian dialectic process. In this process change requires conflict, and conflict requires the clash of opposites. You can't just have a "right," you must have a "right" **and** a "left." You can't have just a pro-Vietnam War policy, you must also have an anti-Vietnam War policy. Else the dialectical process won't bring about change. An interesting thought.

To move on, in 1960 Bundy, while still at CIA, became Staff Director for the newly formed Presidential Commission on National Goals. Such a commission, even in its title, assumes conscious direction. If you have goals, you logically need a device to achieve these goals. In a society like the U.S. it should be a superfluous sort of commission unless there is some "guiding hand," something more than the voting booth and the market place at work.

The Report of this Commission came up with some quotes which are almost pure Hegelianism:

(a) "a role of government is to stimulate changes of attitude"

(b) "in the 1960s every American is summoned to extraordinary personal responsibility, sustained effort, and sacrifice"

(c) "The American citizen in the years ahead ought to devote a larger portion of his time and energy directly to solution of the nation's problems . . . many ways are open for citizens to participate in the attainment of national goals."

Now the basic set of rules governing our society is the Constitution and the Bill of Rights. There is nothing in these constitutional documents to support any of these demands. What the demands imply is that an American citizen has a DUTY to advance the will of the State. But such an assumption is definitely NOT implicit in the philosophy under which the United States was founded and presumably operates today.

In 1972, after a stint of government service, Bundy took over *Foreign Affairs*, the most prestigious and influential foreign affairs journal in the U.S.: the bible for policy makers.

So William Bundy is a **very** influential man. Enough that three aspects of his career require further investigation:

• The Hegelian tinge, that a citizen has a **duty** to the State,

— 50 —

- The operation of the Hegelian dialectic and whether any "left" operations can be traced more directly to Covington and Burling,
- Whether Bundy's service in Government shows promotion of "right" operations, needed to balance off the "left" operations.

McGeorge Bundy

Preferential treatment has been accorded McGeorge Bundy all the way along the line.

Graduating Yale and joining The Order in 1940, Bundy spent a while at Harvard and then joined the U.S. Army "as a private."

Within 12 months Bundy had rocketed to captain and staff officer working on Operation Husky (the invasion of Sicily) and Operation Overlord (the invasion of Normandy).

If there is one job in this world that requires **experience,** it must be a staff planning officer for an amphibious operation. Only experience can make the calculations of timing and logistics for personnel and supplies come out right. And men's lives depend on this experience. Can a 23-year-old, with no military experience, undertake planning for amphibious operations? The answer is obviously no even if his father (The Order) is in the Pentagon as an aide to the Secretary of War (The Order).

The war in Europe finished, Bundy now a veteran of 27 years, went straight to the Pentagon as assistant to the Secretary of War, Henry Stimson. We have already noted Bundy worked on the manuscript of *On Active Service In Peace And War* and was rewarded with coauthorship, a definite leg up in his career.

Then, in quick succession, Bundy became consultant to the Economic Cooperation Administration, although he presumably knew no more about economics than amphibious landing, then foreign policy analyst for Presidential candidate Thomas Dewey, then analyst for the Council on Foreign Relations. By 1949 Bundy was invited to Harvard University and in four years (1953) was made Dean of the Faculty of Arts and Sciences.

We are asked to believe that out of hundreds, perhaps thousands, of experienced academics with decades of hard-won credentials, an assistant professor who has been skipping around the non-academic world for ten years is the most talented for the post of Harvard Dean! We might accept the lack of experience in amphibious warfare planning and economic programs planning, but Dean of a presitigious Harvard department in four years! No, that's too much. It smells of "pull" and few readers will dispute that conclusion.

From 1961 to 1966 Bundy was Special Assistant for National Security Affairs to Presidents Kennedy and Johnson. There is a significant aspect of this sensitive post which only surfaced under Henry Kissinger. The post can be used to screen information reaching the President: in fact, that is one of its major purposes, to stop a flood of paper reaching the Presidential desk.

The other side to this screening process is that it could place the President in an artificial information environment. If the options presented to the President are controlled, so are the decisions. Selected information can control the options.

McGeorge Bundy was National Security Adviser in the early years of the Vietnam debacle. While McGeorge Bundy (The Order) was in the White House his brother, William P. Bundy (The Order) was in key positions relating to the Far East in Defense and State Departments. By acting jointly, the Bundy brothers could have controlled absolutely the flow of information relating to Vietnam from Intelligence, State **and** DOD. We are not saying this happened. We believe it to be a hypothesis worthy of examination. As they are blood brothers in a secret organization of which we know very little — and nothing voluntarily — we have reason to make this further examination.

In 1966 McGeorge Bundy was appointed President of the Ford Foundation, a post he retained until 1979. While at Ford, Bundy brought in as Vice President in charge of Education and Research Division another member of The Order — Harold Howe II.

Howe's qualifications, apart from a Yale undergraduate degree, can be described in Howe's own words:

". . . in the old scheme of things I would not have qualifications to be a professor — I have no PhD degree, no scholarly research publications to my credit. I once applied to the Yale Graduate School but was turned down as academically unpromising." (Apparently The Order doesn't reach everywhere, even at Yale).

Some of the half-baked ideas Howe and Bundy promoted with Ford Foundation money probably stem from Howe's philosophy. In Howe's own words, "When in doubt, do it." For example, we have this gem from Howe:

". . . we will have to re-think American values regarding cooperation and competition . . . many schools (particularly secondary schools) would define as "cheating" the kinds of cooperative activities whereby students help each other instead of competing for places on the ladder of academic success."

This is pure Hegelian collectivism. It undoubtedly works to the advantage of The Order: this moves the citizen to a dependency role and away from reliance on individual faculties.

It is noteworthy that both Fords on the board resigned in disgust with Ford Foundation policies.

Memorandum Number Ten:
Keeping The Lid On The Pot

The Order's control of history, through foundations and the American Historical Association, has been effective. Not so much because of outright censorship, although that is an important element, but more because of the gullibility of the American "educated public."

From time to time their plans go awry. The bubbling pot of political manipulation — it's called conflict management on the inside — threatens to spill over into public view. It is extraordinary how newspaper editors, columnists, TV and radio commentators, and publishers either lack insight to see beyond the superficial or are scared witless to do so. Even worse, the educated public, the 30-40 million degree holders, lets these opinion molders get away with it.

Outright censorship has not been too effective. There has certainly been a campaign to suppress revisionist interpretations of history. Witness Harry Elmer Barnes in *The Struggle Against The Historical Blackout*:

> It may be said, with great restraint, that, never since the Dark and Middle Ages, have there been so many powerful forces organized and alerted against the assertion and acceptance of historical truth as are active today to prevent the facts about the responsibility for the second World War and its results from being made generally accessible to the American public. Even the great Rockefeller Foundation frankly admits (*Annual Report*, 1946, p. 188) the subsidizing of a corps of historians to anticipate and frustrate the development of any neo-Revisionism in our time. And the only difference between this Foundation and several others is that it has been more candid and forthright about its politics.

This author's personal experience of attempted outright censorship was at the Hoover Institution, Stanford University, when the Director attempted to suppress publication of my then forthcoming *National Suicide: Military Aid To The Soviet Union*. The facts weren't in question. Unfortunately, the book offended the Nixon-Kissinger program to aid the Soviets while **they** were aiding the North Vietnamese — so in effect, Americans were being killed by our own technology. In this case neither author nor publisher was in a mood to listen, and the Establishment put tail between legs and called it a day.

More effective than outright censorship is use of the left-right political spectrum to neutralize unwelcome facts and ideas or just condition citizens to think along certain lines.

The "left" leaning segment of the press can always be relied upon to autmatically assault ideas and information from the "right" and vice versa. In fact, media outlets have been artificially set up just for this purpose: both *Nation* and *New Republic* on the "left" were financed by Willard Straight, using Payne Whitney (The Order) funds. On the "right" *National Review* published by William Buckley (The Order) runs a perpetual deficit, presumably made up by Buckley.

Neither the independent right nor the independent left sees the trap. They are so busy firing at each other they've mostly forgotten to look behind the scenes. And The Order smugly claims control of the "moderate" center. A neat game, and it's worked like a charm. But the establishment has a problem . . .

In Fact, It Has Several Problems

They are on the inside looking out. We are on the outside looking in. They may call us "peasants" but we have the advantage of knowing about the real world and its infinite diversity. Their global objectives are dreams based on skewed information. Dangerous dreams, but still dreams.

(1) The Order Lives In A Cultural Straightjacket

All the power in the world is useless without accurate information. If you meet these people, as this author has more or less casually over 30 years, one impression comes to the forefront — they are charming but with a limited perception of the world. They may have global ambitions, they may act politically like miniature power houses, but their knowledge of the world comes from an in-group and those who play along with the in-group. And the in-group lacks morality and diversity. It's a kind of Jet Set Politburo. Charming, power-hungry and myopic simultaneously.

All it can offer to the outsider is an invitation, almost an ultimatum, **"You** are part of the establishment." Which has as much interest for many as a Frederick Bundy fish fillet. Perhaps one of the exceptions is house conservative William Buckley, Jr. — at least his cynicism is marked by witty incisiveness. The rest are a pretty sad bunch.

(2) An Easy Prey For the Ambitious

Limited perception makes members of The Order a target and an easy prey for the ambitious outsider . . . who needs only the ability to say the right things at the right time to the right people, coupled with a sense of unscrupulousness. Henry Kissinger is a prime example — an outsider who wants desperately to stay on the inside. More devious than clever, but expert at using deviousness for his own ends.

Conservative readers may not agree, but Secretary of State Dean Acheson, who defended a guilty Alger Hiss to the bitter end, was probably more stupid than culpable. Which leads us to,

(3) Genetic Problems

Extensive intermarriage among the families raises a serious question of genetic malfunctions. Membership lists are heavily laced with Dodge, Whitney, Phelps, Perkins, Norton, Putnam used as middle (maternal) names. Cultural inhibitions are obvious, the intellectual limitations from genetic factors are more difficult to analyze and describe.

(4) Shallow Power Base

It may be as Rosenbaum comments, that The Order is "incredibly powerful". On the other hand, it is also incredibly weak — there is no philosophic or cultural depth to The Order.

Diversity is strength and The Order lacks diversity.

The vast bulk of the American people, that giant melting pot of Anglo, Germanic, Slavic, Hispanic, black, yellow, and who knows what else has been suckered. Many of them know it. Some are now going to know by whom.

When they've overcome the disbelief, the shock and perhaps some fear, they are surely going to say "What do we do?."

The great strength of individualism, an atomistic social order where the individual holds utlimate sovereignty, is that any counter revolution to an imposed social order where the State is boss, can take a million roads and a million forms.

No one is going to create an anti-The Order movement. That would be foolish and unnecessary. It could be infiltrated, bought off, or diverted all too easily. Much too easily.

Why play by the rules set by the enemy?

The movement that will topple The Order will be extremely simple and most effective. It will be ten thousand or a million Americans who come to the conclusion that they don't want the State to be boss, that they prefer to live under the protection of the Constitution. They will make their own **independent** decision to thwart The Order, and it will take ten thousand or a million forms.

The only weakness is communication. The Order has so wrecked education that reading comprehension is difficult for many — that's part of the brainwashing program. But there are more than enough readers. Most people prefer to talk, anyway.

The program of The Order might work in Russia, which has a history of obedience to the State; it's barely working in Poland, while in England "The Group" survives because enough of class structure and attitude remain. It can never work in the United States.

Conclusions

In the first introductory volume we have laid out the preliminary groundwork and suggested some hypotheses we need to examine. An understanding of The Order, the havoc it has wreaked on American society, its plans for future havoc — perpetual war for perpetual peace — is a logical step by step process.

The next step is to look at education. Our present educational chaos can be traced to three members of The Order: Daniel Coit Gilman (First President of University of California and First President of Johns Hopkins University), Timothy Dwight (twelfth President of Yale University) and Andrew Dickson White (First President of Cornell University).

Gilman imported the experimental psychology of Hegelian physiologist Wilhelm Wundt from Germany. This psychology was grafted onto the American education system through the educational laboratories at Columbia and Chicago University. And they moved a familiar name, John Dewey, a pure Hegelian in philosophy, along the fast track in his carerr. This has been aptly termed "The Leipzig Connection" by Lance J. Klass and Paolo Lionni.

Then we shall look at the Foundations, how these were captured by The Order and their gigantic funds used to finance a Hegelian educational system designed to condition future society. It is doubtful if John D. Rockefeller or Mrs. Russell Sage, and certainly the Ford family, ever quite understood how their philanthropies were used for a long-term conditioning plan.

It is also doubtfrul if The Order forecast the public backlash of the 1970s and 1980s — not all children have succumbed to the social conditioning brainwashing, parents have more than once risen in part revolt, private schools have sprouted like spring flowers in the desert and perhaps enough academics have slipped through a net designed to contain and neutralize independent research and thinking.

After we have looked at education and foundations we still have to work our way through the system of "perpetual war for perpetual peace." How The Order has financed revolution and profited from war. The objective? To keep the conflict boiling because conflict for Hegel is essential for change and the forward motion of society. Then we have to look at the financial system and the Federal Reserve. The Order was there right from the start.

In conclusion we must emphasize one point. An understanding of The Order and its modus operandi is impossible unless the reader holds in mind the Hegelian roots of the game plan. Hegelianism is alien to grass roots America. The national character is straightforward and to the point, not devious and tortuous. The grass roots are still closer to the American Revolution, the Jeffersonian Democrats, the classical liberal school of Cobden and Bright in England, and the Austrian School of Economics where Ludwig von Mises is the undisputed leader.

These schools of thought have been submerged in the public eye by the pirate-like onslaught of The Order and its many minions, but they still very much represent the daily operation of American society. From oil billionaire Bunker Hunt in Dallas, Texas to the seventeen year old black trying to "survive" in the Los Angeles ghetto, individual initiative is still more than obvious in American society.

A Statist system is the objective of The Order. But in spite of constant prattling about "change" by zombie supporters — such a system is foreign to deeply held beliefs in this country.

Above all the reader must — at least temporarily while reading this work — put to one side the descriptive cliches of left and right, liberal and conservative, communist and fascist, even republican and democrat. These terms may be important for self recognition, they do provide a certain reassurance, but they are confusing in our context unless seen as essential elements in a game plan. You will **never** understand The Order if you try to label it right or left.

A Robert Taft and a William Buckley on the right are just as important for the forward motion of society, the fundamental change desired by The Order, as a William Sloan Coffin and a Harry Payne Whitney (who financed the left). Their conflict is essential for change.

Which brings us to HYPOTHESIS NUMBER THREE: THE ORDER USES THE HEGELIAN DIALECTIC PROCESS TO BRING ABOUT A SOCIETY IN WHICH THE STATE IS ABSOLUTE, i.e., ALL POWERFUL.

This hypothesis, of course, reflects the gulf between The Order and American society. The gulf stems from the differing views of the relationship between the State and the individual.

Which is superior? Our whole way of life is based on the assumption that the individual is superior to the State. That the individual is the ultimate holder of sovereignty. That the State is the servant of the people. It's deeply engrained within us.

The Order holds the opposite — that the State is superior, that the common man (the peasant) can find freedom only by obedience to the State.

Now, of course, the State is a fiction. So who or what controls the State?

Obviously, The Order.

How The Order
CONTROLS
EDUCATION

322

Further Influence Of The Order — Post-1900

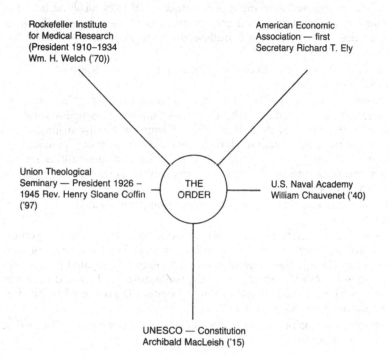

Rockefeller Institute
for Medical Research
(President 1910–1934
Wm. H. Welch ('70))

American Economic
Association — first
Secretary Richard T. Ely

Union Theological
Seminary — President 1926 –
1945 Rev. Henry Sloane Coffin
('97)

THE
ORDER

U.S. Naval Academy
William Chauvenet ('40)

UNESCO — Constitution
Archibald MacLeish ('15)

Memorandum Number One:
It All Began At Yale

The first volume of this series introduced The Order, presented three preliminary hypotheses with examples of the evidence to come.

We also asserted that any group that wanted to control the future of American society had first to control education, i.e., the population of the future. This volume will outline the way in which education has been controlled by The Order.

It all began at Yale. Even the official Yale history is aware of Yale's power and success:

"The power of the place remain(s) unmistakable. Yale was organized. Yale inspired a loyalty in its sons that was conspicuous and impressive. Yale men in after life made such records that the suspicion was that even there they were working for each other. In short, Yale was exasperatingly and mysteriously successful. To rival institutions and to academic reformers there was something irritating and disquieting about old Yale College."[1]

"Yale was exasperatingly and mysteriously successful," says the official history.

And this success was more than obvious to Yale's chief competitor, Harvard University. So obvious, in fact, that in 1892 a young Harvard instructor, George Santanyana, went to Yale to investigate this "disturbing legend" of Yale power. Santanyana quoted a Harvard alumnus who intended to send his son to Yale — because in real life "all the Harvard men are working for Yale men."[2]

But no one has previously asked an obvious question — Why? What is this "Yale power"?

A Revolutionary Yale Trio

In the 1850s, three members of The Order left Yale and working together, at times with other members along the way, made a revolution that changed the face, direction and purpose of American education. It was a rapid, quiet revolution, and eminently successful. The American people even today, in 1983, are not aware of a coup d'etat.

The revolutionary trio were:

- Timothy Dwight ('49) Professor in the Yale Divinity School and then 12th President of Yale University.
- Daniel Coit Gilman ('52), first President of the University of California, first President of the Johns Hopkins University and first President of the Carnegie Institution.
- Andrew Dickson White ('53), first President of Cornell University and first President of the American Historical Association.

This notable trio were all initiated into The Order within a few years of each other (1849, 1852, 1853). They immediately set off for Europe. All three went to study philosophy at the University of Berlin, where post-Hegelian philosophy had a monopoly.

- Dwight studied at the Universities of Berlin and Bonn between 1856 and 1858,
- Gilman was at the University of Berlin between 1854 and 55 under Karl von Ritter and Friedrich Trendelenberg, both prominent "Right" Hegelians, and
- White studied at the University of Berlin between 1856 and 1858.

Notably also at the University of Berlin in 1856 (at the Institute of Physiology) was none other than Wilhelm Wundt, the founder of experimental psychology in Germany and the later source of the dozens of American PhDs who came back from Leipzig, Germany to start the modern American education movement.

Why is the German experience so important? Because these were the formative years, the immediate post graduate years for these three men, the years when they were planning the future, and at this period Germany was dominated by the Hegelian philosophical ferment.

There were two groups of these Hegelians. The right Hegelians, were the roots of Prussian militarism and the spring for the unification of Germany and the rise of Hitler. Key names among right Hegelians were Karl Ritter (at the University of Berlin where our trio studied), Baron von Bismarck, and Baron von Stockmar, confidential adviser to Queen Victoria over in England. Somewhat before this, Karl Theodor Dalberg (1744-1817), arch-chancellor in the German Reich, related to Lord Acton in England and an Illuminati (Baco v Verulam in the Illuminati code), was a right Hegelian.

There were also Left Hegelians, the promoters of scientific socialism. Most famous of these, of course, are Karl Marx, Friedrich Engels, Heinrich Heine, Max Stirner and Moses Hess.

The point to hold in mind is that both groups use Hegelian theory of the State as a start point, i.e., the State is superior to the individual. Prussian militarism, Naziism and Marxism have the **same** philosophic roots.

And it left its mark on our trio.

---

[1]George Wilson Pierson. YALE COLLEGE 1871-1922 (Yale University Press. New Haven. 1952) Volume One. p. 5.
[2]E.E. Slosson. GREAT AMERICAN UNIVERSITIES (New York. 1910) pp. 59-60.

Daniel Coit Gilman

Gilman wrote his sister in 1854 that what he most desired to do on returning home to America was to "influence New England minds." An extract from one Gilman letter is worth quoting at length.

Daniel C. Gilman in 1852 as a senior in Yale College.

Daniel C. Gilman in the early seventies as president of the University of California.

Gilman wrote his sister from St. Petersburg in April, 1854:

And what **do you think I am "keeping" for?** Tell me, some day when you write, for every year makes me feel that I must draw nearer to a point. When I go home to America I must have some definite notions. Day and night I think of that time, and in all I see and do I am planning for being useful at home. I find my wishes cling more and more towards a home in New England, and I long for an opportunity to influence New England minds. If I am an editor, New York is the place; but, to tell the truth, I am a little afraid of its excitements, its politics, its money-making whirl. I look therefore more and more to the ministry as probably the place where I can do more good than anywhere else; that is to say, if I can have a congregation which will let me preach such things as we have talked over so many times in our up-stairs confabs. I am glad you remember those talks with pleasure, for I look upon them as among the greatest "providences" of my life. If ever I make anything in this world or another I shall owe it to the blessed influences of **home.** For me, it seems as though new notions and wider views of men and things were crowding upon me with wonderful rapidity, and every day and almost every hour I think of some new things which I wish to have accomplished in America. . . . I find my thoughts, unconsciously, almost, dwelling on the applications of Christianity or the principles of the New Testament to business, study, public education, political questions, travel, and so forth. I had a long talk with Mr. Porter in Berlin (it was three days long with occasional interruptions) on topics related to such as I have named, and he assures me that there are many places in New England ripe for the advocacy of some such views upon these questions as I have often hinted to you at home. I told him a great deal about my thoughts on such things, talking quite as freely and perhaps more fully than I have ever done with you girls at home. He seemed exceedingly interested . . . . He told me that the kind of preaching I spoke of was the kind now needed — the kind which would be most influential of good — and on the whole he encouraged me to attempt it. I feel more and more desirous to do so, and shall keep on, in all I see and hear abroad, with the examination of every influence now working upon men — churches and schools, politics and literature . . .[1]

Daniel Coit Gilman is the key activist in the revolution of education by The Order. The Gilman family came to the United States from Norfolk, England in 1638. On his mother's side, the Coit family came from Wales to Salem, Massachusetts before 1638.

[1]Fabian Franklin, THE LIFE OF DANIEL COIT GILMAN (Dodd. Mead. New York, 1910). pp. 28-9.

Gilman was born in Norwich, Connecticut July 8, 1831, from a family laced with members of The Order and links to Yale College (as it was known at that time).

Uncle Henry Coit Kingsley (The Order '34) was Treasurer of Yale from 1862 to 1886. James I. Kingsley was Gilman's uncle and a Professor at Yale. William M. Kingsley, a cousin, was editor of the influential journal *New Englander*.

On the Coit side of the family, Joshua Coit was a member of The Order in 1853 as well as William Coit in 1887.

Gilman's brother-in-law, the Reverend Joseph Parrish Thompson ('38) was in The Order.

Gilman returned from Europe in late 1855 and spent the next 14 years in New Haven, Connecticut — almost entirely in and around Yale, consolidating the power of The Order.

His first task in 1856 was to incorporate Skull & Bones as a legal entity under the name of The Russell Trust. Gilman became Treasurer and William H. Russell, the cofounder, was President. It is notable that there is no mention of The Order, Skull & Bones, The Russell Trust, or any secret society activity in Gilman's biography, nor in open records. The Order, so far as its members are concerned, is designed to be secret, and apart from one or two inconsequential slips, meaningless unless one has the whole picture. The Order has been remarkably adept at keeping its secret. In other words, The Order fulfills our first requirement for a conspiracy — i.e., IT IS SECRET.

The information on The Order that we are using surfaced by accident. In a way similar to the surfacing of the Illuminati papers in 1783, when a messenger carrying Illuminati papers was killed and the Bavarian police found the documents. All that exists publicly for The Order is the charter of the Russell Trust, and that tells you nothing.

On the public record then, Gilman became assistant Librarian at Yale in the fall of 1856 and "in October he was chosen to fill a vacancy on the New Haven Board of Education." In 1858 he was appointed Librarian at Yale. Then he moved to bigger tasks.

The Sheffield Scientific School

The Sheffield Scientific School, the science departments at Yale, exemplifies the way in which The Order came to control Yale and then the United States.

In the early 1850s, Yale science was insignificant, just two or three very small departments. In 1861 these were concentrated into the Sheffield Scientific School with private funds from Joseph E. Sheffield. Gilman went to work to raise more funds for expansion.

Gilman's brother had married the daughter of Chemistry Professor Benjamin Silliman (The Order, 1837). This brought Gilman into contact with Professor Dana, also a member of the Silliman family, and this group decided that Gilman should write a report on reorganization of Sheffield. This was done and entitled "Proposed Plan for the Complete Reorganization of the School of Science Connected with Yale College."

While this plan was worked out, friends and members of The Order made moves in Washington, D.C., and the Connecticut State Legislature to get state funding for the Sheffield Scientific School. The Morrill Land Bill was introduced into Congress in 1857, passed in 1859, but vetoed by President Buchanan. It was later signed by President Lincoln. This bill, now known as the Land Grant College Act, donated public lands for State colleges of agriculture and sciences . . . . and of course Gilman's report on just such a college was ready. The legal procedure was for the Federal government to issue land scrip in proportion to a state's representation, but state legislatures first had to pass legislation accepting the scrip. Not only was Daniel Gilman first on the scene to get Federal land scrip, he was first among **all** the states and grabbed all of Connecticut's share for Sheffield Scientific School! Gilman had, of course, tailored his report to fit the amount forthcoming for Connecticut. No other institution in Connecticut received even a whisper until 1893, when Storrs Agricultural College received a land grant.

Of course it helped that a member of The Order, Augustus Brandegee ('49), was speaker of the Connecticut State Legislature in 1861 when the state bill was moving through, accepting Connecticut's share for Sheffield. Other members of The Order, like Stephen W. Kellogg ('46) and William Russell ('33), were either in the State Legislature or had influence from past service.

The Order repeated the same grab for public funds in New York State. All of New York's share of the Land Grant College Act went to Cornell University. Andrew Dickson White, a member of our trio, was the key activist in New York and later became first President of Cornell. Daniel Gilman was rewarded by Yale and became Professor of Physical Geography at Sheffield in 1863.

In brief, The Order was able to corner the total state shares for Connecticut and New York, cutting out other scholastic institutions. This is the first example of scores we shall present in this series — how The Order uses public funds for its own objectives.

And this, of course, is the great advantage of Hegel for an elite. The State is absolute. But the State is also a fiction. So if The Order can manipulate the State, it in effect becomes the absolute. A neat game. And like the Hegelian dialectic process we cited in the first volume, The Order has worked it like a charm.

Back to Sheffield Scientific School. The Order now had funds for Sheffield and proceeded to consolidate its control. In February 1871 the School was incorporated and the following became trustees:

Charles J. Sheffield

Prof. G.J. Brush (Gilman's close friend)

Daniel Coit Gilman (The Order, '52)

W.T. Trowbridge

John S. Beach (The Order, '39)

William W. Phelps (The Order, '60)

Out of six trustees, three were in The Order. In addition, George St. John Sheffield, son of the benefactor, was initiated in 1863, and the first Dean of Sheffield was J.A. Porter, also the first member of Scroll & Key (the supposedly competitive senior society at Yale).

How The Order Came To Control Yale University

From Sheffield Scientific School The Order broadened its horizons.

The Order's control over all Yale was evident by the 1870s, even under the administration of Noah Porter (1871-1881), who was not a member. In the decades after the 1870s, The Order tightened its grip. *The Iconoclast* (October 13, 1873) summarizes the facts we have presented on control of Yale by The Order, without being fully aware of the details:

"They have obtained control of Yale. Its business is performed by them. Money paid to the college must pass into their hands, and be subject to their will. No doubt they are worthy men in themselves, but the many whom they looked down upon while in college, cannot so far forget as to give money freely into their hands. Men in Wall Street complain that the college comes straight to them for help, instead of asking each graduate for his share. The reason is found in a remark made by one of Yale's and America's first men: 'Few will give but Bones men, and they care far more for their society than they do for the college.' The Woolsey Fund has but a struggling existence, for kindred reasons."

"Here, then, appears the true reason for Yale's poverty. She is controlled by a few men who shut themselves off from others, and assume to be their superiors . . ."

The anonymous writer of *Iconoclast* blames The Order for the poverty of Yale. But worse was to come. Then-President Noah Porter was the last of the clerical Presidents of Yale (1871-1881), and the last without either membership or family connections to The Order.

After 1871 the Yale Presidency became almost a fiefdom for The Order.

From 1886 to 1899, member Timothy Dwight ('49) was President, followed by another member of The Order, Arthur Twining Hadley (1899 to 1921). Then came James R. Angell (1921-37), not a member of The Order, who came to Yale from the University of Chicago where he worked with Dewey, built the School of Education, and was past President of the American Psychological Association.

From 1937 to 1950 Charles Seymour, a member of The Order, was President followed by Alfred Whitney Griswold from 1950 to 1963. Griswold was not a member, but both the Griswold and Whitney families have members in The Order. For example, Dwight Torrey Griswold ('08) and William Edward Schenk Griswold ('99) were in The Order. In 1963 Kingman Brewster took over as President. The Brewster family has had several members in The Order, in law and the ministry rather than education.

We can best conclude this memorandum with a quotation from the anonymous Yale observer:

"Whatever want the college suffers, whatever is lacking in her educational course, whatever disgrace lies in her poor buildings, whatever embarrassments have beset her needy students, so far as money could have availed, the weight of blame lies upon this ill-starred society. The pecuniary question is one of the future as well as of the present and past. Year by year the deadly evil is growing. The society was never as obnoxious to the college as it is today, and it is just this ill-feeling that shuts the pockets of nonmembers. Never before has it shown such arrogance and self-fancied superiority. It grasps the College Press and endeavors to rule in all. It does not deign to show its credentials, but clutches at power with the silence of conscious guilt."

APPENDIX TO MEMORANDUM NUMBER ONE:
THE ORDER IN THE YALE FACULTY

Member	Date Initiated	Position at Yale
BEEBE, William	1873	Professor of Mathematics (1882-1917)
BEERS, Henry A.	1869	Professor of English Literature (1874-1926)
BELLINGER, Alfred R.	1917	Professor of Greek (1926-
DAHL, George	1908	Professor Yale Divinity School (1914-1929)
DARLING, Arthûr B.	1916	Professor of History (1925-1933)
DAY, Clive	1892	Professor of Economic History (1902-1938)
DEXTER, Franklin B.	1861	Secretary, Yale University (1869-99)
DWIGHT, Timothy	1849	President of Yale University (1886-98)
FARNAM, Henry	1874	Professor of Economics (1880-1933)
FARNAM, William	1866	Trustee Sheffield Scientific School (1894-1923)
FRENCH, Robert D.	1910	Professor of English (1919-1950)
GILMAN, Daniel C.	1852	See text.
GRAVES, Henry S.	1892	Dean, Yale School of Forestry (1900-1939)
GRUENER, G.	1884	Professor of German (1892-1928)
HADLEY, Arthur T.	1876	President of Yale (1899-1921)
HILLES, Frederick W.	1922	Professor of English (1931-
HOLDEN, Reuben A.	1940	Assistant to President (1947-
HOPPIN, James M.	1840	Professor of History of Art (1861-99)
INGERSOLL, James W.	1892	Professor of Latin (1897-1921)
JONES, Frederick S.	1884	Dean, Yale College 1909-1926)
LEWIS, Charlton M.	1886	Professor of English (1898-1923)
LOHMAN, Carl A.	1910	Secretary, Yale University (1927-
LYMAN, Chester	1837	Professor of Mechanics (1859-1890)
McLAUGHLIN, Edward T.	1883	Professor of English (1890-93)
NORTHROP, Cyrus	1857	Professor of English (1863-84)
PACKARD, Lewis R.	1856	Professor of Greek (1863-84)
PECK, Tracy	1861	Professor of Latin (1889-1908)
PERRIN, Bernadotte	1869	Professor of Greek (1893-1909)
PIERCE, Frederick E.	1904	Professor of English (1910-35)
ROOT, Reginald D.	1926	Yale football coach (1933-48)
SCHWAB, John C.	1886	Professor of Political Economy (1893-1906)
SEYMOUR, Charles	1908	Professor of History (1915-37) President (1936-1950)
SEYMOUR, Charles Jr.	1935	Professor of Art (1949-
SILLIMAN, Benjamin Jr.	1837	Professor of Chemistry (1846-85)
STOKES, Anson P.	1896	Secretary of Yale (1899-1921)
SUMNER, William G.	1863	Professor of Economics (1872-1909)
TAFT, William H.	1878	Professor of Law (1913)
TARBELL, Frank B.	1873	Professor of Greek (1882-87)
THACHER, Thomas A.	1835	Professor of Latin (1842-86)
THOMPSON, John R.	1938	Professor of Law (1949-
WALKER, Charles R.	1916	Assistant Secretary (1943-45)
WOOLSEY, Theodore S.	1872	Professor of International Law (1878-1929)
WRIGHT, Henry B.	1898	Professor of History (1907-11)
WRIGHT, Henry P.	1868	Professor of Latin (1871-1918) Dean, Yale College (1884-1909)

Memorandum Number Two:
The Look-Say Reading Scam

A tragic failure of American education in this century has been a failure to teach children how to read and write and how to express themselves in a literary form. For the educational system this may not be too distressing. As we shall see later, their prime purpose is not to teach subject matter but to condition children to live as socially integrated citizen units in an organic society — a real life enactment of the Hegelian absolute State. In this State the individual finds freedom only in obedience to the State, consequently the function of education is to prepare the individual citizen unit for smooth entry into the organic whole.

However, it is puzzling that the educational system allowed reading to deteriorate so markedly. It could be that The Order wants the citizen components of the organic State to be little more than automated order takers; after all a citizen who cannot read and write is not going to challenge The Order. But this is surmise. It is not, on the basis of the evidence presently at hand, a provable proposition.

In any event, the system adopted the look-say method of learning to read, originally developed for deaf mutes. The system has produced generations of Americans who are functionally illiterate. Yet, reading is essential for learning and learning is essential for most occupations. And certainly those who **can** read or write lack vocabulary in depth and stylistic skills. There are, of course, exceptions. This author spent five years teaching at a State University in the early 1960s and was appalled by the general inability to write coherent English, yet gratified that some students had not only evaded the system, acquired vocabulary and writing skills, but these exceptions had the most skepticism about The Establishment.

The Order comes into adoption of the look-say method directly and indirectly. Let's start at the beginning.

The Founder Of Deaf Mute Instruction

Look-say reading methods were developed around 1810 for deaf mutes by a truly remarkable man, Thomas Hopkins Gallaudet. Thomas H. Gallaudet was the eldest son of Peter Wallace Gallaudet, descended from a French Huguenot family, and Jane Hopkins. Jane Hopkins traced her ancestry back to John Hopkins and the Reverend Thomas Hooker in the seventeenth century, who broke away from the Congregational Church to help found Hartford, Connecticut. This parallels the story of the Lord family (see Volume One). The Lords also traced their ancestry back to Hopkins and Hooker and the Lords founded Hartford, Connecticut. And it was in Hartford, Connecticut in 1835 that a printer named Lord produced Thomas Gallaudet's first look-say primer, *Mother's Primer*.

Gallaudet's original intention was to use the look-say method only for deaf mutes who have no concept of a spoken language and are therefore unaware of phonetic sounds for letters. For this purpose, Gallaudet founded the Hartford School for the Deaf in 1817. The Gallaudet system works well for deaf mutes, but there is no obvious reason to use it for those who have the ability to hear sounds.

Anyway, in 1835 *Mother's Primer* was published and the Massachusetts Primary School Committee under Horace Mann immediately adopted the book on an experimental basis. Later we shall find that Horace Mann ties directly to The Order — in fact, the co-founder of The Order. On pages 73-74 we reproduce two pages from the second edition of 1836, with the following directions to the teacher:

". . . pointing to the whole word Frank, but not to the letters. Nothing is yet to be said about letters. . ."

a printer named Lord produced Thomas Gallaudet's first look-say primer, *Mother's Primer*.

Gallaudet's original intention was to use the look-say method only for deaf mutes who have no concept of a spoken language and are therefore unaware of phonetic sounds for letters. For this purpose, Gallaudet founded the Hartford School for the Deaf in 1817. The Gallaudet system works well for deaf mutes, but there is no obvious reason to use it for those who have the ability to hear sounds.

Anyway, in 1835 *Mother's Primer* was published and the Massachusetts Primary School Committee under Horace Mann immediately adopted the book on an experimental basis. Later we shall find that Horace Mann ties directly to The Order — in fact, the co-founder of The Order. On pages 73-74 we reproduce two pages from the second edition of 1836, with the following directions to the teacher:

". . . pointing to the whole word Frank, but not to the letters. Nothing is yet to be said about letters. . ."

THE

MOTHER'S PRIMER,

TO

TEACH HER CHILD ITS LETTERS,

AND

HOW TO READ.

DESIGNED ALSO FOR THE

LOWEST CLASS IN PRIMARY SCHOOLS.

ON A NEW PLAN.

BY REV. T. H. GALLAUDET,
Late Principal of the Deaf and Dumb Asylum, Hartford.

SECOND EDITION.

HARTFORD.
DANIEL BURGESS & CO.
1836.

THE MOTHER'S PRIMER.   9

frank   jane

frank   jane
jane   frank
frank
jane

Directions to the Teacher.—Say to the child, pointing to the first picture, "What is that? Do you know his name? I wonder if he has a name. Suppose we call him *Frank*. O there is his name, right under him," pointing to the *whole word*, Frank, but not to the letters. *Nothing is yet to be said about letters.* "Here is his name again. And here it is again. And here it is once more. What is that?" pointing to the other picture. "Perhaps it is Frank's sister. What is her name? O here is her name. It is Jane. Can you show me her name again?—again—once more." Repeat till the child can tell the words readily.

10   THE MOTHER'S PRIMER.

dog   cat

dog   cat
cat   dog
dog
cat
frank
jane

Point to the first picture, "What is that? Here is the word *dog* under the picture. Can you show me the word *dog* again?—again,—once more. That is Frank's dog. Well here is Jane's"——(pointing to the second picture,) "What? Can you tell me? What word do you think that is right under Jane's cat? Can you show me the word *cat* again?—again,—once more." Pointing to the word *Frank,* "What word is this?" So with the word *Jane.* Repeat till the words are thoroughly learned.

Why did Horace Mann push a method designed for deaf mutes onto a school system populated with persons who were not deaf mutes?

There are two possible reasons. The reader can take his or her pick.

First, in 1853 Mann was appointed President of Antioch College. The most influential Trustee of Antioch College was the co-founder of The Order — Alphonso Taft.

Second, Mann never had a proper education and consequently was unable to judge a good method from a bad method for reading. Here's a description of Mann's school days:

"The opportunities for the lad's schooling were extremely meagre. The locality enjoyed the reputation of being the smallest school district, with the poorest school house and the cheapest teacher in the State."

Mann's teacher was Samuel Barratt and we quote: "In arithmetic he was an idiot. He could not recite the multiplication table and could not tell the time of day by the clock . . . Six months of the year he was an earnest and reliable teacher, tasting nothing stronger than tea, then for another six months he gave himself up to a state of beastly drunkeness . . ."

By 1840 there was a backlash, and the look-say system was dropped in Massachusetts.

The Second Attempt

Towards the end of the 19th century The Order came on the scene — and the look-say method was revived. The youngest son of Thomas Hopkins and Sophia Gallaudet was Edward Miner Gallaudet. Two of his sons went to Yale and became members of The Order:

- Edson Fessenden Gallaudet ('93), who became an instructor of physics at Yale, and
- Herbert Draper Gallaudet ('98), who attended Union Theological Seminary and became a clergyman.

Then the method was adopted by Columbia Teachers' College and the Lincoln School. The thrust of the new Dewey-inspired system of education was away from learning and towards preparing a child to be a unit in the organic society. Look-say was ideal for Deweyites. It skipped one step in the learning process. It looked "easy," and de-emphasized reading skills.

The educational establishment rationalized look-say be claiming that up to the turn of the century reading was taught by "synthetic" methods, i.e., children were taught letters and an associated sound value. Then they learned to join syllables to make words. This was held to be uninteresting and artificial. Educational research, it was claimed, demonstrated that in reading words are not analyzed into component letter parts but seen as complete units. Therefore, learning to read should start with complete units.

Education

Of course, there is a gigantic nonsequitur in this reasoning process. Certainly a skilled reader does see words as complete units. And a really skilled reader does see lines and paragraphs at a glance. But the accuracy of perceiving the whole is based on the degree of understanding and knowledge of the component parts.

The educational establishment argues today in the 1980s that, based on further experimental testing, it is easier for a child to read the line "the rocket zoomed into space" than "the cat sat on the mat." The first line has "constrasting visual structure" and the second quote has a "similar visual pattern."

What they have done now is to make a mountain out of a molehill, convert the relatively simple task of learning to read into an unnecessarily complex system.

Why? That we shall see as the story progresses.

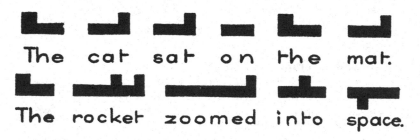

The visual patterns of words in two sentences

How children are taught to read - and why they can't.

Memorandum Number Three:
The Illuminati Connection

We need to trace three historical lines in modern education: the first we looked at in Memorandum Number Two, the development of the look-say method of reading, its abandonment and its later adoption around the turn of the century.

Another line is the import of the experimental psychology of Wilhelm Wundt into the United States by The Order. This we shall examine in Memorandum Number Four.

For the moment we want to briefly trace the influence of Johann Friedrich Herbart, a major German philosopher of the early 19th century. There was at one time in the United States a National Herbart Society for the Scientific Study of Education to adapt Herbartian principles to American education. Later, this became just National Society for the Study of Education. You don't hear too much about Johann Herbart today, but his influence survives in the so-called "enriched" school curricula and in current educational methodology.

Our purpose in this memorandum is twofold: to show the Hegelian aspects of Herbartian theory and to trace the Illuminati connection. There is no direct connection to The Order. However, in a subsequent book, we will trace The Order to the Illuminati and this section will then fall into a logical place.

Herbart was an educational theorist as well as philosopher and psychologist, and strongly influenced Wilhelm Wundt. For Herbart, education had to be presented in a scientifically correct manner, and the chief purpose of education for Herbart is to prepare the child to live properly in the social order of which he is an integral part. Following Hegel, the individual is not important. The mere development of individual talent, of individual fitness, mental power and knowledge is not the purpose of education. The purpose is to develop personal character and social morality, and the most important task of the educator is to analyze the activities and duties of men within society.

The function of instruction is to fulfill these aims and impart to the individual socially desirable ideas. Morality for Herbart, therefore, is what is good for society, following Hegelian theory.

Herbartians favor grouping of subjects around a core topic, i.e., the grouping of history, social science and English literature. This enables the teacher to more easily draw out those notions useful to the objective.

All of these ideas we can recognize in today's educational philosophy came into American education through the Herbartian groups.

INTERNATIONAL EDUCATION SERIES

HERBART'S A B C

OF SENSE-PERCEPTION

AND MINOR PEDAGOGICAL WORKS

TRANSLATED, WITH INTRODUCTION, NOTES, AND COMMENTARY, BY

WILLIAM J. ECKOFF

Ph. D. (Columbia), Pd. D. (N. Y. U.)

FORMERLY PROFESSOR OF PHILOSOPHY AND PEDAGOGY IN THE UNIVERSITY OF COLORADO, AND OF PEDAGOGY IN THE UNIVERSITY OF ILLINOIS AUTHOR OF "KANT'S INAUGURAL DISSERTATION"

NEW YORK

D. APPLETON AND COMPANY

1896

The Illuminati Connection

Johann Herbart studied at the University of Jena, and came under the influence of Johann Herder, Friedrich Schiller, Johann Fichte and Johann Goethe. Later, in Switzerland, Herbart came into contact with Johann Pestalozzi.

What is interesting about these names, and they comprise the most important influence on Herbart, is that they are either known members of the Illuminati or reputed to be close to the Illuminati Order.

Let's take each name in turn:

- Johann Gottfried Herder (1744-1803) was "Damascus pontifex" in the Illuminato.
- Johann Fichte, we have already noted in the previous volume, was close to the Illuminati and pushed by Goethe ("Abaris") for the post at the University of Jena, where Johann Herbart was studying.
- Friedrich Schiller (1759-1805) was known in the circle but not reliably recorded as an Illuminati member.
- Johann Wolfgang Goethe (1749-1832) was "Abaris" in the Illuminati.

We have an even more precise connection for another prominent Illuminati, Johann Heinrich Pestalozzi (1746-1827), a Swiss teacher of some renown living at Interlaken, and known as "Alfred" in the Illuminati code.

Before Herbart completed his doctorate, just after the turn of the 19th century, he spent three years at Interlaken in Switzerland. Out of his contact with Pestalozzi came a book on Pestalozzi's educational theories, much of which rubbed off onto Herbart. The book is *Pestalozzi's Idee Eines ABC Der Anschaung Untersucht Und Wissenschaftlich Asugefuhrt* (Pestalozzi's idea of an ABC of sense impression). This book has been translated and we reproduce a copy of the title page of the 1896 New York edition. This is not insignificant. It is a commentary by a prominent influence on today's education upon an Illuminati book.

Why Is The Illuminati Connection Significant?

The Illuminati was founded May 1, 1776 by Professor Adam Weishaupt of the University of Ingolstadt. It was a secret society, but in 1785 and 1787 several batches of internal documents came to the Bavarian Government. Subsequent investigation determined that the aim of the Illuminati was world domination, using any methods to advance the objective, i.e., the end always justifies the means. It was anti-Christian, although clergymen were found in the organization. Each member had a pseudonym to disguise his identity.

During its time, the Illuminati had widespread and influential membership. After suppression by the Bavarian Government in 1788 it was quiet for some years and then reportedly revived.

The significance for this study is that the methods and objectives parallel those of The Order. In fact, infiltration of the Illuminati into New England is known and will be the topic of a forthcoming volume.

So far as education is concerned, the Illuminati objective was as follows:

"We must win the common people in every corner. This will be obtained chiefly by means of the schools, and by open, hearty behaviour, show, condescension, popularity and toleration of their prejudices which we shall at leisure root out and dispel."

As Rosenbaum has pointed out in his *Esquire* article, the Illuminati ceremony has similarities to The Order. For example, John Robison in *Proofs Of A Conspiracy:*[1] "The candidate is presented for reception in the character of a slave; and it is demanded of him what has brought him to this most miserable of all conditions. He answers — Society - the State - Submissiveness - False Religion. A skeleton is pointed out to him, at the feet of which are laid a Crown and a Sword. He is asked whether that is the skeleton of a King, a Nobleman or a Beggar?

As he cannot decide, the President of the meeting says to him, "the character of being a man is the only one that is of importance."

Finally, in conclusion, we can trace the foundation of three secret societies, in fact the most influential three secret societies that we know about, to Universities. The Illuminati was founded at University of Ingolstadt. The Group was founded at All Souls College, Oxford University in England, and The Order was founded at Yale University in the United States.

The paradox is that institutions supposedly devoted to the search for truth and freedom have given birth to institutions devoted to world enslavement.

---

[1]John Robinson. PROOFS OF A CONSPIRACY (Americanist Classics. Belmont. 1967). p. 110.

Memorandum Number Four:
The Leipzig Connection*

The link between German experimental psychology and the American educational system is through American psychologist G. Stanley Hall, in his time probably the foremost educational critic in the U.S.

The Hall family is Scotch and English and goes back to the 1630s, but Hall was not a Yale graduate, and **at first sight** there is no connection between Hall and The Order.

On the other hand, Hall is a good example of someone whose life has major turning points and on probing the turning points, we find The Order with its guiding hand. The detail below is important to link Hall with The Order. It is an open question how much Hall knew, if he knew anything at all, about The Order and its objectives.

After graduation from Williams College, Hall spent a year at the Union Theological Seminary, New York. Our "Addresses" books for The Order do not give church affiliations for members citing the ministry as their occupation. We do know that Rev. Henry Sloane Coffin ('97) was Associate Professor of Practical Theology at Union from 1904-1926 and President of Union Seminary from 1926 to 1945, but we cannot trace any members at Union before 1904.

Fortunately, Hall was an egocentric and wrote two long, tedious autobiographies: *Recreations Of A Psychologist* and *Life And Confessions Of A Psychologist*. This is how Hall described his entry to Union in the latter book (pp. 177-8):

> "Recovering from a severe attack of typhoid fever the summer after graduation and still being very uncertain as to what I would be and do in the world, I entered Union Theological Seminary in September 1867."

Later Hall adds,

> "The man to whom I owe far more in this group than any other was Henry B. Smith, a foreign trained scholar, versed more or less not only in systematic theology, which was his chair, but in ancient and modern philosophy, on which he gave us a few lectures outside the course. Of him alone I saw something socially. He did me perhaps the greatest intellectual service one man can render another by suggesting just the right reading at the right time. It was he, too, who seeing my bent advised me to go to Europe."

*The Leipzig Connection is the title of an excellent little booklet by Lance J. Klass and Paoli Lionni, published by The Delphian Press, Route 2, Box 195, Sheridan, Oregon 97378 ($4.00 postpaid). The book came out in 1967 and was the first to trace the Wundt link. It has more detail on Wundt than this memorandum, but, of course, is not concerned with The Order.

The Rev. Henry Boynton Smith cited by Hall was Professor of Church History at Union Seminary from 1850 to 1874, and in the "liberal" wing of the Presbyterian Church, he edited *Theological Review* from 1859-1874 and translated several German theological works. Smith was not a member of The Order.

How did Hall, who says he was broke, get from New York to Europe, specifically to Germany?

Here's the interesting twist. Someone he didn't know (but whom today we can trace to The Order) gave him $1,000 — a lot of money in those days. Here's how it happened. While preaching in Pennsylvania in 1868, Hall received a letter from Rev. Henry Ward Beecher, whose church he attended in New York:

". . . asking me to call on him. I immediately took the train and Beecher told me that through the Manns (friends) he had learned that I wished to study philosophy in Germany but lacked the means . . . (he) gave me a sealed note to the lumber magnate Henry Sage, the benefactor of Cornell, which I presented at his office without knowing its contents. To my amazement, after some scowling and a remark to the effect that his pastor took amazing liberties with his purse, he gave me a check for one thousand dollars. Taking my note to repay it with interest, he told me to sail for Germany the next day" (*Confessions*, p. 182).

Who was "lumber magnate Henry Sage, the benefactor of Cornell"?

The Sage family had several "Henrys" involved with Yale and Cornell Universities in those days. The "Henry Sage" cited is probably William Henry Sage (1844-1924) who graduated Yale 1865 and then joined the family lumber company, H.W. Sage & Company in New York. Henry Sage was a member of Scroll & Key — the sister Senior Society to Skull & Bones at Yale. Furthermore, two of Henry Sage's nephews were in The Order, but well after 1868:

• Dean Sage ('97)

• Henry Manning Sage ('90)

Both Sages entered the family lumber business, by then renamed Sage Land & Lumber.

In brief: the funds to get Hall to Germany on his first trip came from a member of Scroll & Key, i.e., Henry Sage, while Sage's two nephews joined The Order later in the century.

In Germany, Hall studied philosophy at the University of Berlin for two years under Hegelians Trendelenberg (Gilman of The Order also studied under Trendelenberg) and Lepsius. There were few American students in Berlin at this time. So few that the American Minister George Bancroft could entertain them at the U.S. Embassy to meet German Chancellor von Bismarck.

Hall At Antioch College

Hall returned to the U.S. from Germany in 1871 and by design or accident found himself under the wing of The Order.

Again, the detail is important. There are two versions of Hall's life immediately after returning from his first trip to Germany. According to Hall's *Confessions*, he became tutor for the Seligman banking family in New York and was then contacted by James K. Hosmer, Professor at Antioch College, Yellow Springs, Ohio. Hosmer asked, and this is **very** unusual, if Hall would like his professorial post at Antioch. Said Hall, "I gladly accepted."

There is another version in *National Cyclopaedia Of American Biography* which states, "In 1872 he (Hall) accepted a professorship at Antioch College, Ohio, that formerly was held by Horace Mann."

In any event Hall went to Antioch, a "liberal" Unitarian college with a more than "liberal" view of education. And at Antioch College, G. Stanley Hall was at the core of The Order.

Horace Mann, whom we met in Memorandum Two as the promoter of "look-say" reading, was the first President of Antioch (1853-1860). The most prominent trustee of Antioch College was none other than the co-founder of The Order, Alphonso Taft. According to Hall, "(I) occasionally spent a Sunday with the Tafts. Ex-President Taft was then a boy and his father, Judge Alonzo (sic) Taft was a trustee of Antioch College" (*Confessions*, p. 201).

Furthermore, Cincinnati, Ohio, at that time was the center for a Young Hegelian movement including famous left Hegelian August Willich, and these were well known to Judge Alphonso Taft.

The Americanization Of Wilhelm Wundt

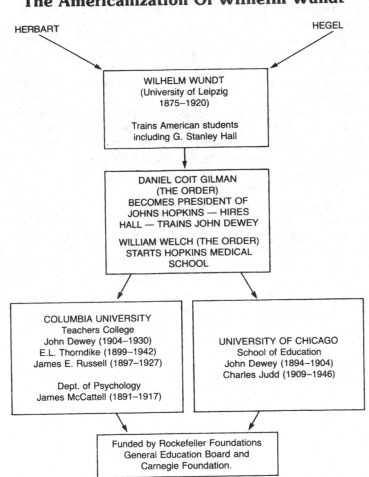

HERBART

HEGEL

WILHELM WUNDT
(University of Leipzig
1875–1920)

Trains American students
including G. Stanley Hall

DANIEL COIT GILMAN
(THE ORDER)
BECOMES PRESIDENT OF
JOHNS HOPKINS — HIRES
HALL — TRAINS JOHN DEWEY

WILLIAM WELCH (THE ORDER)
STARTS HOPKINS MEDICAL
SCHOOL

COLUMBIA UNIVERSITY
Teachers College
John Dewey (1904–1930)
E.L. Thorndike (1899–1942)
James E. Russell (1897–1927)

Dept. of Psychology
James McCattell (1891–1917)

UNIVERSITY OF CHICAGO
School of Education
John Dewey (1894–1904)
Charles Judd (1909–1946)

Funded by Rockefeller Foundations
General Education Board and
Carnegie Foundation.

In brief, while at Antioch College in Yellow Springs, Ohio, Hall came under the influence of four groups:

(a) the legend of Horace Mann, a hero of the modern education movement.

(b) the Unitarian Church, which will enter our later reports,

(c) a Hegelian discussion group comprised of left Hegelians, and

(d) the co-founder of The Order, Alphonso Taft. And Hall knew William Howard Taft, also a member of The Order ('78) and future President and Chief Justice of the United States.

Hall stayed four years at Antioch, then took off again for Europe, while Alphonso Taft went to Washington, D.C. as Secretary of War, then as Attorney General in the Grant Administration. Hall paused a while in England and then went on to Germany, to Leipzig and Wilhelm Wundt. He became the first of a dozen Americans to receive a Ph.D. in psychology (a new field) under Wundt.

The Hegelian Influence On Hall

So between 1870 and 1882, a span of twelve years, Hall spent six years in Germany. As Hall himself comments,

"I do not know of any other American student of these subjects (i.e., philosophy and psychology) who came into even the slight personal contact it was my fortune to enjoy with Hartmann and Fechner, nor of any psychologist who had the experience of attempting experimental work with Helmholtz and I think I was the first American pupil of Wundt. The twelve years included in this span, more than any other equal period, marked and gave direction to modern psychology . . ."[1]

Who were these four German philosophers who so influenced Stanley Hall?

Eduard von Hartmann (1842-1906), a prominent philosopher. Hartmann's views on individual rights are entirely contrary to our own, i.e., "The principle of freedom is negative . . . in every department of life, save religion alone, compulsion is necessary . . . What all men need is rational tyranny, if it only holds them to a steady development, according to the laws of their own nature."

There isn't too much difference between Hegel and Hartmann on the idea of social progress. Individual freedom is not acceptable to these philosophers, man must be guided by "rational tyranny."

Gustav Theodor Fechner (1801-1887). Fechner disliked Hegel, who Fechner said, "unlearned men to think." However, Fechner was mainly interested in psycho-physics, i.e., parapsychology:

[1]G. Stanley Hall, FOUNDERS OF MODERN PSYCHOLOGY. Appleton & Co., London, 1912, pp. v-vi.

". . . he was particularly attracted to the unexplored regions of the soul and so he became interested in somnambulism, attended seances when table tapping came into vogue."

Herman L. F. von Helmholtz (1821-1894) was undoubtedly Germany's greatest scientist in the 19th century and was rooted in Kant, the predecessor of Hegel.

For Helmholtz:

"The sensible world is a product of the interaction between the human organism and an unknown reality. The world of experience is determined by this interaction but the organism itself is only an object of experience and is to be understood by psychology and physiology."

Wilhelm Maximilian Wundt

Wilhelm Wundt (1832-1920), Professor of Philosophy at University of Leipzig, was undoubtedly the major influence on G. Stanley Hall. Modern education practice stems from Hegelian social theory combined with the experimental psychology of Wilhelm Wundt. Whereas Karl Marx and von Bismarck applied Hegelian theory to the political field, it was Wilhelm Wundt, influenced by Johann Herbart, who applied Hegel to education, which in turn, was picked up by Hall and John Dewey and modern educational theorists in the United States.

Wilhelm Maximilian Wundt was born August 16, 1832 at Neckarau, a suburb of Mannheim, Germany. His father Maximilian (1787-1846) was a minister. Wundt's grandfather on the paternal side is of significant interest: Kirchenrat Karl Kasimir Wundt (1744-84) was Professor at Heidelberg University in the history and geography of Baden and pastor of the church at Wieblingen, a small neighborhood town.

The Illuminati-Order documents show that "Raphael" in the Illuminati is identified as this same Professor Karl Kasimir Wundt and is referred to in the Illuminati Provincial Report from Utica (i.e., Heidelberg) dated September 1782.[1]

The magnum opus of Wilhelm Wundt, i.e., *Volkerpsychologie*, is also today a recommended book in *Internationales Freimaurer Lexikon* (page 50).

Historical links aside, Wundt is important in the history of American education for the following reasons:

(1) He established in 1875 the world's first laboratory in experimental psychology to measure individual responses to stimuli.

---

[1]Richard van Dulman, *Der Geheimbund Der Illuminaten* (Stuttgart, 1977, p. 269).

(2) Wundt believed that man is only the summation of his experience, i.e., the stimuli that bear upon him. It follows from this that, for Wundt, man has no self will, no self determination. Man is in effect only the captive of his experiences, a pawn needing guidance.

(3) Students from Europe and the United States came to Leipzig to learn from Wundt the new science of experimental psychology. These students returned to their homelands to found schools of education or departments of psychology, and trained hundreds of Ph.D.s in the new field of psychology.

The core of our problem is that Wundt's work was based on Hegelian philosophical theory and reflected the Hegelian view of the individual as a valueless cog in the State, a view expanded by Wundt to include man as nothing more than an animal influenced solely by daily experiences.

This Wundtian view of the world was brought back from Leipzig to the United States by G. Stanley Hall and other Americans and went through what is known among psychologists as "The Americanization of Wundt."

Although Hall was primarily psychologist and teacher, his political views were partially Marxist, as Hall himself writes: ". . . (I) had wrestled with Karl Marx and half accepted what I understood of him" (*Confessions*, p. 222).

In the next Memorandum, Number Five, we will link Hall with Gilman and trace their joint influence on American education.

Memorandum Number Five:
The Baltimore Scheme

While G. Stanley Hall was in Leipzig working under Wilhelm Wundt, the revolutionary trio Gilman-Dwight-White were moving events back home — and The Order ran into its first organized opposition.

The protesting "neutrals" at Yale had no hope of winning. Even under independent President Noah Porter in the 1870s, The Order had Yale University under its control. But while Yale students were watching, protesting and writing bad verse, Daniel Gilman ran into opposition 3000 miles away — and if the leaders of this counter revolution had known the story we are recounting here, they might just have stopped The Order dead in its tracks.

In 1867 Daniel Gilman received an offer as President of the University of Wisconsin. This he declined. In 1872 Gilman was offered the Presidency of the newly established University of California. This offer he accepted.

In California Gilman found a political hornets' nest. For some years there had been increasing popular concern about the railroad monopolies, government subsidies to railroads and — oddly enough — the Morrill Bill which gave federal land grants to agricultural and scientific colleges. The reader will recall that in Connecticut and New York, The Order had grabbed the total state's share for Yale and Cornell respectively. Californians believed that the University of California, a land grant college, should teach agriculture and science, whereas Gilman had different ideas. Unrest over corruption, including corruption among University of California Regents and the railroads (in which members of The Order had widespread interests), led to formation of a new California political party.

In 1873 the party was known as the Patrons of Husbandry or the Grangers. Then members of the Republican Party broke away and joined with the Grangers to form the Peoples Independent Party (known also as the Dolly Varden Party). They won a decisive victory in the 1873 California elections and following investigations by the Grangers, a petition was sent to the Legislature concerning operation of the University of California under Daniel Gilman.

At that time Henry George was editor of the San Francisco *Daily Evening Post* and George used his considerable journalistic skills to attack the University, the Regents, Gilman, and the land grants. Although Henry George is known as a socialist, we classify him as an independent socialist, not part of the Hegelian right-left spectrum. His main target was land **monopoly,** whereas the "scientific" Hegelian socialism of Karl Marx is geared to establishing monopolies of all kinds under state control, following the Hegelian theory of the supremacy of the State.

This populist furor scared Gilman, as he freely admits:

". . . there are dangers here which I could not foresee. . . . This year the dangers have been averted but who can tell what will happen two years hence? I feel that we are building a superior structure but it rests over a powder mill which may blow it up any day. All these conditions fill me with perplexity."

Reading between the lines, Daniel Gilman was not too anxious to face the populist west. He needed a more stable base where prying journalists and independent politicians could be headed off. And this base presented itself in the "Baltimore scheme."

Daniel Gilman Becomes President Of Johns Hopkins

Johns Hopkins, a wealthy Baltimore merchant, left his fortune to establish a University for graduate education (the first in the United States along German lines) and a medical school.

Hopkins' trustees were all friends who lived in Baltimore. How then did they come to select Daniel Coit Gilman as President of the new University?

In 1874 the trustees invited three university presidents to come to Baltimore and advise on the choice of a President. These were Charles W. Eliot of Harvard, Andrew Dickson White of Cornell, and James B. Angell of Michigan. Only Andrew Dickson White was in The Order. After meeting independently with each of these presidents, half a dozen of the trustees toured several American Universities in search of further information — and Andrew D. White accompanied the tour. The result was, in the words of James Angell:

"And now I have this remarkable statement to make to you, that without the least conference between us three, we all wrote letters telling them that the one man was Daniel C. Gilman of California."[1]

The truth is that Gilman not only knew what was going on in Baltimore, but was in communication with Andrew White on the "Baltimore scheme," as they called it.

In a letter dated April 5, 1874, Gilman wrote as follows to Andrew D. White:

"I could not conclude on any new proposition without conferring upon it with some of my family friends, and I have not felt at liberty to do so. I confess that the **Baltimore** (italics in original) scheme has ofttimes suggested itself to me, but I have no personal relations in that quarter."[2]

[1]John C. French. A HISTORY OF THE UNIVERSITY FOUNDED BY JOHNS HOPKINS (The Johns Hopkins Press. Baltimore. 1946). p. 26.
[2]LIFE OF DANIEL COIT GILMAN. p. 157.

Here's the interesting point: the board appointed by Johns Hopkins to found a university did not even meet to adopt its by-laws and appoint committees until **four weeks** before this letter i.e., March 7, 1874. Yet Gilman tells us "the **Baltimore** scheme has ofttimes suggested itself to me . . ."

In brief: Gilman knew what was happening over in Baltimore BEFORE HIS NAME HAD BEEN PRESENTED TO THE TRUSTEES!

Gilman became first President of Johns Hopkins University and quickly set to work.

Johns Hopkins had willed substantial amounts for both a University and a medical school. Dr. William H. Welch ('70), a fellow member of The Order, was brought in by Gilman to head up the Hopkins medical school. (Welch was President of the Board of Directors of the Rockefeller Institute of Medical Research for almost 25 years, 1910-1934. This we shall expand upon later in the series when we examine how The Order came to control medicine). For the moment let's return to G. Stanley Hall who was in Leipzig while Johns Hopkins was acquiring its new President.

Gilman Starts The Revolution in American Education

When he returned to the United States Hall was feeling pretty low:

"I came home, again in the depths because of debt and with no prospects, took a small flat on the edge of Somerville, where my two children were born, and waited, hoped and worked. One Wednesday morning President Eliot (of Harvard University) rode up to the house, rapped on the door without dismounting from his horse and asked me to begin Saturday of that week a course of lectures on education . . ."

As Hall recounts it, he had a "very impressive audience" for these lectures. Sometime later,

"In 1881 I was surprised and delighted to receive an invitation from the Johns Hopkins University, then the cynosure of all aspiring young professors, to deliver a course of twelve semi-public lectures on psychology."

At the end of the lecture series, Gilman offered Hall the chair of Professor of Psychology and Pedagogy. This puzzled Hall because others at Johns Hopkins were "older and abler" than himself and

"Why the appointment for which all of them had been considered fell to me I was never able to understand unless it was because my standpoint was thought to be a little more accordant with the ideals which then prevailed there."

Hall was given a psychological laboratory, a thousand dollars a year for equipment and, with the encouragement of Gilman, founded *The American Journal Of Psychology.*

And what did Hall teach? Again in his own words:

"The psychology I taught was almost entirely experimental and covered for the most part the material that Wundt had set forth in the later and larger edition of *Physiological Psychology.*"

The rest is known. The chart demonstrates how doctoral students from Wundt and Hall fanned out through the United States, established departments of psychology and education by the score; 117 psychological laboratories just in the period up to 1930. Prominent among these students were John Dewey, J.M. Cattell and E.L. Thorndike — all part of the founding of Columbia Teachers' College and Chicago's School of Education — the two sources of modern American education.

Their activities can be measured by the number of doctorates in educational psychology and experimental psychology granted in the period up to 1948. The following list includes psychologists with training in Germany under Wilhelm Wundt before 1900, and the number of doctorates they in turn awarded up to 1948:

American Students of Wundt Teaching at U.S. Universities	Career At	Number of Doctorates They Awarded up to 1948
G. Stanley Hall	Johns Hopkins and Clark University	149 doctorates
J. McKeen Cattell	Columbia University	344 doctorates
E.W. Scripture	Yale University	138 doctorates
E.B. Titchener	Cornell University	112 doctorates
H. Gale	Minnesota University	123 doctorates
G.T.W. Patrick	Iowa University	269 doctorates
C.H. Judd	University of Chicago	196 doctorates

Of these only E.B. Titchener at Cornell could be called a critic of the Wundt school of experimental psychology. The rest followed the party line: an amalgamation of Hegelian philosophy and Wundtian animal psychology.

So from the seed sown by Daniel Coit Gilman at Johns Hopkins grew the vast network of interlocking schools of education and departments of psychology that dominates education today.

Memorandum Number Six:
The Troika Spreads Its Wings

Around the turn of the century The Order had made significant penetration into the educational establishment. By utilizing the power of members in strategic positions they were able to select, groom and position non-members with similar philosophy and activist traits.

In 1886 Timothy Dwight (The Order) had taken over from the last of Yale's clerical Presidents, Noah Porter. Never again was Yale to get too far from The Order. Dwight was followed by member Arthur T. Hadley ('76). Andrew Dickson White was secure as President of Cornell and alternated as U.S. Ambassador to Germany. While in Berlin, White acted as recruiting agent for The Order. Not only G. Stanley Hall came into his net, but also Richard T. Ely, founder of the American Economic Association. Daniel Gilman, as we noted in the last memorandum, was President of Johns Hopkins and used that base to introduce Wundtian psychology into U.S. education. After retirement from Johns Hopkins, Gilman became the first President of the Carnegie Institution of Washington, D.C.

The chart overleaf summarizes the achievements of this remarkable troika.

Now let's see how The Order moved into more specialized fields of education, then we need to examine how The Order fits with John Dewey, the source of modern American educational philosophy, then how The Order spread Dewey throughout the system.

Founding Of The American Economic Association

Academic associations are a means of conditioning or even policing academics. Although academics are great at talking about academic freedom, they are peculiarly susceptible to peer group pressures. And if an academic fails to get the word through his peer group, there is always the threat of not getting tenure. In other words, what is taught at University levels is passed through a sieve. The sieve is faculty conformity. In this century when faculties are larger, conformity cannot be imposed by a President. It is handled equally well through faculty tenure committees and publications committees of academic associations.

Achievements Of The Troika

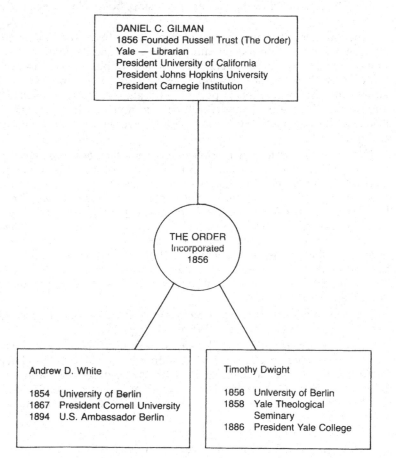

DANIEL C. GILMAN
1856 Founded Russell Trust (The Order)
Yale — Librarian
President University of California
President Johns Hopkins University
President Carnegie Institution

THE ORDER
Incorporated
1856

Andrew D. White

1854 University of Berlin
1867 President Cornell University
1894 U.S. Ambassador Berlin

Timothy Dwight

1856 University of Berlin
1858 Yale Theological
Seminary
1886 President Yale College

We have already noted that member Andrew Dickson White founded and was first President of the American Historical Association and therefore was able to influence the constitution and direction of the AHA. This has generated an official history and ensured that existence of The Order is never even whispered in history books, let alone school texts.

An economic association is also of significance because it conditions how people who are not economists think about the relative merits of free enterprise and state planning. State economic planning is an essential part of State political control. Laissez faire in economics is the equivalent of individualism in politics. And just as you will never find any plaudits for the Ninth and Tenth Amendments to the Constitution in official history, neither will you find any plaudits for individual free enterprise.

The collectivist nature of present day college faculties in economics has been generated by the American Economic Association under influence of The Order. There are very few outspoken preachers of the Austrian School of Economics on American campuses today. They have been effectively weeded out. Even Ludwig von Mises, undisputed leader of the school, was unable to find a teaching post in the United States. So much for academic freedom in economics. And it speaks harshly for the pervasive, deadening, dictatorial hand of the American Economics Association. And the controlling hand, as in the American Psychological Association and the American Historical Association, traces back to The Order.

The principal founder and first Secretary of the American Economic Association was Richard T. Ely. Who was Ely?

Ely descended from Richard Ely of Plymouth, England who settled at Lyme, Connecticut in 1660. On his grandmother's side (and you have heard this before for members of The Order) Ely descended from the daughter of Rev. Thomas Hooker, founder of Hartford, Connecticut. On the paternal side, Ely descended from Elder William Brewster of Plymouth Colony.

Ely's first degree was from Dartmouth College. In 1876 he went to University of Heidelberg and received a Ph.D. in 1879. Ely then returned to the United States, but as we shall describe below, had already come to the notice of The Order.

When Ely arrived home, Daniel Gilman invited Ely to take the Chair of Political Economy at Johns Hopkins. Ely accepted at about the same time Gilman appointed G. Stanley Hall to the Chair of Philosophy and Pedagogy and William Welch, a member of The Order we have yet to describe, to be Dean of the Johns Hopkins medical school.

Fortunately, Richard Ely was an egocentric and left an

autobiography, *Ground Under Our Feet*, which he dedicated to none other than Daniel Coit Gilman (see illustration). Then on page 54 of this autobiography is the caption "I find an invaluable friend in Andrew D. White." And in Ely's first book, *French And German Socialism*, we find the following:

> "The publication of this volume is due to the friendly counsel of the Honorable Andrew D. White, President of Cornell University, a gentleman tireless in his efforts to encourage young men and alive to every opportunity to speak fitting words of hope and cheer. Like many of the younger scholars of our country, I am indebted to him more than I can say."

Ely also comments that he never could understand why he always received a welcome from the U.S. Embassy in Berlin, in fact from the Ambassador himself. But the reader has probably guessed what Ely didn't know — White was The Order's recruiter in Berlin.

Ely recalls his conversations with White, and makes a revealing comment: "I was interested in his psychology and the way he worked cleverly with Ezra Cornell and Mr. Sage, a benefactor and one of the trustees of Cornell University." The reader will remember it was Henry Sage who provided the first funds for G. Stanley Hall to study in Germany.

Then Ely says, "The only explanation I can give for his special interest in me was the new ideas I had in relation to economics." And what were these new ideas? Ely rejected classical liberal economics, including free trade, and noted that free trade was "particularly obnoxious to the German school of thought by which I was so strongly impressed." In other words, just as G. Stanley Hall had adopted Hegelianism in psychology from Wundt, Ely adopted Hegelian ideas from his prime teacher Karl Knies at University of Heidelberg.

TO THE MEMORY OF
DANIEL COIT GILMAN

First President of Johns Hopkins University, creative genius in the field of education; wise, inspiring and courageous chief under whom I had the good fortune to begin my career and to whom I owe an inestimable debt of gratitude, I dedicate this book.

And both Americans had come to the watchful attention of The Order. The staff of the U.S. Embassy in Berlin never did appreciate why a young American student, not attached to the Embassy, was hired by Ambassador White to make a study of the Berlin City Government. That was Ely's test, and he passed it with flying colors. As he says, "It was this report which served to get me started on my way and later helped me get a teaching post at the Johns Hopkins."

The rest is history. Daniel Coit Gilman invited Richard Ely to Johns Hopkins University. From there Ely went on to head the department of economics at University of Wisconsin. Through the ability to influence choice of one's successor. Wisconsin has been a center of statist economics down to the present day.

Before we leave Richard Ely we should note that financing for projects at University of Wisconsin came directly from The Order — from member George B. Cortelyou ('13), President of New York Life Insurance Company.

Ely also tells us about his students, and was especially enthralled by Woodrow Wilson: "We knew we had in Wilson an unusual man. There could be no question that he had a brilliant future."

And for those readers who are wondering if Colonel Edward Mandell House, Woodrow Wilson's mysterious confidant, is going to enter the story, the answer is Yes! He does, but not yet.

The clue is that young Edward Mandell House went to school at Hopkins Grammar School, New Haven, Connecticut. House knew The Order from school days. In fact one of House's closest classmates at Hopkins Grammar School was member Arthur Twining Hadley ('76), who went on to become President of Yale University (1899 to 1921). And it was Theodore Roosevelt who surfaced Hadley's hidden philosophy: "Years later Theodore Roosevelt would term Arthur Hadley his fellow anarchist and say that if their true views were known, they would be so misunderstood that they would both lose their jobs as President of the United States and President of Yale."[1]

House's novel, *Philip Dru*, was written in New Haven, Connecticut and in those days House was closer to the Taft segment of The Order than Woodrow Wilson. In fact House, as we shall see later, was The Order's messenger boy. House was also something of a joker because part of the story of The Order is **encoded** within *Philip Dru*!

We are not sure if The Order knows about House's little prank. It's just like House to try to slip one over on the holders of power.

American Medical Association

Your doctor knows nothing about nutrition? Ask hom confidentially and he'll probably confess he had only one course in nutrition. And there's a reason.

Back in the late 19th century American medicine was in a deplorable state. To the credit of the Rockefeller General Education Board and the Institute for Medical Research, funds were made available to staff teaching hospitals and to eradicate some pretty horrible diseases. On

[1] Morris Hadley. ARTHUR TWINING HADLEY. Yale University Press. 1948. p. 33.

the other hand, a chemical-based medicine was introduced and the medical profession cut its ties with naturopathy. Cancer statistics tell you the rest.

For the moment we want only to note that the impetus for reorganizing medical education in the United States came from John D. Rockefeller, but the funds were channeled through a single member of The Order.

Briefly, the story is this. One day in 1912 Frederick T. Gates of Rockefeller Foundation had lunch with Abraham Flexner of Carnegie Institution. Said Gates to Flexner: "What would you do if you had one million dollars with which to make a start in reorganizing medical education in the United States?"[1]

As reported by Fosdick, this is what happened:

"The bluntness was characteristic of Mr. Gates, but the question about the million dollars was hardly in accord with his usual indirect and cautious approach to the spending of money. Flexner's reply, however, to the effect that any funds — a million dollars or otherwise — could most profitably be spent in developing the Johns Hopkins Medical School, struck a responsive chord in Gates who was already a close friend and devoted admirer of Dr. William H. Welch, the dean of the institution."

Welch was President of the Rockefeller Institute for Medical Research from 1901, and a Trustee of the Carnegie Institution from 1906.

William H. Welch was also a member of the Order and had been brought to Johns Hopkins University by Daniel Coit Gilman.

Other Areas Of Education

We should note in conclusion other educational areas where The Order had its influence. In theology we have already noted that The Order controlled Union Theological Seminary for many years, and was strong within the Yale School of Divinity.

The constitution for UNESCO was written largely by The Order, i.e., member Archibald MacLeish. And member William Chauvenet (1840) was "largely responsible for establishing the U.S. Naval Academy on a firm scientific basis." Chauvenet was director of the Observatory, U.S. Naval Academy, Annapolis from 1845 to 1859 and then went on to become Chancellor of Washington University (1869).

Finally, a point on methodology. The reader will remember from Memorandum One (Voume One) that we argued the most "general" solution to a problem in science is the most acceptable solution. In brief, a useful hypothesis is one that explains the most events. Pause a minute and reflect. We are not developing a theory that includes numerous

[1]Raymond D. Fosdick, ADVENTURE IN GIVING (Harper & Row, New York, 1962), p. 154.

superficially unconnected events. For example, the founding of Johns Hopkins University, the introduction of Wundtian educational methodology, a psychologist G. Stanley Hall, an economist Richard T. Ely, a politician Woodrow Wilson — and now we have included such disparate events as Colonel Edward House and the U.S. Naval Observatory. The Order links to them all . . . . and several hundred or thousand other events yet to be unfolded.

In research when a theory begins to find support of this pervasive nature it suggests the work is on the right track.

So let's interpose another principle of scientific methodology. How do we finally know that our hypothesis is valid? If our hypothesis is correct, then we should be able to **predict** not only future conduct of The Order but also events where we have yet to conduct research. This is still to come. However, the curious reader may wish to try it out. Select a major historical event and search for the guiding hand of The Order.

Members Of The Order In Education

(For Yale University see list at end of Memorandum Number One)

Name	Date Initiated	Affiliations
BURTT, Edwin A.	1915	Professor of Philosophy, University of Chicago (1924-1931) and Cornell University (1931-1960)
ALEXANDER, Eben	1873	Professor of Greek and Minister to Greece (1893-97)
BLAKE, Eli Whitney	1857	Professor of Physics, Cornell (1868-1870) and Brown University (1870-95)
CAPRON, Samuel M.	1853	Not known
CHAUVENET, William	1840	U.S. Naval Academy (1845-59) and Chancellor Washington University (1862-9)
COLTON, Henry M.	1848	Not known
COOKE, Francis J.	1933	New England Conservatory of Music
COOPER, Jacob	1852	Professor of Greek, Center College (1855-1866), Rutgers University (1866-1904)
CUSHING, William	1872	Not known
CUSHMAN, Isaac LaFayette	1845	Not known
CUTLER, Carroll	1854	President, Western Reserve University (1871-1886)
DALY, Frederick J.	1911	Not known
DANIELS, Joseph L.	1860	Professor of Greek, Olivert College, and President (1865-1904)
EMERSON, Joseph	1841	Professor of Greek, Beloit College (1848-1888)
EMERSON, Samuel	1848	Not known
ESTILL, Joe G.	1891	Connecticut State Legislature (1932-1936)
EVANS, Evan W.	1851	Professor of Mathematics, Cornell University (1868-1872)

EWELL, John L.	1865	Professor of Church History, Howard University (1891-1910)
FEW SMITH, W.	1844	Not known
FISHER, Irving	1888	Professor of Political Economy, Yale (1893-1935)
FISK, F.W.	1849	President, Chicago Theological Seminary (1887-1900)
GREEN, James Payne	1857	Professor of Greek, Jefferson College (1857-59)
GRIGGS, John C.	1889	Vassar College (1897-1927)
GROVER, Thomas W.	1874	Not known
HALL, Edward T.	1941	St. Mark's School Southborough, Mass.
HARMAN, Archer	1913	St. Paul's School, Concord, N.H.
HARMAN, Archer, Jr.	1945	St. Paul's School, Concord, N.H.
HEBARD, Daniel	1860	Not known
HINCKS, John H.	1872	Professor of History, Atlanta University (1849-1894)
HINE, Charles D.	1871	Secretary, Connecticut State Board of Education (1883-1920)
HOLLISTER, Arthur N.	1858	Not known
HOPKINS, John M.	1900	Not known
HOXTON, Archibald R.	1939	Episcopal High School
HOYT, Joseph G.	1840	Chancellor, Washington University (1858-1862)
IVES, Chauncey B.	1928	Adirondack-Florida School
JOHNSON, Charles F.	1855	Professor of Mathematics, U.S. Naval Academy (1865-1870), Trinity College (1884-1906)
JOHNSTON, Henry Phelps	1862	Professor of History, N.Y. City College (1883-1916)
JOHNSTON, William	1852	Professor of English Literature, Washington & Lee (1867-1877) and Louisiana State University (1883-1889)
JONES, Theodore S.	1933	Institute of Contemporary Art
JUDSON, Isaac N.	1873	Not known
KELLOGG, Fred W.	1883	Not known
KIMBALL, John	1858	Not known
KINGSBURY, Howard T.	1926	Westminster School
KINNE, William	1948	Not known
KNAPP, John M.	1936	Princeton University
KNOX, Hugh	1907	Not known
LEARNED, Dwight Whitney	1870	Professor of Church History, Doshiba College, Japan (1876-1928)
McCLINTOCK, Norman	1891	Professor of Zoology, University of Pittsburgh (1925-30), Rutgers (1932-6)
MACLEISH, Archibald	1915	Library of Congress (1939-1944), UNESCO, State Dept., OWI, Howard University

MACLEISH, William H.	1950	Not known
MACLELLAN, George B.	1858	Not known
MOORE, Eliakim H.	1883	Professor of Mathematics, University of Chicago (1892-1931)
MORSE, Sidney N.	1890	Not known
NICHOLS, Alfred B.	1880	Professor of German, Simmons College (1903-1911)
NORTON, William B.	1925	Professor of History, Boston Univ.
OWEN, Edward T.	1872	Professor of French, University of Wisconsin (1879-1931)
PARSONS, Henry McI	1933	Columbia University
PERRY, David B.	1863	President, Douana College (1881-1912)
PINCKARD, Thomas C.	1848	Not known
POMEROY, John	1887	Professor of Law, University of Illinois (1910-1924)
POTWIN, Lemuel S.	1854	Professor, Western Reserve University (1871-1906)
REED, Harry L.	1889	President, Auburn Theological Seminary (1926-1939)
RICHARDSON, Rufus B.	1869	Director of American School of Classical Studies, Athens (1893-1903)
RUSSELL, William H.	1833	Collegiate School, Hartford
SEELY, Wm. W.	1862	Dean, Medical Faculty, University of Cincinnati (1881-1900)
SHIRLEY, A.	1869	Not known
SOUTHWORTH, George CS	1863	Bexley Theological Seminary (1888-1900)
SPRING, Andrew J.	1855	Not known
STAGG, Amos A.	1888	Director Physical Education, University of Chicago
STILLMAN, George S.	1935	St. Paul's School
SUTHERLAND, Richard O.	1931	Not known
THACHER, William L.	1887	Not known
TIGHE, Lawrence G.	1916	Treasurer of Yale
TWICHELL, Charles P.	1945	St. Louis Country Day School
TYLER, Charles M.	1855	Professor of History, Cornell University (1891-1903)
TYLER, Moses Coit	1857	Professor at Cornell (1867-1900)
VOGT, T.D.	1943	Not known
WALKER, Horace F.	1889	Not known
WATKINS, Charles L.	1908	Director, Phillips Art School
WHITE, John R.	1903	Not known
WHITNEY, Emerson C.	1851	Not known
WHITNEY, Joseph E.	1882	Not known
WILLIAMS, James W.	1908	Not known
WOOD, William C.	1868	Not known
YOUNG, Benham D.	1848	Not known
YARDLEY, Henry A.	1855	Berkeley Divinity School (1867-1882)

Memorandum Number Seven:
The Order's Objectives For Education

We can deduce The Order's objectives for education from evidence already presented and by examining the work and influence of John Dewey, the arch creator of modern educational theory.

How do we do this? We first need to examine Dewey's relationship with The Order. Then compare Dewey's philosophy with Hegel and with the philosophy and objectives of modern educational practice.

These educational objectives have not, by and large, been brought about by governmental action. In fact, if the present state of education had been brought about by legislation, it would have been challenged on the grounds of unconstitutionality.

On the contrary, the philosophy and practice of today's system has been achieved by injection of massive private funds by foundations under influence, and sometimes control, of The Order. This implementation we will describe in a future volume, *How The Order Controls Foundations*. In fact, the history of the implementation of Dewey's objectives is also the history of the larger foundations, i.e., Ford, Carnegie, Rockefeller, Peabody, Sloan, Slater and Twentieth Century.

How John Dewey Relates To The Order

John Dewey worked for his doctorate at Johns Hopkins University from 1882-86 under Hegelian philosopher George Sylvester Morris. Morris in turn had his doctorate from University of Berlin and studied under the same teachers as Daniel Gilman, i.e., Adolph Trendelenberg and Hermann Ulrici.

Neither Morris nor Dewey were members of The Order, but the link is clear. Gilman hired Morris, knowing full well that Hegelianism is a totally integrated body of knowledge and easy to recognize. It is as different from the British empirical school of John Stuart Mill as night and day.

John Dewey's psychology was taken from G. Stanley Hall, the first American student to receive a doctorate from Wilhelm Wundt at University of Leipzig. Gilman knew exactly what he was getting when he hired Hall. With only a dozen faculty members, all were hired personally by the President.

In brief, philosophy and psychology came to Dewey from academics hand-picked by The Order.

From Johns Hopkins Dewey went as Professor of Philosophy to University of Michigan and in 1886 published *Psychology*, a blend of Hegelian philosophy applied to Wundtian experimental psychology. It sold well. In 1894 Dewey went to University of Chicago and in 1902 was appointed Director of the newly founded — with Rockefeller money — School of Education.

The University of Chicago itself had been founded in 1890 with Rockefeller funds — and in a future volume we will trace this through Frederick Gates (of Hartford, Connecticut), and the Pillsbury family (The Order). The University of Chicago and Columbia Teachers' College were the key training schools for modern education.

The Influence Of Dewey

Looking back at John Dewey after 80 years of his influence, he can be recognized as the pre-eminent factor in the collectivisation, or Hegelianization, of American Schools. Dewey was consistently a philosopher of social change. That's why his impact has been so deep and pervasive. And it is in the work and implementation of the ideas of John Dewey that we can find the objective of The Order.

When The Order brought G. Stanley Hall from Leipzig to Johns Hopkins University, John Dewey was already there, waiting to write his doctoral dissertation on "The Psychology of Kant." Already a Hegelian in philosophy, he acquired and adapted the experimental psychology of Wundt and Hall to his concept of education for social change. To illustrate this, here's a quote from John Dewey in *My Pedagogic Creed*:

> "The school is primarily a social institution. Education being a social process, the school is simply that form of community life in which all those agencies are concentrated that will be most effective in bringing the child to share in the inherited resources of the race, and to use his own powers for social ends. Education, therefore, is a process of living and not a preparation for future living."

What we learn from this is that Dewey's education is not **child** centered but **State** centered, because for the Hegelian, "social ends" are always State ends.

This is where the gulf of misunderstanding between modern parents and the educational system begins. Parents believe a child goes to school to learn skills to use in the adult world, but Dewey states specifically that education is "not a preparation for future living." The Dewey educational system does not accept the role of developing a child's talents but, contrarily, only to prepare the child to function as a unit in an organic whole — in blunt terms a cog in the wheel of an organic society. Whereas most Americans have moral values rooted in the individual, the values of the school system are rooted in the Hegelian concept of the State as the absolute. No wonder there is misunderstanding!

The Individual Child

When we compare Hegel, John Dewey, and today's educational thinkers and doers, we find an extraordinary similarity.

For Hegel the individual has no value except as he or she performs a function for society:

"The State is the absolute reality and the individual himself has objective existence, truth and morality only in his capacity as a member of the State."

John Dewey tried to brush the freedom of the individual to one side. In an article, "Democracy and Educational Administration" (School & Society, XVL, 1937, p. 457) Dewey talks about the "lost individual," and then restates Hegel in the following way: "freedom is the participation of every mature human being in formation of the values that regulate the living of men together." This is pure Hegel, i.e., man finds freedom only in obedience to the State. As one critic, Horace M. Kallen stated, John Dewey had a "blindness to the sheer individuality of individuals."

In other words, for Dewey man has no individual rights. Man exists only to serve the State. This is directly contradictory to the Declaration of Independence and the Constitution with the preamble "We the people." They then go on to define the rights of the **state** which are **always** subordinate and subject to the will of "We the people."

This, of course, is why modern educationists have great difficulty in introducing the Constitution into school work. Their ideas follow Hegel and Dewey and indirectly the objectives of The Order. For example:

"An attempt should be made to redress the present overemphasis on individualism in current programs . . . students need to develop a sense of community and collective identity." (Educational Leadership, May 1982, William B. Stanley, Asst. Professor, Dept. of Curriculum and Instruction, Louisiana State University).

The Purpose Of Education

What then is the purpose of education, if the individual has no rights and exists only for the State?

There was no need for Hegel to describe education, and so far as we know there is no statement purely on education in Hegel's writings. It is unnecessary. For Hegel **every** quality of an individual exists only at the mercy and will of the State. This approach is reflected in political systems based on Hegel whether it be Soviet Communism or Hitlerian national socialism. John Dewey follows Hegel's organic view of society. For example:

"Education consists either in the ability to use one's powers in a social direction or else in ability to share in the experience of others and thus widen the individual conscienceness to that of the race" (*Lectures For The First Course In Pedagogy*).

This last sentence is reminiscent of the Hitlerian philosophy of race (i.e., right Hegelianism).

And today's educators reflect this approach. Here's a quote from Assemblyman John Vasconcellos of California, who also happens to be Chairman of the Joint Committee on the Master Plan for Higher Education and the Education Goals Committee for the California State Assembly — a key post:

"It is now time for a new vision of ourselves, of man, of human nature and of human potential, and a new theory of politics and institutions premised upon that vision. What is that vision of Man? That the natural, whole, organismic human being is loving . . . that man's basic thrust is towards community" (quoted in Rex Myles, *Brotherhood and Darkness*, p. 347).

What is this "widen(ing) the individual conscienceness" (Dewey) and "thrust . . . towards community" (Vasconcellos)?

Stripped of the pedantic language it is new world order, a world organic society. But there is no provision for a global organic order within the Constitution. In fact, it is illegal for any government officer or elected official to move the United States towards such an order as it would clearly be inconsistent with the Constitution. To be sure, Dewey was not a government official, but Vasconcellos has taken an oath of allegiance to the Constitution.

The popular view of a global order is probably that we had better look after our problems at home before we get involved in these esoteric ideas. Political corruption, pitifully low educational standards, and insensitive bureaucracy are probably of more concern to Americans.

It's difficult to see what the new world order has to do with education of children, but it's there in the literature. Fichte, Hegel's predecessor from whom many of his philosophical ideas originated, had a definite concept of a League of Nationas (Volkerbund) and the idea of a league to enforce peace. Fichte asserted "As this federation spreads further and gradually embraces the whole earth, perpetual peace begins, the only lawful relation among states . . ."

The National Education Association, the lobby for education, produced a program for the 1976 Bicentennial entitled "*A Declaration Of Interdependence: Education For A Global Community.*"

On page 6 of this document we find:

"We are committed to the idea of Education for Global Community. You are invited to help turn the commitment into action and mobilizing world education for development of a world community."

An objective almost parallel to Hegel is in *Self Knowledge And Social Action* by Obadiah Silas Harris, Associate Professor of Educational

Management and Development New Mexico State University, Las Cruces, New Mexico:

> "When community educators say that community education takes into consideration the total individual and his total environment, they mean precisely this: the field of community education includes the individual in his total psycho-physical structure and his entire ecological climate with all its ramifications — social, political, economical, cultural, spiritual, etc. It seeks to integrate the individual within himself (sic) and within his community until the individual becomes a cosmic soul and the community the world."

And on page 84 of the same book:

> "The Cosmic soul . . . the whole human race is going to evolve an effective soul of its own — the cosmic soul of the race. That is the future of human evolution. As a result of the emergence of the universal soul, there will be a great unification of the entire human race, ushering into existence a new era, a new dawn of unique world power."

This last quote sounds even more like Adolph Hitler than Assemblyman John Vasconcellos. It has the same blend of the occult, the ethnic and absolutism.

In conclusion we need only quote the Constitution, the basic body of law under which the United States is governed.

The generally held understanding of the Constitution on the relationship between the individual and the State is that the individual is supreme, the State exists **only** to serve individuals and the State has no power except by express permission of the people.

This is guaranteed by Amendments IX and X of the Constitution.

Amendment IX reads,

> "The enumeration in the Constitution of certain rights shall not be construed to deny or disparage others retained by the People."

Note, the "retained". And,

Amendment X reads,

> "The powers not delegated to the United States by the Constitution, nor prohibited by it to the States, are reserved to the States respectively, or to the people."

In brief, the proposals of John Dewey and his followers are unconstitutional. They would never have seen the light of day in American schoolrooms unless they had been promoted by The Order with its enormous power.

Mind Blank — The Order's Objective For Education

Memorandum Number Eight: Summary

Up to this point we have established the following:

(1) By the 1870s The Order had Yale University under its control. Every President of Yale since Timothy Dwight has either been a member of The Order or has family connections to The Order.

It also appears that some Yale graduates who are not members of The Order will act towards objectives desired by The Order. Some of these, for example Dean Acheson, we can identify as members of Scroll & Key, or with relatives in The Order. Others yet to be brought into our discussion are members of Wolf's Head (for example, Reeve Schley, who worked for the Rockefellers). Still others, for example Robert Maynard Hutchins (Fund for the Republic), are Yale graduates but not yet identified as members of any Yale senior society. It appears at this point that Ron Rosenbaum's assertion (in *Esquire*, 1977), that members of the Eastern Establishment who are not members of Skull & Bones will be members of either Scroll & Key or Wolf's Head is holding up.

(2) So far as education is concerned, look-say reading originated with Thomas Gallaudet and was designed for deaf mutes. The elder Gallaudet was not a member of The Order, but his two sons (Edson and Herbert Gallaudet) were initiated in 1893 and 1898. Horace Mann, a significant influence in modern educational theory and the first promoter of "look-say," was not a member. However, Mann was President of Antioch College, and the Tafts (The Order) were the most powerful trustees of Antioch.

(3) We traced John Dewey's philosophy, that education is to prepare a person to fit into society rather than develop individual talents, to Herbart who was influenced by the Swiss Pestalozzi. Personal development cannot be achieved by developing individual talents, it must take the form of preparation to serve society, according to Herbart, Dewey and Pestalozzi. Pestalozzi was a member of the Illuminati, with the code name "Alfred."

This raises new perspectives for future research, specifically whether The Order can be traced to the Illuminati.

(4) The scene shifts in the late 19th century from Yale to Johns Hopkins University. Member Daniel Coit Gilman is the first President of Johns Hopkins and he has handpicked either members of The Order (Welch) or Hegelians for the new departments. G. Stanley Hall, the first of Wilhelm Wundt's American students, began the process of Americanization of Wundt, established the first experimental psychology laboratory for education in the United States with funds from Gilman, and later started the *Journal Of Psychology*.

John Dewey was one of the first doctorates from Johns Hopkins (under Hall and Morris), followed by Woodrow Wilson, who was President of Princeton University before he became President of the United States.

We noted that at key turning points of G. Stanley Hall's career the guiding hand of The Order can be traced. Hall also links to another member of The Order, Alphonso Taft. We noted that Wilhelm Wundt's family had Illuminati connections.

(5) The Order was able to acquire all the Morrill Act land grant entitlements for New York and Connecticut for Cornell and Yale respectively. However, member Gilman ran into trouble as President of University of California on the question of the California land grants and corruption among the University regents. The first organized opposition to The Order came from the San Francisco *Times*, but editor Henry George was not fully aware of the nature of his target.

(6) The core of The Order's impact on education can be seen as a troika: Gilman at Johns Hopkins, White at Cornell (and U.S. Minister to Germany) and Dwight, followed by member Hadley, at Yale. Andrew White was first President of the American Historical Association. Richard T. Ely (not a member but aided by The Order) became a founder and first secretary of the American Economic Association. Members can also be traced into such diverse areas as the U.S. Naval Observatory and the Union Theological Seminary.

(7) John Dewey, the originator of modern educational theory, took his doctorate at Johns Hopkins under Hegelians. Dewey's work is pure Hegel in theory and practice, and is totally inconsistent with the Constitution of the U.S. and rights of the individual. A comparison of German Hegelians, John Dewey and modern educational theorists demonstrates the parallelism. Children do not go to school to develop individual talents but to be prepared as units in an organic society.

Experimental schools at University of Chicago and Columbia University fanned the "new education" throughout the United States.

In brief, The Order initiated and controlled education in this century by controlling its CONTENT. The content is at variance with the traditional view of education, which sees each child as unique and the school as a means of developing this uniqueness.

Criticism of the educational system today bypasses the fundamental philosophic aspect and focuses on omissions, i.e., that the kids can't read, write, spell or undertake simple mathematical exercise. If we look at the educational system through the eyes of The Order and its objectives, then the problems shift.

If teachers are not teaching basics, then what **are** they doing?

They appear to be preparing children for a **political** objective which also happens to be the objective of The Order. The emphasis is on global living, preparing for a global society. It is apparently of no concern to the educational establishment that children can't read, can't write, and can't do elementary mathematics . . . . but they **are** going to be ready for the Brave New World.

Summary Of The Order's Influence In Education

Institution/Field	DIRECT (Major impact only)	INDIRECT (via a member of) The Order
Yale University	Gilman/Dwight/Hadley/White	— —
Cornell University	White	
Johns Hopkins University	Gilman/Welch/White	Hall/Ely/Dewey/Wilson/Morris
University of Chicago	—	Hall/Dewey+foundation financial aid (Volume III)
Columbia Teachers College	—	Hall/Dewey+foundation financial aid (Volume III)
Look-say reading	Gallaudet (Edson and Herbert)	Mann/Gallaudet (Thomas)
Influence of:		
Horace Mann	Taft	— —
Herbart	Illuminati :Pestalozzi i.e. "Alfred")	— —
Wundt	Gilman/Taft/White	— —
American Historical Assoc.	White	
American Economic Assoc.	—	Ely

Refer to membership at end of Memoranda #1 and #6 for lesser influences.

Memorandum Number Nine:
Conclusions And Recommendations

A general conclusion is that The Order has been able to convert the educational system from one aimed at developing the individual child to one aimed at conditioning the child to be a unit in an organic, i.e., Hegelian, society.

When we look at philanthropic foundations in the next volume we shall see the way this has been implemented by private foundation funds.

There is not sufficient evidence to argue whether the decline in educational standards is an accidental by-product of this "new education" or a deliberate subsidiary policy. In any event, the Reagan Administration policy of merit pay will compound, not solve, the problem.

Recommendations for reform have been forthcoming at intervals since the late 1950s when educational problems first surfaced. At the time of Sputnik there was a hue and cry about the backward nature of U.S. training in mathematics and science, which at the University level are not at all backward. Anyway the educational establishment recognized an opportunity and cried, "more, more money." They got it, and there was a massive expansion in the '60s. But the funds have been poured into social conditioning. Mathematics and sciences have taken back seat in the last 30 years.

Then in 1981, James S. Coleman of the University of Chicago produced a study of public schools for the U.S. Department of Education. In this study Coleman used the National Opinion Research Center to contact 58,728 sophomores and seniors in 1,016 public, parochial, and private schools across the United States. His findings were:

- private and parochial schools provide an education closer to the common school ideal than do public schools,
- private school students learned more than public school counterparts,
- Coleman wrote it was paradoxical that "catholic schools function much closer to the American ideal of the common school . . . than do public schools."
- private schools provide "a safer, more disciplined and more ordered environment" than public schools,
- "blacks and Hispanics perform better at private schools."

The reason? Private schools are less under the influence of the Dewey educational philosophy. They still have to use accredited teachers, but these teachers — quite bluntly — have been able to survive the teacher training conditioning.

Yet the educational establishment does not see the writing on the wall.

In Fall 1983 a report by John Goodlad, Dean of the School of Education at University of Southern California, will be published. John I. Goodlad wrote the Foreword to *Schooling For A Global Age* (McGraw Hill, 1979) which includes these comments:

"Enlightened social engineering is required to face situations that demand global action now" (page xiii).

"Parents and the general public must be reached . . . otherwise children and youth enrolled in globally oriented programs may find themselves in conflict with values assumed in the home."

And more. Another 345 pages of globalony follows.

Nothing about the child as an individual. Nothing about the child as a repository of talents that need to be encouraged. Nothing about basic education: the 3 R's.

Yet this Goodlad report is being pushed in *The New York Times* (July 19, 1983) as the most "comprehensive report" ever made on American schools. These are some Goodlad proposals:

- education should start at 4 years old
- schools should be smaller
- head teachers with doctorates should have more pay.

And this does nothing, of course, to stop what a former Commissioner of Education called "a rising tide of mediocrity."

If the United Stqates is to survive in the coming technologically intensive age, then certain recommendations follow. These are:

- the function of the school is to develop individual talent. Social engineering as an objective has to be discarded.
- A thorough grounding in the 3 R's is essential for a good education. In other words, "content" is all important.
- It follows that Schools of Education should be abolished (this is under serious discussion at Duke University and has been proposed at University of Michigan and even Cal Berkeley).
- Teacher credentials should be based on subject matter entirely, not educational theory.
- All restrictions on private schools should be abolished.
- Public schools should be returned to local control.

How The Order
CREATES
WAR and REVOLUTION

Preface

The operational history of The Order can only be understood within a framework of the **Hegelian dialectic** process. Quite simply this is the notion that **conflict creates history.**

From this axiom it follows that **controlled** conflict can **create** a predetermined history. For example: When the Trilateral Commission discusses "managed conflict", as it does extensively in its literature, the Commission implies the managed use of conflict for long run predetermined ends — not for the mere random exercise of manipulative control to solve a problem.

The dialectic takes this Trilateral "managed conflict" process one step further. In Hegelian terms, an existing force (the thesis) generates a counterforce (the antithesis). Conflict between the two forces results in the forming of a synthesis. Then the process starts all over again: Thesis vs. antithesis results in synthesis.

The synthesis sought by the Establishment is called the New World Order. Without controlled conflict this New World Order will not come about. Random individual actions of persons in society would not lead to this synthesis, it's artificial, therefore it has to be created. And this is being done with the calculated, managed, use of conflict. And all the while this synthesis is being sought, there is no profit in playing the involved parties against one another. This explains why the International bankers backed the Nazis, the Soviet Union, North Korea, North Vietnam, ad nauseum, against the United States. The "conflict" built profits while pushing the world ever closer to One World Government. The process continues today.

We apologize for the poor quality of some documents included in this volume. These are the best copies in existence today. In fact, it is a miracle they survived at all . . . For example, letters between Patriarch Amos Pinchot (Club D. 95) and Patriarch William Kent (Club D. 85) would almost certainly have been destroyed if a New York State Commission had not seized the documents as part of an investigation into subversion in the United States.

However, even where contents cannot be clearly identified, the very existence of even a fragmentary text proves a vital point: There is a joint calculated effort among Patriarchs to bring about a specific objective. Furthermore, the diverse conflicting nature of these efforts, commented upon even in letters between Patriarchs, can only be explained in the terms of the Hegelian dialectic.

In brief, the existence of these documents is just as important as the nature of the contents. It demonstrates joint planned actions, ergo: A Conspiracy!

Antony C. Sutton

April, 1984

Memorandum Number One:
Created Conflict And The Dialectic Process

I. INTRODUCTION

The first volume of this series (*Introduction To The Order* described in broad terms the nature and objectives of The Order.

Our first hypothesis, that the U.S. was ruled by an elite, secret society, was supported by documentary evidence: such a secret society **does** exist, its membership is concealed, and disclosure of membership is not a voluntary effort. Further, since publication of the first volume, the Sterling Library at Yale University which has major holdings of their records has refused to allow researchers further access to Russell Trust papers (the legal name for The Order).

We also argued in the first volume that the operations of The Order must be seen and explained in terms of the Hegelian dialectic process. Their operations cannot be explained in terms of any other philosophy; therefore The Order cannot be described as "right" or "left," secular or religious, Marxist or Capitalist. The Order, and its objectives, is all of these and none of these.

In Hegelian philosophy the conflict of political "right" and political "left," or thesis and antithesis in Hegelian terms, is essential to the forward movement of history and historical change itself. Conflict between thesis and antithesis brings about a synthesis, i.e., a new historical situation.

Our descriptive world history in the West and Marxist countries consists only of description and analysis within a political framework of "right" **or** "left." For example, historical work published in the West looks at communism and socialism either through the eyes of financial capitalism or Marxism. Historical work published in the Soviet Union looks at the West only through Marxist eyes. However, there is another frame for historical analysis that has never (so far as we can determine) been utilized, i.e., to use a framework of Hegelian logic, to determine if those elites who control the State use the dialectic process to **create** a predetermined historical synthesis.

Only tantalizing glimpses of any such creative process can be found in modern historical works. The most convincing glimpses are in the late Carroll Quigley's *Tragedy And Hope* which we shall quote below. Rarely some politicians on the periphery of elitist power have allowed brief insights into the public eye. For example, President Woodrow Wilson made the revealing statement: "Some of the biggest men in the U.S. in the fields of commerce and manufacturing know that there is a power so organized, so subtle, so complete, so pervasive that they had better not speak above their breath when they speak in condemnation of it."

Who or what is this power? And how is it used?

This series argues that the current world situation has been deliberately created by this elitist power more or less by manipulation of "right" and "left" elements. We argue that the most powerful of all world elites has during the past 100 years or so developed **both** right **and** left elements to bring about a New World Order.

There is no question that the so-called establishment in the U.S. uses "managed conflict." The practice of "managing" crises to bring about a favorable outcome, that is, favorable to the elite, is freely admitted in the literature of, for example, The Trilateral Commission. Furthermore, there is no question that decisions of war and peace are made by a few in the elite and not by the many in the voting process through a political referendum. This volume explores some major conflict decisions made by the few in The Order and the way in which right-left situations have been deliberately created and then placed in a conflict mode to bring about a synthesis.

Finally, we will tie these decisions and operations back to the elite and specifically to The Order.

II. HOW THE DIALECTIC PROCESS WORKS

Throughout the last 200 years, since the rise of Kant in German philosophy, we can identify two conflicting systems of philosophy and so opposing ideas of the State, society and culture. In the U.S., the British Commonwealth and France, philosophy is based on the individual and the rights of the individual. Whereas in Germany from the time of Kant, through Fichte and Hegel up to 1945, the root philosophy has been universal brotherhood, rejection of individualism and general opposition to Western classical liberal thought in almost all its aspects. German idealism, as we noted in earlier volumes of this series, was the philosophical basis for the work of Karl Marx and the Left Hegelians as well as Bismarck, Hitler and the Right Hegelians. This is the paradox: that Hegel gave a theoretical basis not only to the most conservative of German movements, but also to most of the revolutionary movements of the 19th century. **Both Marx and Hitler have their philosophical roots in Hegel.**

From the Hegelian system of political thought, alien to most of us in the West, stem such absurdities as the State seen as the "march of God through history," that the State is also God, that the only duty of a citizen is to serve God by serving the State, that the State is Absolute Reason, that a citizen can only find freedom by worship and utter obedience to the State. However, we also noted in How The Order Controls Education that Hegelian absurdities have thoroughly penetrated the U.S. educational system under pressure from such

— 118 —

organizations as the National Education Association and major foundations.

From this system of Hegelian philosophy comes the historical dialectic, i.e., that all historical events emerge from a **conflict** between opposing forces. These emerging events are above and different from the conflicting events. Any idea or implementation of an idea may be seen as THESIS. This thesis will encourage emergence of opposing forces, known as ANTITHESIS. The final outcome will be neither thesis nor antithesis, but a synthesis of the two forces in conflict.

Karl Marx, in *Das Kapital,* posed capitalism as thesis and communism as antithesis. What has been completely ignored by historians, including Marxists, is that any clash between these forces cannot lead to a society which is either capitalist **or** communist but must lead to a society characterized by a synthesis of the two conflicting forces. The clash of opposites must in the Hegelian system bring about a society neither capitalist nor communist. Moreover, in the Hegelian scheme of events, this new synthesis will reflect the concept of the State as God and the individual as totally subordinate to an all powerful State.

What then is the function of a Parliament or a Congress for Hegelians? These institutions are merely to allow individuals to **feel** that their opinions have some value and to allow a government to take advantage of whatever wisdom the "peasant" may accidentally demonstrate. As Hegel puts it:

"By virtue of this participation, subjective liberty and conceit, with their general opinion, (individuals) can show themselves palpably efficacious and enjoy the satisfaction of feeling themselves to count for something."

War, the organized conflict of nations for Hegelians, is only the visible outcome of the clash between ideas. As John Dewey, the Hegelian darling of the modern educational system, puts it:

"War is the most effective preacher of the vanity of all merely finite interests, it puts an end to that selfish egoism of the individual by which he would claim his life and his property as his own or as his family's." (John Dewey, *German Philosophy And Politics,* p. 197)

Of course, this war-promoting Dewey paragraph is conveniently forgotten by the National Education Association, which is today busy in the "Peace Movement" — at precisely that time when a "peace" movement most aids the Hegelian Soviets.

Above all, the Hegelian doctrine is the divine right of States rather than the divine right of kings. The State for Hegel and Hegelians is God on earth:

"The march of God in history is the cause of the existence of states, their foundation is the power of Reason realizing itself as will. Every state, whatever it be, participates in the divine essence. The State is not the work of human art, only Reason could produce it." (*Philosophy Of Right*)

For Hegel the individual is nothing, the individual has no rights, morality consists solely in following a leader. For the ambitious individual the rule is Senator Mansfield's maxim: "To get along you have to go along."

Compare this to the spirit and letter of the Constitution of the United States: "We the people" grant the state **some** powers and reserve all others to the people. Separation of church and state is built into the U.S. Constitution, a denial of Hegel's "the State is God on earth." Yet, compare this legal requirement to the actions of The Order in the United States, The Group in England, the Illuminati in Germany, and the Politburo in Russia. For these elitists the State is supreme and a self-appointed elite running the State acts indeed as God on earth.

III. J.P. MORGAN USES THE DIALECTIC PROCESS

The concept of the Hegelian dialectic is obviously beyond the comprehension of modern textbook writers. No historical or political theory textbook that we know of discusses the possible use of the Hegelian dialectic in American politics. Yet its use has been recorded by Professor Carroll Quigley in *Tragedy And Hope,* a trade book based on documents of the Council on Foreign Relations. Quigley not only describes banker J.P. Morgan's use of the "right" and the "left" as competitive devices for political manipulation of society, but adds an eye-opening comment:

"Unfortunately we do not have space here for this great and untold story, but it must be remembered that what we do say is part of a much larger picture." (*Tragedy And Hope*, p. 945)

This much larger picture is partly revealed in this book. First let's briefly note how J.P. Morgan used the dialectic process as a means of political control for financial ends. The only college attended by Morgan was 2-3 years in the mid-1850s at University of Gottingen, Germany, which was a center of Hegelian activism. We have no record that Morgan joined any secret society, no more than the KONK-NEIPANTEN, one of the student corps. Yet German Hegelianism is apparent in J.P. Morgan's approach to political parties — Morgan used them **all.**

As Quigley comments:

"The associations between Wall Street and the Left, of which Mike Straight is a fair example, are really survivals of the associations between the Morgan Bank and the Left. To Morgan all political parties were simply organizations to be used, and the firm always was careful to keep a foot in all camps. Morgan himself, Dwight Morrow, and other partners were allied with Republicans; Russell C. Leffingwell was allied with the Democrats; Grayson Murphy was allied with the extreme Right; and Thomas W. Lamont was allied with the Left. Like the Morgan interest in libraries, museums, and art, its inability to distinguish between loyalty to the United States and loyalty to England, its recognition of the need for social work among the poor, the multipartisan political views of the Morgan firm in domestic politics went back to the original founder of the firm, George Peabody (1795-1869). To this same seminal figure may be attributed the use of tax-exempt foundations for controlling these activities, as may be observed in many parts of America to this day, in the use of Peabody foundations to support Peabody libraries and museums. Unfortunately, we do not have space here for this great and untold story, but it must be remembered that what we do say is part of a much larger picture." (*Ibid*)

Quigley did not know of the link between the Morgan firm, other New York financial interests and The Order. As we have noted before, Quigley did publish a valuable expose of the British Establishment known as "The Group." And we know from personal correspondence that Quigley suspected more than he published, but identification of an American elite was not part of Quigley's work. The names Harriman, Bush, Acheson, Whitney — even Stimson — do not appear in *The Anglo American Establishment*.

We can therefore take the above paragraph from Quigley's *Tragedy And Hope* and insert identification of The Order. The paragraph then becomes more revealing. Although Morgan himself was not a member of The Order, some of his partners were, and after Morgan's death the firm became Morgan, Stanley & Co. The "Stanley" was Harold Stanley (The Order 1908). In Morgan's time the influence of The Order came through partner Henry P. Davison, whose son H.P. Davison, Jr. was initiated in 1920. The elder Henry P. Davison brought Thomas Lamont and Willard Straight into the Morgan firm. These partners were instrumental in building the left wing of Morgan's dialectic, including the Communist Party U.S.A. (with Julius Hammer, whose son is today Chairman of Occidental Petroleum).

Morgan partner Thomas Cochran was initiated in 1904. However, it was in the network of Morgan dominated and affiliated firms, rather than in the partnership itself, that one finds members of The Order. In firms like Guaranty Trust and Bankers Trust, somewhat removed from the J.P. Morgan financial center, although under Morgan control, we find concentrations of initiates (as we shall describe below).

This practice by The Order of supporting both "right" and "left" persists down to the present day. We find in 1984, for example, that Averell Harriman (The Order '13) is elder statesman of the Democratic Party while George Bush (The Order '49) is a Republican Vice President and leader of the misnamed "moderate" (actually extremist) wing of the Republican Party. In the center we have so-called "independent" John Anderson, who in fact receives heavy financial support from the elite.

IV. THE CREATION OF WAR AND REVOLUTION

This manipulation of "left" and "right" on the domestic front is duplicated in the international field where "left" and "right" political structures are artificially constructed and collapsed in the drive for a one-world synthesis.

College textbooks present war and revolution as more or less accidental results of conflicting forces. The decay of political negotiation into physical conflict comes about, according to these books, after valiant efforts to avoid war. Unfortunately, this is nonsense. War is always a deliberate creative act by individuals.

Western textbooks also have gigantic gaps. For example, after World War II the Tribunals set up to investigate Nazi war criminals were careful to censor any materials recording Western assistance to Hitler. By the same token, Western textbooks on Soviet economic development omit any description of the economic and financial aid given to the 1917 Revolution and subsequent economic development by Western firms and banks.

Revolution is always recorded as a spontaneous event by the politically or economically deprived against an autocratic state. Never in Western textbooks will you find the evidence that revolutions need finance and the source of the finance in many cases traces back to Wall Street.

Consequently it can be argued that our Western history is every bit as distorted, censored, and largely useless as that of Hitler's Germany or the Soviet Union or Communist China. No Western foundation will award grants to investigate such topics, few Western academics can "survive" by researching such theses and certainly no major publisher will easily accept manuscripts reflecting such arguments.

In fact, there is another largely unrecorded history and it tells a story quite different than our sanitized textbooks. It tells a story of the **deliberate** creation of war, the **knowing** finance of revolution to change governments, and the use of conflict to **create** a New World Order.

In the following Memorandum Number Two we will describe the operational vehicles used to create two revolutions and one world conflict. Then, in Memoranda Three and Four, we will explore thesis and antithesis in one major historical episode — the development and construction of the Soviet Union (thesis) and Hitler's Germany (antithesis).

In Memorandum Five we will explore the continuation of this dialectic conflict into the last few decades, specifically Angola and China today. We will show that the purpose of The Order is to create a new synthesis, a New World Order along Hegelian lines where the State is the Absolute and the individual can find freedom only in blind obedience to the State.

Memorandum Number Two:
Operational Vehicles For Conflict Creation

I. A UNIVERSAL MIND SET

Our first task is to break an almost universally held mind set, i.e., that communists and elitist capitalists are bitter enemies. This Marxist axiom is a false statement and for a century has fooled academics and investigators alike.

To illustrate this mind set, let's look at a report on revolutionaries in the U.S. compiled by the respected Scotland Yard (London) in 1919. London police investigators were then tracking the Bolshevik Revolution and attempting to identify its Western supporters. When it came to men with long beards and even longer overcoats, most police departments had no problem — they **looked like** revolutionaries, therefore, they must **be** revolutionaries. But when it came to respectable black-suited bankers, Scotland Yard was unable to rise above its mind set and recognize that bankers might equally be revolutionaries. Witness this extract from a Scotland Yard Intelligence Report.[1]

"Martens is very much in the limelight. There appears to be no doubt about his connection with the Guarantee (sic) Trust Company. Although it is surprising that so large and influential an enterprise should have dealings with a Bolshevik concern."

Scotland Yard had picked up an accurate report that the Soviets were deeply involved with Guaranty Trust of New York, **but they couldn't believe it,** and dropped this line of investigation.

Even today the FBI has a similar mind set. For example, David Rockefeller has met regularly with a KGB agent in the United States — weekly lunch meetings is a close description. Yet the FBI presumably can't bring itself to investigate David Rockefeller as a potential Soviet agent, but if Joe Smith of Hoboken, N.J. was lunching weekly with the KGB, you can be sure the FBI would be on his tail. And, of course, our domestic U.S. Marxists find it absolutely inconceivable that a capitalist would support communism.

Organizations like Scotland Yard and the FBI, and almost all academics on whom investigators rely for their guidelines, have a highly important failing: they look at known verifiable historical facts with a mind set. They convince themselves that they have the explanation of a problem even before the problem presents itself.

The key to modern history is in these facts: **that elitists have close working relations with both Marxists and Nazis.** The only questions are who and why? The common reaction is to reject these facts.

---

[1] A copy is in U.S. State Department Decimal File, Microcopy 316, Roll 22, Frame 656.

On the other hand, national security alone demands that we face these unwelcome relations before any more damage is done to our way of life.

In this memorandum we will present the concept that world history, certainly since about 1917, reflects deliberately created conflict with the objective of bringing about a synthesis, a New World Order.

The operation actually began before 1917. In later volumes we will explore the Spanish-American War and the Anglo-Boer War of 1899. The first was created by The Order, i.e., the U.S. elite, and the second by "The Group," i.e., the British elite (with some U.S. assistance). We might aptly term these the First and Second Hegelian Wars, but this is another story. In this volume we are limited to the rise of Hitler in Germany and the rise of the Marxist state in the Soviet Union. The clash between these two powers or the political systems they represent was a major source of World War II.

After World War II the world stage was changed. After 1945 it became the Soviet Union on one side versus the United States on the other. The first dialectical clash led to the formation of the United Nations, an elementary step on the road to world government. The second dialectical clash led to the Trilateral Commission, i.e., regional groupings and more subtly to efforts for a merger of the United States and the Soviet Union.

In *Introduction To The Order* we established the existence of a secret society, The Order. We are now going to demonstrate how The Order created and developed two global arms needed for Hegelian conflict. Since 1917 the operational vehicles for this global battle have been:

    (a) Guaranty Trust Company of New York, the same firm cited in the 1919 Scotland Yard report, and

    (b) Brown Brothers, Harriman, private bankers of New York.

Before 1933 Brown Brothers, Harriman consisted of two firms: W.A. Harriman Company and Brown Brothers. Numerous members of The Order have been in both firms, but **one individual stands out above all others as the key to the operation of The Order: W. Averell Harriman** (The Order '13).

Creation Of Global Conflict -
The Operational Vehicles

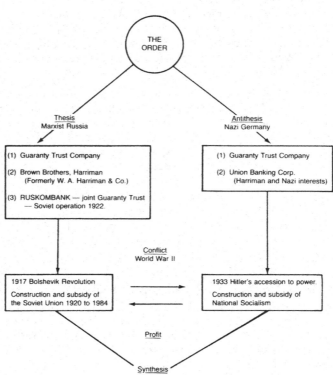

THE
ORDER

Thesis
Marxist Russia

Antithesis
Nazi Germany

(1) Guaranty Trust Company

(2) Brown Brothers, Harriman
    (Formerly W. A. Harriman & Co.)

(3) RUSKOMBANK — joint Guaranty Trust
    — Soviet operation 1922.

(1) Guaranty Trust Company

(2) Union Banking Corp.
    (Harriman and Nazi interests)

Conflict
World War II

1917 Bolshevik Revolution

Construction and subsidy of
the Soviet Union 1920 to 1984

1933 Hitler's accession to power.

Construction and subsidy of
National Socialism

Profit

Synthesis
(Post World War II United Nations as a first step to New World Order)

II. W. AVERELL HARRIMAN (THE ORDER '13)[1]

The name William Averell Harriman turns up behind world political scenes more frequently than any other member of The Order. Possibly it's because Harriman is a remarkably active man. Born in 1891, graduated Yale 1913, Harriman is still newsworthy in the 1980s. In June 1983 Harriman had a private meeting with Yuri Andropov in Moscow and in December 1983, at 92, broke his right leg while swimming in the sea off Barbados. Whatever else we say here about Averell, we must record his truly remarkable energy and longevity.

In official Harriman biographies, however, there is no mention of The Order, Skull & Bones, or the Russell Trust. Like other initiates Harriman has carefully expunged membership from the public record. We have not yet determined if this membership was ever made known to the FBI for use in background checks needed for government positions, or maybe no one ever bothered to ask for a background check on Averell Harriman.

To understand Averell Harriman we need to go back to his father, Edward H. Harriman, the 19th century "robber baron." Edward Harriman's biography (*E.H. Harriman: A Biography*) is as self-serving as all hired biographies. It was written by George Kennan (published by Houghton Mifflin in 1922) who was active in the Dean Acheson State Department. The author of the famous — some say infamous — National Security Council document 68 was none other than George Kennan. (See page 175)

Edward Harriman started work at 14 with little education, but married Mary Averell, daughter of a New York banker and railroad president. At 22, Harriman bought a seat on the New York Stock Exchange and got lucky or smart with Union Pacific after the crash of 1893.

Even the widely accepted *Dictionary of American Biography* states that Harriman was subsequently guilty of a combination in restraint of trade (1904 Northern Securities case), that his dubious financial activities netted him $60 million in a manner which led to investigation by the Interstate Commerce Commission. This source cites Harriman as "an example of how a road may be drained of its resources for the benefit of insiders."

Harriman printed securities with a nominal value of $80 million to expand capitalization of his railroads. On the other hand, Harriman neglected to acquire improvements and property for more than $18 million. In other words, $60 million of the securities was water, mostly sold through Kuhn Loeb & Co., his backers and bankers. The $60 million went into Harriman's pocket.

[1]Names of Brown Brothers, Harriman partners in 1972 were included in *Introduction To The Order*, pages 20-21. About 100 Harriman related documents from the 1920s may be found in U.S. State Department Decimal File, Microcopy 316, Roll 138 (861.6364-6461).

The 1904 ICC report stated:

"It was admitted by Mr. Harriman that there was about $60 million of stock and liabilities issued, against which no property had been acquired and this is undoubetdly an accurate estimate."[1]

In brief, Mr. Edward H. Harriman was apparently a thief, a crook, and a felon, because fraudulent conversion of $60 million is a felony. Harriman stayed out of jail by judicious expenditures to politicians and political parties. Biographer George Kennan relates how Harriman responded to President Theodore Roosevelt's 1904 plea for $250,000 for the Republican National Committee.[2]

These funds were turned over to the Committee by Harriman's friend and attorney, Judge Robert Scott Lovett. Lovett was also general counsel for the Union Pacific Railroad and could be described as Harriman's bagman. Judge Lovett's son, Robert Abercrombie Lovett (The Order '18) went to Yale and with the two Harriman boys, Roland and Averell, was initiated into The Order. We shall catch up again with Robert Abercrombie Lovett in the 1950s as Secretary of Defense, partner in Brown Brothers, Harriman, and a key force to have President Harry Truman recall General Douglas MacArthur from Korea. By itself the Lovett family is incidental. When we link it to the Harriman family we have an example of how these families help each other along the way for a common objective.

In any event, $250,000 hardly changed Theodore Roosevelt's view of Harriman. Two years after the gift, Roosevelt wrote Senator Sherman and described Harriman as a man of "deep seated corruption," an "undesirable citizen" and "an enemy of the Republic."[3]

Another description of Averell Harriman's father is in *Concise Dictionary Of National Biography* (page 402): "Self confident, dominant, cold and ruthless, he spared neither friend nor foe if they blocked his plans."

Now we cannot visit the sins of the father onto his sons, but we should keep this background in mind when we look at the careers of the Harriman boys, Averell and Roland. At least we have reasons to probe behind the public relations facade and perhaps suspect the worst.

---

[1]Gustavus Myers, *History Of The Great American Fortunes* (Modern Library, New York, 1937) p. 500

[2]George Kennan, op. cit., p. 192

[3]Augustus Myers, op. cit., p. 214

**The Harriman Family And Its Satellites
In *The Order***

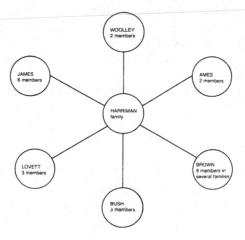

Superficially, Averell Harriman's life has been quite different than his father's. Here's an official summary of Averell Harriman's long career:
• Married three times —
    (1) 1915 Kitty Lanier Lawrence
    (2) 1930 Marie Norton Whitney[4]
    (3) 1971 Pamela Churchill Hayward[5]
• Groton Prep School, then Yale. Initiated into The Order in 1913.
• Started with his father's company, Union Pacific Railroad

• 1917 organized the Merchant Shipbuilding Corporation, sold all
    shipping interests in 1925

Superficially, Averell Harriman's life has been quite different than his father's. Here's an official summary of Averell Harriman's long career:
• Married three times —
    (1) 1915 Kitty Lanier Lawrence
    (2) 1930 Marie Norton Whitney[4]
    (3) 1971 Pamela Churchill Hayward[5]
• Groton Prep School, then Yale. Initiated into The Order in 1913.
• Started with his father's company, Union Pacific Railroad

• 1917 organized the Merchant Shipbuilding Corporation, sold all
    shipping interests in 1925
• 1917 Director of Guaranty Trust. Family holdings of about one-third
    of Guaranty stock were put into a J.P. Morgan voting trust in
    1912

[4]For Marie Norton Whitney, see Volume One. p. 29. The Order, p. 29.

[5]Pamela Hayward was formerly married to Randolph Churchill, thus linking Harriman to the British establishment.

- 1920 established W.A. Harriman Company, with his brother Roland as Vice-President
- 1923 formed Georgian Manganese Company
- 1933 W.A. Harriman merged with Brown Brothers to become Brown Brothers, Harriman
- 1934 Special assistant administrator of Roosevelt's National Recovery Act
- 1941 Minister to Great Britain in charge of Lend Lease for Britain and Russia
- 1941 Ambassador to the Soviet Union
- 1946 Ambassador to Great Britain
- 1946 Secretary of Commerce
- 1948 U.S. representative to ECA in Europe
- 1950 Special Assistant to President Truman
- 1951 U.S. representative at NATO defense meetings
- 1951 Director of Mutual Security Agency
- 1955 Governor of State of New York
- 1961 Ambassador at Large
- 1961 Assistant Secretary of State for Far East
- 1963 Under Secretary of State for Political Affairs
- 1968 U.S. representative at Paris "peace" talks on Vietnam
- 1974 Chairman Democratic Party Foreign Policy Task Force
- 1975 Limited Partner Brown Brothers, Harriman
- 1983 Visits Yuri Andropov in Moscow

With this lengthy global experience one might suspect that Harriman has developed a deep knowledge, understanding and perception of the world. But in fact his writings suggest he is either rather stupid or one of the most deceptive men ever to walk the face of our earth. Let's take one example: an article written by Averell Harriman, published in *Look*, October 3, 1967 and entitled "From Stalin to Kosygin: the myths and the realities."

Here are two extracts:

(1) "Therefore in the early twenties my firm participated in credits to finance trade with Russia. We found as others did that the new government was most meticulous in meeting its financial commitments."

In fact, the Soviets **expropriated** the concessions of the 1920s including Harriman's, usually without reimbursement. Harriman was doublecrossed by the Soviets in his Georgian manganese concession, then persuaded to take $3 million **in Soviet bonds** as compensation

(See documents printed on pages 154-155). This Soviet "compensation" in effect put Harriman in a position of making the first U.S. loan to Russia, so breaching United States law against such loans.

But this is what Harriman told John B. Stetson, Jr. of the State Department (861.637-Harriman) "Mr. Harriman said that they expect to drop about three million dollars which they would charge off to experience." This, Harriman calls "most meticulous in meeting its financial obligations."

(2) "On the Russian side, one of the most troublesome myths is that America is run by a 'ruling circle,' made up of Wall Streeters and industrialists who have an interest in continuing the cold war and the arms race to prop up the 'capitalist' economy. Anybody who knows American politics knows what nonsense this is."

Unfortunately, the Russians are largely right on the **political** aspects of this one. In making the above statement Harriman not only confirms Russian paranoia, i.e., that capitalists can't be trusted to tell the truth, but also deceives the American reading audience in Look that they do, in fact, have a participation in running political affairs. Compare this paragraph to this series on The Order and you will see the devious way the Harriman mind works, perhaps not so different than Harriman senior.

The previously described official Harriman biography suggests that Harriman, given his decades on the political inside, must be well aware of the dependence of the Soviet Union on Western technology: that the Soviet Union can make no economic progress without Western enterprise technology. In fact, Stalin himself told Harriman as much back in 1944. Here's an extract from a **report by Ambassador Harriman** in Moscow to the State Department, dated June 30, 1944:

"Stalin paid tribute to the assistance rendered by the United States to Soviet industry before and during the war. He said that about two-thirds of all the large industrial enterprises in the Soviet Union had been built with United States help or technical assistance."[1]

Stalin could have added that the other one-third of Soviet industry had been built by British, German, French, Italian, Finnish, Czech and Japanese companies.

In brief, Harriman knew **first hand** back in 1944 at least that the West had built the Soviet Union. Now examine Harriman's official biography with its string of appointments relating to NATO, Mutual Security Agency, State Department, foreign policy, and so on. In these posts Harriman actively pushed for a military build-up of the United States. But if the Soviet Union was seen to be an enemy in 1947, then

[1]Original in U.S. State Department Decimal File 033.1161 Johnston Eric/6-3044 Telegram June 30, 1944.

we had no need to build a massive defense. What we **should** have done was cut off technology. There was no Soviet technology — and HARRIMAN KNEW THERE WAS NO SOVIET TECHNOLOGY.

Furthermore, Harriman has been in the forefront of the cry for "more trade" with the Soviet Union — and trade is the transfer vehicle for technology. In other words, Harriman has been pushing two CONFLICTING POLICIES SIMULTANEOUSLY.

(a) a build-up of Soviet power by export of our technology, and

(b) a Western defense against that power.

Isn't this the Hegelian dialectic? Thesis versus antithesis, then conflict which leads to a new synthesis. In the following memoranda we will show how Harriman and his fellows in the Brotherhood of Power went about this program of conflict creation.

Moreover, Harriman is understandably highly sensitive when challenged on his pious "I am always right about the Soviets" attitude.

One memorable occasion was back in 1971 when author Edward (Teddy) Weintal was at a dinner party with Harriman when Harriman trotted out his well worn line: "I was the first to warn of Soviet dangers . . ."

Weintal stopped him cold. In research for a book, Weintal had found documents incriminating Harriman in the National Archives (similar to those reproduced later in this book). In particular, Weintal cited a State Department telegram dated February 12, 1944 from Harriman to Roosevelt. Said Weintal,

"You told Roosevelt that you were convinced that the Soviets did not want to introduce a Communist government into Poland."

So up jumped 79-year-old Harriman from the dinner table and waved his fists at 70-year-old Weintal. Shouted Harriman, "If you print anything like that in your book, I'll break your jaw."

Reportedly, the agitated host separated the two men, but not before a *Washington Post* reporter noted the details (See *Washington Post*, March 17, 1971, VIP Column by Maxine Cheshire).

III. THE GUARANTY TRUST COMPANY

Guaranty Trust was founded 1864 in New York. Over the next 100 years the banking firm expanded rapidly by absorbing other banks and trust companies; in 1910 it merged Morton Trust Company, in 1912 the Standard Trust Company, and in 1929 the National Bank of Commerce. The J.P. Morgan firm has effectively controlled Guaranty Trust since 1912 when Mrs. Edward Harriman (mother of Roland and Averell Harriman) sold her block of 8,000 shares of the total outstanding 20,000 shares to J.P. Morgan. By 1954 Guaranty Trust had become the most important banking subsidiary of the J.P. Morgan firm and since 1954 the merged firms have been known as Morgan-Guaranty Company.

The original capital for Guaranty Trust came from the Whitney, Rockefeller, Harriman and Vanderbilt families, **all represented in The Order,** and on the Board of Guaranty Trust by family members throughout the period we are discussing.

Harry Payne Whitney (The Order'94) inherited two Standard Oil fortunes from the Payne and the Whitney families. H.P. Whitney was a director of Guaranty Trust, as was his father, William C. Whitney (The Order '63). Alfred Gwynne Vanderbilt (The Order '99) represented the Vanderbilt family until he drowned at sea in the sinking of the *Lusitania* in 1915. (His sister Gertrude married Harry Payne Whitney, above). The power of The Order is reflected in a bizarre incident as Alfred Gwynne Vanderbilt boarded the *Lusitania* in New York on its fateful voyage. A telegram warning Vanderbilt not to sail was delivered to the *Lusitania* before it sailed — but never reached Vanderbilt. Consequently, Vanderbilt went down with the ship.

The Harriman investment in Guaranty Trust has been represented by W. Averell Harriman.

The Rockefeller investment in Guaranty Trust was represented by Percy Rockefeller (The Order '00).

In brief, The Order was closely associated with Guaranty Trust and Morgan-Guaranty long before 1912 when Mrs. Edward Harriman sold her interest to J.P. Morgan. Averell Harriman remained on the Board of Guaranty Trust after the transfer. The following members of The Order have also been officers and directors of Guaranty Trust Company:

Harold Stanley (The Order 1908): Harold Stanley, born 1885, was the son of William Stanley, an inventor associated with General Electric Company. Stanley prepared for Yale University at the elitist Hotchkiss School, Lakeville, Connecticut. An excellent athlete, Stanley graduated Yale in 1908 and was initiated into The Order.

After Yale, Stanley joined National Bank of Albany and then, between 1913-1915, was with J.G. White (prominent in construction of the Soviet First Five Year Plan). In 1915 Stanley joined Guaranty Trust as Vice President. From 1921 to 1928 he was President of Guaranty Trust and then a partner in the firm of J.P. Morgan, replacing William Morrow. From 1935 to 1941 he was President of Morgan, Stanley & Company, then a partner from 1941 to 1955 and a limited partner after 1956, until his death in 1963.

In brief, a member of The Order was Vice President, then President of Guaranty Trust Company in the years 1915 to 1928 — the years which record the Bolshevik Revolution and the rise of Hitler to power in Germany.

Joseph R. Swan (The Order '02). The Guaranty Company was a subsidiary of Guaranty Trust Co. Joseph Rockwell Swan (The Order '02) was President of the Guaranty Company as well as a director of Guaranty Trust Company.

Percy Rockefeller (The Order '00). Percy Rockefeller, born 1878, was the son of William D. Rockefeller (brother of John D. Rockefeller) and inherited part of the Standard Oil fortune. Percy was a director of Guaranty Trust in the 1915-1930 period.

How The Order Relates To Guaranty Trust Company And Brown Brothers, Harriman

THE
ORDER

GUARANTY TRUST COMPANY

HAROLD STANLEY (The Order '08)
W. MURRAY CRANE (The Order '04)
HARRY P. WHITNEY (The Order '94)
W. AVERALL HARRIMAN (The Order '13)
KNIGHT WOOLLEY (The Order '17)
FRANK P. SHEPARD (The Order '17)
JOSEPH R. SWAN (The Order '02)
THOMAS COCHRANE (The Order '94)
PERCY ROCKEFELLER (The Order '00)

POST WORLD WAR II PARTNERS
GEORGE H. CHITTENDEN (The Order '39)
WILLIAM REDMOND CROSS (The Order '41)
HENRY P. DAVISON, JR. (The Order '20)
THOMAS RODD (The Order '35)
CLEMENT D. GILE (The Order '39)
DANIEL P. DAVISON (The Order '49)

BROWN BROTHERS, HARRIMAN,
formerly
W.A. HARRIMAN

W. AVERELL HARRIMAN (The Order '13)
E. ROLAND HARRIMAN (The Order '17)
ELLERGY S. JAMES (The Order '17)
RAY MORRIS (The Order '01)
PRESCOTT SHELDON BUSH (The Order '17)
KNIGHT WOOLLEY (The Order '17)
MORTIMER SEABURY (The Order '09)
ROBERT A. LOVETT (The Order '18)

POST WORLD WAR II PARTNERS
EUGENE WM. STETSON, JR. (The Order '34) (1937-42)
WALTER H. BROWN (The Order '45)
STEPHEN Y. HORD (The Order '21)
JOHN BECKWITH MADDEN (The Order '41)
GRANGE K. COSTIKYAN (The Order '29)

PARTNER NOT IN THE ORDER:
MATTHEW C. BRUSH (32° Mason)

IV. BROWN BROTHERS, HARRIMAN

The other operational vehicle used by The Order was the private banking firm of Brown Brothers, Harriman. Before 1933 W.A. Harriman Company was the vehicle, and Brown Brothers did not enter the picture. After 1933, the merged firm continued Harriman Company activities.

In *Introduction To The Order* we presented details of the merged firm (pp. 29-33). There is, however, one aspect we want to identify: the extraordinary role of the Yale Class of '17 in Brown Brothers, Harriman and the events to be described in Memoranda Three and Four.

The following **five** members in the class of '17 (only fifteen were initiated) were involved:

Knight Woolley (The Order '17) was with Guaranty Trust from 1919-1920, Harriman Company from 1927-1931, then Brown Brothers, Harriman from 1933 to the present time. Woolley was also a director of the Federal Reserve Bank.

Frank P. Shepard (The Order '17) also joined Guaranty Trust in 1919 and was a Vice President from 1920 to 1934, the period concerned with development of both Soviet Russia and Hitler's Nazi Party. From 1934 onwards Shepard was with Bankers Trust Company, a member of the Morgan group of banks.

Ellery Sedgewick James (The Order '17) was a partner in Brown Brothers, Harriman.

And finally, two interesting characters: Edward Roland Noel Harriman (The Order '17) and Sheldon Prescott Bush (The Order '17), the father of President George Herbert Walker Bush (The Order '49), and grandfather of President George Walker Bush (The Order '68).

V. THE ORDER'S "FRONT MAN": MATTHEW C. BRUSH

From World War I until well into the 1930s The Order's "front man" in both Guaranty Trust and Brown Brothers, Harriman was Matthew C. Brush.

Brush was not Yale, nor a member of The Order, but through an accidental meeting in the 1890s his talents were used by The Order. Brush became a Knight Templar, a 32nd degree Mason and a Shriner, but not — so far as we can trace — more closely linked to the power center.

Brush was born in Stillwater, Minnesota in 1877 and was a graduate of the Armour Institute of Technology and MIT. By accident his first job in the 1890s was as a clerk with Franklin MacVeagh & Company of Chicago. Franklin MacVeagh was a member (The Order '62) and later Secretary of the Treasury (1909-1913) under President William Taft (The Order '78).

MacVeagh himself, as distinct from Brush, is a little difficult to classify. In 1913 MacVeagh left the Treasury and resigned as trustee of the University of Chicago. By 1919 he had become delinquent in his fees to Russell Trust. We have a copy of a dunning notice sent to MacVeagh by Otto Bannard (The Order '76), President of New York Life and Treasurer for The Order in 1919. The notice asked MacVeagh to pay up his dues.

While the trail of MacVeagh fades out after 1913, that of Matthew Brush, his one-time clerk, blossoms forth. After a series of posts in railroad companies, Brush was made Vice President of American International Corporation in 1918 and President in 1923. He was also Chairman of the Equitable Office Building, also known as 120 Broadway, illustrated on page 139.

Moreover, Brush was President of Barnsdall Corporation and Georgian Manganese Company; the significance of these posts will be seen in the next memorandum.

The purpose of this memorandum has been to demonstrate control of two banking houses by members of The Order. Both Guaranty Trust and Brown Brothers, Harriman can truly be said to have been dominated and substantially owned by individuals identified as members. Furthermore, both Guaranty Trust and the original W.A. Harriman Company were **established** by members of The Order. Brown Brothers was not absorbed until 1933.

Now, let's examine the evidence that these two banking firms have been vehicles for creation of war and revolution.

Memorandum Number Three: Thesis — *The Order* Creates The Soviet Union

In an earlier book, published in 1974, we presented major evidence of Wall Street assistance for the Bolshevik Revolution. This assistance was mainly cash, guns and ammunition, and diplomatic support in London and Washington, D.C. *Wall Street And The Bolshevik Revolution* also introduced the concept which Quigley described, i.e., that Morgan and other financial interests financed and influenced **all** parties from left to right in the political spectrum.

This Memorandum continues the story, but now links The Order to the earlier evidence of Wall Street involvement.

On the following pages we reproduce a map of the Wall Street area and a list of firms connected with the Bolshevik Revolution and financing of Hitler located in this area. We can now identify the influence, in fact the dominant influence, of The Order in these firms.

Revolutionary activity was centered at Equitable Trust Building, 120 Broadway, in the building in the photograph on page 139. This had been E.H. Harriman's address. The American International Corporation was located at 120 Broadway. The Bankers' Club, where Wall Street bankers met for lunch, was at the very top of the building. It was in this plush club that plans were laid by William Boyce Thompson for Wall Street participation in the 1917 Russian Revolution. Guaranty Securities was in 120 Broadway, while Guaranty Trust was next door at 140 Broadway (the building can be seen to the left of 120).

I. THE ORDER PUSHES FOR ASSISTANCE TO THE SOVIET ARMY

Fortunately we have a copy of the memorandum written by a member of The Order, summarizing intentions for the 1917 Bolshevik Revolution. The memorandum was written by Thomas D. Thacher (The Order '04), a partner in the Wall Street law firm of Simpson, Thacher & Bartlett. Thacher's address was 120 Broadway. Today this law firm, now in Battery Plaza, has the largest billing on Wall Street and has former Secretary of State Cyrus Vance (Scroll & Key) as a partner.

In 1917 Thacher was in Russia with William Boyce Thompson's Red Cross Mission. After consultations in New York, Thacher was then sent to London to confer with Lord Northcliffe about the Bolshevik Revolution and then to Paris for similar talks with the French Government.

The Thacher memorandum not only urges recognition of the barely surviving Soviet Government, which in early 1918 controlled only a very small portion of Russia, but also military assistance for the Soviet Army and intervention to keep the Japanese out of Siberia until the Bolsheviks could take over.

120 Broadway, 1915

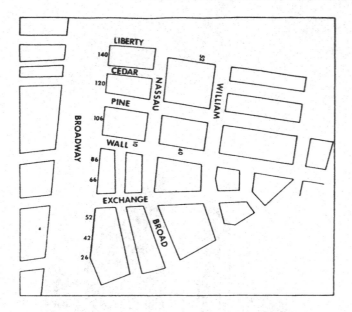

FIRMS WITH LINKS TO THE ORDER AT, OR NEAR, 120 BROADWAY IN 1917

120 Broadway	Edward H. Harriman (before his death)
59 Broadway	W.A. Harriman Company
120 Broadway	American International Corporation
23 Wall	J.P. Morgan firm
120 Broadwat	Federal Reserve Bank of New York
120 Broadway	Bankers Club (top floor)
120 Broadway	Thomas D. Thacher (of Simpson, Thacher & Bartlett)
14 Wall	William Boyce Thompson
120 Broadway	Guggenheim Exploration
15 Broad	Stetson, Jennings & Russell
120 Broadway	C.A.K. Martens of Weinberg & Posner (the first Soviet "ambassador")
110 W. 40th Street	Soviet Bureau
60 Broadway	Amos Pinchot's office
120 Broadway	Stone & Webster
120 Broadway	General Electric
120 Broadway	Sinclair Gulf Corp.
120 Broadway	Guaranty Securities
140 Broadway	Guaranty Trust Company
233 Boradway	Anglo-Russian Chamber of Commerce

INDIVIDUAL MEMBERS OF THE ORDER AT 120 Broadway:
George Webster Adams (The Order '04)
Allen Wallace Ames (The Order '18)
Philip Lyndon Dodge (The Order '07)

Here are the main sections from the Thacher memorandum:
"First of all . . . the Allies should discourage Japanese intervention in Siberia. In the second place, the fullest assistance should be given to the Soviet Government in its efforts to organize a volunteer revolutionary army. Thirdly, the Allied Governments should give their moral support to the Russian people in their efforts to work out their own political systems free from the domination of any foreign power . . . Fourthly, until the time when open conflict shall result between the German Government and the Soviet Government of Russia there will be opportunity for peaceful commercial penetration by German agencies in Russia. So long as there is no open break, it will probably be impossible to entirely prevent such commerce. Steps should therefore be taken to impede, so far as possible, the transport of grain and raw materials to Germany from Russia."[1]

The reader should note in particular paragraph two: "In the second place, the fullest assistance should be given to the Soviet Government in its efforts to organize a volunteer revolutionary army." This assistance has been recorded in my *National Suicide: Military Aid To The Soviet Union.*

It was in fact the **hidden** policy adopted at the highest levels, in absolute secrecy, by the United States and to some extent by The Group (especially Milner) in Great Britain. Thacher apparently did not have too much success with the French Government.

When President Woodrow Wilson sent U.S. troops to hold the Trans-Siberian railroad, secret instructions were given by Woodrow Wilson **in person** to General William S. Graves. We have not yet located these instructions (although we know they exist), but a close reading of the available files shows that American intervention had little to do with anti-Bolshevik activity, as the Soviets, George Kennan and other writers maintain.

So grateful were the Soviets for American assistance in the Revolution that in 1920 — when the last American troops left Vladivostok — the Bolsheviks gave them a friendly farewell.

Reported the *New York Times* (February 15, 1920 7:4):

[1]The full document is in U.S. State Department Decimal File Microcopy 316, Roll 13, Frame 698.

relatives here.

VLADIVOSTOK PRO-AMERICAN.

Revolutionist Staff Thanks Graves for Preserving Neutrality.

VLADIVOSTOK, Feb. 1 (Associated Press).—Parades, street meetings and speechmaking marked the second day today of the city's complete liberation from Kolchak authority. Red flags fly on every Government building, many business houses and homes.

There is a pronounced pro-American feeling evident. In front of the American headquarters the revolutionary leaders mounted steps of buildings across the street, making speeches calling the Americans real friends, who at a critical time saved this present movement. The people insist upon an allied policy of no interference internationally in political affairs.

The General Staff of the new Government at Nikolsk has telegraphed to the American commander, Major Gen. Graves, expressing its appreciation for efforts toward guaranteeing an allied policy of non-interference during the occupation of the city, also in aiding in a peaceful settlement of the local situation.

Note in particular the sentence:

". . . calling the Americans real friends, who at a critical time saves this present movement."

Normally reports inconsistent with the Establishment line are choked, either by the wire services or by the rewrite desks at larger newspapers (small papers unfortunately follow *New York Times*). This is one report that got through intact.

In fact, the United States took over and held the Siberian Railroad until the Soviets gained sufficient power to take it over. Both British and French military missions in Siberia recorded the extraordinary actions of the United States Army, but neither mission made much headway with its own government.

So far as aiding the Soviet Army is concerned, there are State Department records that show guns and ammunition were shipped to the Bolsheviks. And in 1919, while Trotsky was making anti-American speeches in public, he was also asking Ambassador Francis for American military inspection teams to train the new Soviet Army.[1]

[1] See Antony C. Sutton, *National Suicide* (Arlington House, New York, 1974) and *Wall Street And The Bolshevik Revolution* (Arlington House, New York, 1974)

II. THE ORDER PUSHES FOR THE SOVIETS IN THE UNITED STATES

However, it was in Washington and London that The Order **really** aided the Soviets. The Order succeeded not only in preventing military actions against the Bolsheviks, but to so-muddy the policy waters that much needed vital raw materials and goods, ultimately even loans, were able to flow from the United States to the Soviets, in spite of a legal ban.

The following documents illustrate how members of The Order were able to encourage Soviet ambitions in the United States. While the Department of Justice was deporting so-called "Reds" to Russia, a much more potent force was at work WITHIN the U.S. Government to keep the fledgling Soviet Union intact.

Publisher's Note: *To assist readers with the very poor reproductions of the following two letters we print our reading from the copies that we have.*

211
Hon. William Kent,   May 29, 1919
U.S. Tariff Commission,
Washington, D.C.

Dear Billy:

This will introduce to you my friend, Professor Evans Clark, now associated with the Bureau of Information of the Russian Soviet Republic. He wants to talk with you about the recognition of Wolchak, the raising of the blockade, etc., and get your advice in regard to backing up the senators who would be apt to stand up and make a brave fight. Won't you do what you can for him.

As I see it, we are taking a (unreadable) Russia that will leave our, until now, mightily good reputation, badly damaged.

Hope to see you in Washington soon.

Faithfully yours,
A.P.

1543
Mr. Santeri Nourteva,   November 22, 1918
Finnish Information Bureau,
299 Broadway, City

Dear Mr. Nuorteva:

Let me thank you for your very kind letter of November 1st; I apologize for not answering sooner.

I have read your bulletin on the barrage of lies, and I am, needless to say, heartily sympathetic with your view of the situation and with the work you are doing. One of the most sinister things at present is the fact that governments are going into the advertising business. They are organized so that they can make or wreck movements. I am sending you, under separate cover, a copy of a letter I have written, which I hope will interest you.

With kindest regards, I am

Sincerely yours,
Amos Pinchot

211

Office of
Amos Pinchot
101 Park Avenue
New York

Dear Irvine,
Hope you will talk to

··· ··, 1919

Mr. Clark

On...

Hon. William Kent,
U. S. Tariff Commission,
Washington, D. C.

Dear Billy:
This will introduce to you my friend,
Professor Evans Clark, now connected with
the Bureau of Information of the Russian
Soviet Republic.   He wants to talk with
you about the recognition of Bolshevik, the
raising of the blockade, etc., and get your
advice in regard to backing up the senators
who would be apt to stand up and make a
brave fight.   Trust you to do what you can for
him.
As I see it, we are backing a thing in
Russia that will make our...til...,...it's
good reputation, Billy...did.
Hope to see you in Washington...

Faithfully yours,

A.P.

212

Senator Lenroot
Introducing
Prof. Evans Clark.

**Exhibits 211 and 212 From The Lusk Committee
Files, New York.**

|1543|

Office of
Amos Pinchot
60 Broadway } 101 PARK AVE
New York

...ove...er ..., 1918

.r. S..teri ..orteva,
Finnish Information Bureau,
... Broadway, City

Dear .r. ..orteva:
    Let me thank you for your very ki.. letter of
...ove..ber 1st; I apologize for .ot answering sooner.
    I have read your bulletin on the barrage of
lies, and I am, needless to say, heartily sympathetic
with your view of the situation and with the work you
are doing. One of the most sinister things at present
is the ri.ot that governments are going into the a-
vertising business. They are organized so that they
can make or wreck movements. I am sending you,
under separate cover, a copy of a letter I have written,
which I hope will interest you.
    ...ith kindest regards, I am
            Sincerely yours,

                    Amos Pinchot

U.S. State Department Decimal File, 851.516/140
Stockholm Legation October 13, 1922

— 145 —

The above letter is from Amos Pinchot (The Order '97). His brother, conservationist Gifford Pinchot (The Order '89) was also a member. Amos Pinchot was a founder of the American Civil Liberties Union and active in aiding the Soviets during the early days of the Bolshevik Revolution. The above letter, exemplifying this assistance, was sent to Santeri Nourteva, November 22, 1918, just a year after the 1917 Revolution. Pinchot was "heartily sympathetic with your view of the situation and the work you are doing."[1]

Who was Nourteva? This name was an alias for Alexander Nyberg, a Soviet representative in the United States. Nyberg worked for the Soviet Bureau (at first called the Finnish Information Bureau — a cover name), along with Ludwig C.A.K. Martens, the first Soviet Ambassador and formerly a Vice President of Weinberg & Posner. The New York office of Weinberg & Posner was at — 120 Broadway! Nyberg's assistant was Kenneth Durant, an American newspaper man, later TASS correspondent in the U.S. and one time aide to "Colonel" Edward House, mystery man of the Wilson Administration. Director of the Commercial Department in this Soviet Bureau was "Comrade Evans Clark." Clark later became Executive Director of the influential Twentieth Century Foundation, and at Twentieth Century Foundation we find a member of The Order — in this case Charles Phelps Taft (The Order '18), nephew of President and Chief Justice William Howard Taft. In the coming volume on FOUNDATIONS, we shall see how Evans Clark and The Order, working together at Twentieth Century Foundation, had a significant role in the Hegelization of American education.

The document on page 147 is a brief biography of "Comrade Evans Clark", issued by the Soviet Bureau in 1919 on his appointment as Assistant, Director of the Commercial Department of the Bureau, with the task of establishing trade relations with the U.S. Note the Harvard and Princeton associations.

Trade was vital for the survival of the Soviet Union. In 1919 all Russian factories and transportation were at a standstill. There were no raw materials and no skills available.

For assistance Evans Clark turned to The Order. On May 29, 1919, Amos Pinchot wrote fellow Skull & Bones member and strong Republican William Kent about raising the blockade against the Soviets. William Kent (The Order '87) was on the U.S. Tariff Commission and in turn wrote Senator Lenroot to request an interview for "Professor" Evans Clark. (Albert Kent, his father, was a member [The Order '53] and he married the daughter of Thomas Thacher [The Order '35].

In brief, two members of The Order, Pinchot and Kent, cooperated to

---

[1]Exhibit Number 1543 from the Lusk Committee files, New York.

push a known Bolshevik operator onto an unsuspecting Senator. Neither member of The Order advised Senator Lenroot about Clark's affiliation with the Soviet Bureau.

1500

BUREAU OF INFORMATION ON SOVIET RUSSIA
299 Broadway, Room 1812

Statement April 19th

Comrade Evans Clark has resigned his position as Director of the Bureau of Research of the Socialist Aldermanic Delegation in New York, and has been appointed Assistant Director of the Commercial Department of the Bureau of the Representative of the Russian Socialist Federal Soviet Republic with headquarters at the World's Tower Building - 110 West 40th Street.

Comrade Clark has been a member of the Socialist Party since 1911 and has taken an active part in the labor movement in the United States. He is a graduate of Amherst College, Harvard University and the Columbia Law-School. He has been instructor of politics in Princeton University and was one of the organizers of the Intercollegiate Socialist Society of which he was the first President Comrade Clark will assist Comrade Heller in the task of establishing trade relations between the United States and Soviet Russia.

Exhibit Number 1500 From the Lusk Committee Files, New York.

How The Order Controlled The Early Development Of The Soviet Union

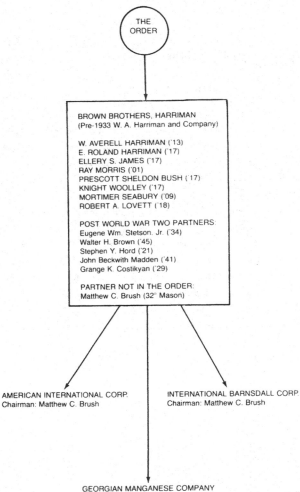

THE ORDER

BROWN BROTHERS, HARRIMAN
(Pre-1933 W. A. Harriman and Company)

W. AVERELL HARRIMAN ('13)
E. ROLAND HARRIMAN ('17)
ELLERY S. JAMES ('17)
RAY MORRIS ('01)
PRESCOTT SHELDON BUSH ('17)
KNIGHT WOOLLEY ('17)
MORTIMER SEABURY ('09)
ROBERT A. LOVETT ('18)

POST WORLD WAR TWO PARTNERS:
Eugene Wm. Stetson. Jr. ('34)
Walter H. Brown ('45)
Stephen Y. Hord ('21)
John Beckwith Madden ('41)
Grange K. Costikyan ('29)

PARTNER NOT IN THE ORDER:
Matthew C. Brush (32° Mason)

AMERICAN INTERNATIONAL CORP.
Chairman: Matthew C. Brush

INTERNATIONAL BARNSDALL CORP.
Chairman: Matthew C. Brush

GEORGIAN MANGANESE COMPANY
Director: Matthew C. Brush

III. HOW THE ORDER DEVELOPED THE STAGNANT SOVIET UNION

Between 1917 and 1921 the Soviets pushed their control of Russia into Siberia and the Caucasus. As we have noted, the United States intervened in Siberia along the Trans-Siberian Railroad. Histories of U.S. intervention by George Kennan and the Soviets maintain this was an anti-Soviet intervention. In fact, it was nothing of the kind. The U.S. spread troops along the Siberian railroad only to keep out the Japanese, not to keep out the Soviets. When they left through Vladivostok, the Soviet authorities gave American forces a resouding send-off. But this is yet another untold story, not in the textbooks.

The immediate problem facing the Soviets was to restore silent Russian factories. This needed raw materials, technical skills and working capital. The key to Russian reconstruction was the oil fields of the Caucasus. The Caucasus oil fields are a major segment of Russian natural resource wealth. Baku, the most important field, was developed in the 1870s. **In 1900 it was producing more crude oil than the United States,** and in 1901 more than half of the total world crude output. The Caucasus oil fields survived Revolution and Intervention without major structural damage and became a significant factor in Soviet economic recovery, generating about 20 percent of all exports by value; **the largest single source of foreign exchange.**

The Bolsheviks took over the Caucasus in 1920-1, but until 1923 oil field drilling almost ceased. During the first year of Soviet rule ". . . not one single new well has started giving oil"[1] and even two years after Soviet occupation, no new oil-field properties had been developed. In addition, deepening of old wells virtually ceased. As a result, water percolated into the wells, and the flow of crude oil became a mixture of oil and water. Drilling records are an excellent indicator of the state of oil field maintenance, development, and production. The complete collapse after the Soviet takeover is clearly suggested by the statistics. In 1900, Russia had been the world's largest producer and exporter of crude oil; almost 50,000 feet of drilling per month had been required in Baku alone to maintain this production. By early 1921, the average monthly drilling in Baku had declined to an insignificant 370 feet or so (0.7 percent of the 1900 rate), although 162 rigs were in working order.

Then, Serebrovsky, Chairman of Azneft (the Soviet oil production trust), put forward a program for recovery in a *Pravda* article. The plan for 1923 was to increase oil well drilling to 35,000 sazhens per year (245,000 feet). This would require 35 rotary drills (to drill 77,000 feet) and 157 percussion drills (to drill 130,000 feet). Serebrovsky pointed out that Azneft had no rotary drills, and that Russian enterprise could

[1]U.S. State Dept. Decimal File, 316-137-221.

not supply them. Rotary drilling, however, was essential for the success of the plan.

He then announced:

"But just here American capital is going to support us. The American firm International Barnsdall Corporation has submitted a plan . . . Lack of equipment prevents us from increasing the production of the oil industry of Baku by ourselves. The American firm . . . will provide the equipment, start drilling in the oil fields and organize the technical production of oil with deep pumps."[1]

During the next few years International Barnsdall, together with the Lucey Manufacturing Company and other major foreign oil well equipment firms, fulfilled Serebrovsky's program. Massive imports of equipment came from the United States. International Barnsdall inaugurated the rotary drilling program, initiated Azneft drilling crews into its operational problems, and reorganized oil well pumping with deep well electrical pumps.

The first International Barnsdall concession was signed in October 1921, and was followed in September of 1922 by two further agreements. There is no doubt that Barnsdall did work under the agreements. *Pravda* reported groups of American oil field workers on their way to the oil fields, and a couple of months previously the United States, Constantinople Consulate, had reported that Philip Chadbourn, the Barnsdall Caucasus representative, had passed through on his way **out** of Russia. The U.S. State Department Archives contain an intriguing quotation from Rykov, dated October 1922:

"The one comparatively bright spot in Russia is the petroleum industry, and this is due largely to the fact that a number of American workers have been brought into the oil fields to superintend their operation."[2]

Who, or what, was International Barnsdall Corporation?

The Chairman of International Barnsdall Corporation was Matthew C. Brush whom we previously identified as The Order's "front man."

Guaranty Trust, Lee, Higginson Company and W.A. Harriman owned Barnsdall Corporation, and International Barnsdall Corporation was owned 75% by the Barnsdall Corporation and 25% by H. Mason Day. The Guaranty Trust interest was represented by Eugene W. Stetson (also a Vice President of Guaranty Trust), whose son, Eugene W. Stetson Jr., was initiated into The Order in 1934. The Lee Higginson interest was represented by Frederick Winthrop Allen (The Order '00).

---

[1]*Pravda*, September 21, 1922.

[2]U.S. State Department Decimal File, Microcopy 316, Roll 107, Frame 1167.

In brief, The Order controlled International Barnsdall Corporation.

The second potentially largest source of Soviet foreign exchange in the 1920s was the large Russian manganese deposits. In 1913, tsarist Russia supplied 52 percent of world manganese, of which about 76 percent, or one million tons, was mined from the Chiaturi deposits in the Caucasus. Production in 1920 was zero, and by 1924 had risen only to about 320,000 tons per year. The basic problem was:

"that further development was seriously retarded by the primitive equipment, which was considered grossly inadequate even according to prewar standards."

The Chiaturi deposits, situated on high plateaus some distance from Batum, were mined in a primitive manner, and the ore was brought on donkeys from the plateaus to the railroads. There was a change of gauge en route, and the manganese had to be transshipped between the original loading point and the port. When at the port, the ore was transferred by bucket: a slow, expensive process.

The Soviets acquired modern mining and transportation facilities for their manganese deposits, acquired foreign exchange, and finally shattered American foreign policy concerning loans to the U.S.S.R., in a series of business agreements with W.A. Harriman Company and Guaranty Trust.[1]

On July 12, 1925, a concession agreement was made between the W.A. Harriman Company of New York and the U.S.S.R. for exploitation of the Chiaturi manganese deposits and extensive introduction of modern mining and transportation methods.

Under the Harriman concession agreement, $4 million was spent on mechanizing the mines and converting them from hand to mechanical operation. A washer and reduction plant were built; and a loading elevator at Poti, with a two million ton capacity and a railroad system were constructed, together with an aerial tramway for the transfer of manganese ore. The expenditure was approximately $2 million for the railroad system and $1 million for mechanization of the mines.

The Chairman of the Georgian Manganese Company, the Harriman operating company on the site in Russia, **was none other than The Order's "front man" Matthew C. Brush.**

---

[1] The interested reader is referred to over 300 pages of documents in the U.S. State Dept. Decimal File 316-138-12/331, and the German Foreign Ministry Archives. Walter Duranty described the Harriman contract as "utterly inept" and von Dirksen of the German Foreign Office as "a rubber contract." The full contract was published [Vysshii sovet nardnogo khoziaistva, *Concession Agreement Between The Government Of The U.S.S.R and W.A. Harriman & Co. Inc. Of New York* (Moscow, 1925)].

In reply refer   November 14, 1924.
to FE

Dear Mr. Atherton:

   Please accept my thanks for your letter of October
30, 1924, transmitting a clipping from the TIMES of
October 28, giving an account of the Prime Minister's
speech in which reference is made to a concession
granted to Americans for the manganese ore in Russia,
and enclosing a confidential memorandum respecting the
nature of the concession.

   I appreciate your courtesy and thoughtfulness in
the matter. The memorandum transmitted by you embodies
the first information received by the Department concerning the concession other than that which has appeared in the public press.

                         Sincerely yours,

                              Evan E. Young.
Ray Atherton, Esquire,
   Secretary, American Embassy,
      London.

EEY:LGS
      4-20.
   Nov. 14 1924.po

State Department Letter To U.S. Embassy
In London (861.637/1)

IV. THE ORDER TOO POWERFUL FOR STATE DEPARTMENT TO INVESTIGATE

While The Order carried out its plans to develop Russia, the State Department could do nothing. Its bureaucrats sat in Washington D.C. like a bunch of mesmerized jackrabbits.

Firstly, in the 1920s loans to the Soviet Union were strictly against U.S. law. While American citizens could enter Russia at their own risk, there were no diplomatic relations and no government support or sanction for commercial activity. Public and government sentiment in the United States was overwhelmingly against the Soviets — not least for the widespread atrocities committed in the name of the Revolution.

Secondly, the Harriman-Guaranty syndicate, which reflected The Order, did **not** inform the State Department of its plans. As the attached letter (page 152) from Washington to the London Embassy describes, the first information of the Harriman manganese deposit came from the American Embassy in London, which picked it up from London newspaper reports.

In other words, Averell Harriman sneaked an illegal project past the U.S. Government. If this is not irresponsible behavior, then nothing is. And this was the man who was later to become the U.S. Ambassador to Russia.

The State Department letter to London is quite specific on this point: "The memorandum transmitted by you embodies the first information received by the Department concerning the concession other than that which has appeared in the public press."

A month or so later came a letter from Department of Commerce asking for confirmation and more information. Apparently, Harriman didn't bother to inform Commerce either.

DIVISION OF
EASTERN EUROPEAN AFFAIRS.
JAN 28 1925

DEPARTMENT OF COMMERCE
BUREAU OF FOREIGN AND DOMESTIC COMMERCE
WASHINGTON

JAN 26 1925

DEPARTMENT OF STATE
January 23, 1925.

January 31, 1925

Hon. Wilbur J. Carr,
Assistant Secretary of State,
Department of State,
Washington, D.C.

IN REPLY REFER TO. 51-m

Dear Mr. Carr:

We have a copy of confidential despatch No. 2565 to the Secretary of State from Minister F.W.B. Coleman at Riga, Latvia, in regard to a conversation with a Mr. P.M. Friedlander on the subject of Russia.

On page 7 of this report there is a paragraph which reads as follows:

"Magraf is the Agent of the Imperial and Foreign Corporation, which represents its own, Harriman and Stinnes interest in the matter of the Chiaturi Manganese Concession. **********
It appears from Mr. Friedlander's account that they have pooled their interest and are presenting a united front".

The subject of the Chiaturi Manganese concession is of great interest to the American Mineral Industry and its control by an American concern will have a notable effect on the steel industry of this country. For this reason, we are interested in obtaining the most reliable information possible on this subject and therefore request that you obtain for us, if possible, confirmation of the above report. We would like to know something more as to the reliability of Mr. Friedlander's statements and any further facts in this case that are procurable.

Very truly yours,

R.C. Miller,
Liaison Officer.

ADDRESS ALL COMMUNICATIONS TO
BUREAU OF FOREIGN AND DOMESTIC COMMERCE
WASHINGTON, D.C.

gpo

Commerce Department To State Asking For Confirmation Of Harriman Manganese Concession (861.637/5)

DEPARTMENT OF STATE

DIVISION OF EASTERN EUROPEAN AFFAIRS

January 25, 1925.

A-C

Dear Mr. Carr:

> Assistant Secretary
> of State
>
> JAN 26 1925
>
> MR. CARR

With respect to the attached letter from Mr. Miller, Liaison Officer with the Department of Commerce, there are certain and very definite reasons why I consider it very unwise for the Department to initiate any investigation with respect to the reported manganese concession. I shall be glad to explain these reasons to you orally if you so desire.

Evan E. Young.

861.637/5

EEY:EBS

I defer to your judgment upon this. WC.

Now we reach the truly exraordinary point. The U.S. Government was not informed by W.A. Harriman or Guaranty Trust that they intended to invest $4 million developing Soviet manganese deposits. Yet this was clearly illegal and a move with obvious strategic consequences for the U.S. Neither was the U.S. Government able to pick up this information elsewhere; in those days there was no CIA. Economic intelligence was handled by the State Department. It is also obvious that Government officials were interested in acquiring information, as they should have been.

The truly extraordinary point is THAT THE U.S. GOVERNMENT WAS NOT ABLE TO PURSUE AN INVESTIGATION.

We reproduce on page 155 a memorandum from Evan E. Young in Division of Eastern European Affairs to Assistant Secretary of State Carr. Note this is a memorandum at the **upper** levels of the State Department. Young specifically writes: ". . . there are certain and very definite reasons why I consider it very unwise for the Department to **initiate** any investigation with respect to the reported manganese concession."

And Assistant Secretary of State Carr scribbles on the bottom, "I defer to your judgment upon this" (presumably after the suggested oral communication).

The distinct impression is that some behind-the-scenes power was not to be challenged.

-2-

Max May, of the Guaranty Trust Company, New York, will take part. In the present arrangement Mr. Max May is designated as director of the foreign division of the Moscow bank.

The above paper gives the following information in regard to the new bank:

"There is a board consisting of five members and five active directors. Among these we note Mr. Schlesinger, former Chief of Moscow's Merchant Bank, Mr. Kalaschkin, Chief of the Junker Bank, and Mr. Ternoffsky, former Chief of the Siberian Bank. Mr. Max May is designated as director of the foreign division of the bank. According to Mr. Asch-berg, the Russian bank, through the Ekonomibolaget, Mr. Asch-berg's bank in Stockholm, will be in closer contact with German and American financial institutions."

The "Svenska Dagbladet", of October 17th, reports that the above mentioned Mr. Scheinmann has succeeded in obtaining the consent of Professor Gustav Cassel to act as adviser to the Russian State Bank, which bank it appears has a representative in the administration of the new Commercial Bank of Moscow and has the right to exercise control of its activities. Professor Cassel is quoted as stating in part:

"That a bank has now been started in Russia to take care of purely banking matters is a great step forward, and it seems to me that this bank was established in order to do something to create a new economic life in Russia. What Russia needs is a bank to create internal and external commerce. If there is to be any business between Russia and other countries there must be a bank to handle it.

"This step forward should be supported in every way by other countries, and when I was asked my advice I stated that I was prepared to give it. I am not in favor of a negative policy and believe that every opportunity should be seized to help in a positive reconstruction.

"The great question is how to bring the Russian exchange back to normal. It is a complicated question and will necessitate thorough investigation. To solve this problem I am naturally more than willing to take part in the work. To leave Russia to her own resources and her own fate is folly."

I have the honor to be, Sir,

Your obedient servant,

[signature]

IRA N. MORRIS.

U.S. State Department Decimal File, 861.516/140
Stockholm Legation October 13, 1922

S.R. Bertron (The Order '84')
Chairman Of American-Russian Chamber Of Commerce

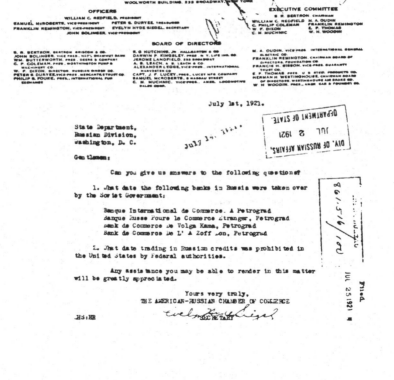

V. THE ORDER MAKES ITS OWN LAW

The Order kept a hold on every non-government strategic position related to the Soviet Union. Nothing appears to have escaped their attention. For example, the Anglo-Russian Chamber of Commerce was created in 1920 to promote trade with Russia — desperately needed by the Soviets to restore idle Tsarist industry. The Chairman of its Executive Committee, the key post in the Chamber, was held by Samuel R. Bertron (The Order '85), a Vice President of Guaranty Trust and formerly a member of the 1917 Root Mission to Russia. Elihu Root, Chairman of the Mission, was, of course, the personal attorney to William Collins Whitney (The Order '63), one of the key members of The Order. The letter from Bertron's Anglo-Russian Chamber of Commerce to State Department, printed on page 158 is noteworthy because it asks the question: "What date trading in Russian credits was prohibited in the United States by Federal authorities?"

This means that The Order was well aware in 1921 that "credits" to the U.S.S.R. were illegal and indeed were not made legal until President Roosevelt took office in 1933. However, illegal or not, within 18 months of this Bertron letter, Guaranty Trust established more than trading in Russian credits. Guaranty Trust made a joint banking agreement with the Soviets and installed a Guaranty Trust Vice President, Max May, as director in charge of the foreign division of this Soviet bank, the RUSKOMBANK (See document on page 157).

In brief, while the U.S. public was being assured by the U.S. Government that the Soviets were dastardly murderers, while "Reds" were being deported back to Russia by the Department of Justice, while every politician (almost without exception) was assuring the American public that the United States would have no relations with the Soviets — while this barrage of lies was aimed at a gullible public, behind the scenes the Guaranty Trust Company was actually running a division of a Soviet bank! And American troops were being cheered by Soviet revolutionaries for helping protect the Revolution.

That, dear readers, is why governments **need** censorship. That's why even 50 years after some events, it is almost impossible for independent researchers (not the bootlickers) to get key documents declassified.

DIVISION OF
EASTERN EUROPEAN AFFAIRS

JUL 26 1927

DEPARTMENT OF STATE

SIMPSON THACHER
120 BROADWAY
NEW YORK

Index Bureau

Dep't of State

July 21, 1927.

Hon. R. E. Olds,
Under-Secretary of State,
Washington, D. C.

Jul 27, 1927

Sir:

    The State Bank of the U.S.S.R., although, as
we are informed, its whole capital is owned by the Treasury
Department (People's Commissariat of Finance) of the Soviet
Government, is not itself the Soviet Government but a jurid-
ical entity, incorporated in November 1921 by edict of the
Soviet Government, and capable of suing and being sued as
an individual in the Soviet courts.

    This Bank already has large sums on deposit in
various banks in this country.

    In view of the growing trade between companies in
this country and the U.S.S.R. and the desire of the latter
to increase this trade, the Bank would like to increase its
deposits with banks in this country. Before advising the
Bank to increase its deposits in the amounts it desires, we
should like, if it is consistent for you so to favor us, to
receive an expression of your opinion as to the traditional
attitude of our Government with respect to such deposits.
As a practical matter, if we understand your views correctly,
it seems to us there can be no reason why the Bank should
not so increase its deposits notwithstanding our Government
has not recognized the U.S.S.R.

              Very respectfully yours,

1927: Simpson Thacher & Bartlett Gets
Around Non Recognition

VI. THE ORDER'S LAW FIRMS

New York establishment law firms, several founded by members of The Order, have close links to banks and specifically those operational vehicles for revolution already cited.

Take the example of Simpson, Thacher & Bartlett which in the 1920s was located at 120 Broadway, New York. The firm was founded by Thomas Thacher (The Order '71) in 1884. His son Thomas Day Thacher (The Order '04) worked for the family law firm after leaving Yale and initiation into The Order. The younger Thomas Thacher went to work for Henry L. Stimson (The Order '88), a very active member of The Order discussed in Volume One of this series. About this time Thacher, who wrote The Order's statement on the Bolshevik Revolution (page 138), became friendly with both Felix Frankfurter and Raymond Robins. According to extensive documentation in the Lusk Committee files, both Frankfurter and Robins were of considerable assistance to the Soviets.

Another link between the 1917 Revolution and Simpson, Thacher & Bartlett is through the daughter of Thomas Anthony Thacher (The Order '35) who married William Kent (The Order '87) who we have linked to member Amos Pinchot in the case of intervention on behalf of the Soviets in Washington, D.C.

Furthermore, readers of *Wall Street And The Bolshevik Revolution* will recall that member Samuel Bertron was on the Root Mission to Russia in 1917. Moreover, Thomas Thacher (The Order '04) was a member of the Red Cross Mission with Allan Wardwell, son of Thomas Wardwell, Standard Oil Treasurer and a partner in another Wall Street law firm, Statson, Jennings & Russell (the links of this firm to The Order will be described in a later volume). Eugene Stetson, Jr., for example, is in The Order ('34).

Simpson, Thacher & Bartlett represented the Soviet State Bank in the U.S. and was the vehicle used by The Order to inform State Department of activities that might otherwise be blocked by low level bureaucrats following the government rulebook.

For example, in 1927 Simpson, Thacher & Bartlett informed the U.S. Government that the Soviets were in the process of substantially increasing deposits in the U.S. This increase was in preparation for the enormous outlays to be channeled to a few favored U.S. firms to build the Soviet First Five Year Plan.

The letter read closely is definite; it puts words in the mouth of the State Department, i.e., this is what we are going to do and in spite of the U.S. Government, there is no reason why we should not go ahead. Note, for example, the last paragraph: ". . . it seems to us there is no reason why the Bank should not so increase its deposits notwithstanding our Government has not recognized the U.S.S.R."

RUSSIA

During the past four years the Government of the United States has maintained the position that it would be both futile and unwise to enter into relations with the Soviet Government so long as the Bolshevik leaders persist in aims and practices in the field of international relations which preclude the possibility of establishing relations on the basis of accepted principles governing intercourse between nations. It is the conviction of the Government of the United States that relations on a basis usual between friendly nations can not be established with a governmental entity which is the agency of a group who hold it as their mission to bring about the overthrow of the existing political, economic and social order throughout the world and who regulate their conduct towards other nations accordingly.

The experiences of various European Governments which have recognized and entered into relations with the Soviet regime have demonstrated conclusively the wisdom of the policy to which the Government of the United States has consistently adhered. Recognition of the Soviet regime has not brought about any cessation of interference by the Bolshevik leaders in the internal affairs of any recognizing country, nor has it led to the acceptance by them of other fundamental obligations of international intercourse. Certain European states have endeavored, by entering into discussions with representatives of the Soviet regime, to reach a settlement of outstanding differences on the basis of accepted international practices. Such conferences and discussions have been entirely fruitless. No state has been able to obtain the payment of debts contracted by Russia under preceding governments or the indemnification of its citizens for confiscated property. Indeed, there is every reason to believe that the granting of recognition and the holding of discussions have served only to encourage the present rulers of Russia in their policy of repudiation and confiscation, as well as in their hope that it is possible to establish a working basis, accepted by other nations, whereby they can continue their war on the existing political and social order in other countries.

Current developments demonstrate the continued persistence at Moscow of a dominating world revolutionary purpose and the practical manifestation of this purpose in such ways as render impossible the establishment of normal relations with the Soviet government. The present rulers of Russia, while seeking to direct the evolution of Russia along political, economic and social lines in such manner as to make it an effective "base of the world revolution", continue to carry on, through the Communist International and other organizations with headquarters at Moscow, within the borders of other nations, including the United States, extensive and carefully planned operations for the *purpose of ultimately bringing about the overthrow of the existing order in such nations.*

A mass of data with respect to the activities carried on in the United States by various Bolshevik organizations, under the direction and control of Moscow, was presented by the Department of State to a subcommittee of the Senate Committee on Foreign Relations in January 1924.

VII. WHAT THE POLITICIANS TOLD AMERICAN CITIZENS . . .

All this Soviet-building activity recorded in the Lusk Committee and State Department files was carefully concealed from the American public. What the public was told can only be described as a pack of lies, from beginning to end.

To demonstrate the degree of falsehood, we reprint here a page on "Russia" from a document "Excerpt from a statement entitled 'Foreign Relations' by the Honorable Frank B. Kellogg, Secretary of State, published by the Republican National Committee, Bulletin No. 5, 1928."

Among the falsehoods promoted by Secretary Kellogg is the following: ". . . the Government of the United States has maintained the position that it would be both futile and unwise to enter into relations with the Soviet Government."

In fact, at this very time the United States, with implicit government approval, was involved in planning the First Five Year Plan in Russia. The planning work was done actively by American firms. [1]

Construction of the Soviet dialectic arm continued throughout the 1930s up to World War II. In 1941 W.A. Harriman was appointed Lend Lease Administrator to assure the flow of United States technology and products to the Soviet Union. Examination of Lend Lease records shows that U.S. law was violated. The law required military goods **only** to be shipped. In fact, industrial equipment in extraordinary amounts was also shipped and Treasury Department currency plates so that the Soviets could freely print U.S. dollars.

Since World War II the United States has kept the Soviets abreast of modern technology. This story has been detailed elsewhere.

In brief, the creation of the Soviet Union stems from The Order. The early survival of the Soviet Union stems from The Order. The development of the Soviet Union stems from The Order.

But above all, this story has been concealed from the American public by politicians . . . more of this later. Now let's turn to the financing of the Nazi Party in Germany.

---

[1]This story has been described in my *Western Technology And Soviet Economic Development* 1917-1930 and 1930-1945, published by the Hoover Institution at Stanford University.

Memorandum Number Four:
Antithesis — Financing The Nazis

The Marxist version of the Hegelian dialectic poses financial capitalism as thesis and Marxist revolution as antithesis. An obvious puzzle in this Marxian statement is the nature of the synthesis presumed to evolve out of the clash of these opposites, i.e., the clash of financial capitalism and revolutionary Marxism.

Lenin's statement that the State will wither away at the synthesis stage is nonsensical. In fact, as all contemporary Marxist states testify, the State in practice becomes all powerful. The immediate task of "the revolution" is to convey all power to the state, and modern Marxist states operate under a constant paranoia that power may indeed pass away from the hands of the State into the hands of the people.

We suggest that world forces may be seen differently, although still in terms of the Hegelian dialectic. If Marxism is posed as the thesis and national socialism as antithesis, then the most likely synthesis becomes a Hegelian New World Order, a synthesis evolving out of the clash of Marxism and national socialism. Moreover, in this statement those who finance and manage the clash of opposites can remain in control of the synthesis.

If we can show that The Order has artificially encouraged and developed **both** revolutionary Marxism **and** national socialism while retaining some control over the nature and degree of the conflict, then it follows The Order will be able to determine the evolution and nature of the New World Order.

R E S T R I C T E D

U. S. GROUP CONTROL COUNCIL
(Germany)
Office of the Director of Intelligence
Field Information Agency, Technical

Mail Address: WS/ff
FIAT
c/o USFET Main
APO 757, U.S. Army

IN FIAT I 350.09-77   4 September 1945

INTELLIGENCE REPORT NO. EF/Me/1

SUBJECT: Report No. 1, Parts I and II, on the Examination of Dr. FRITZ THYSSEN.

TO   : FIAT Distribution.

1. The report consists of two parts:

a. Three statements prepared and signed by THYSSEN, in conjunction
with his interrogations.

(1) THYSSEN's Relations with the Nazi Party.
(2) A second statement on the same subject.
(3) THYSSEN's Interview with GOERING, 29 January 1941.

b. Notes on various subjects, from stenographic transcripts of
his interrogations.

(1) Real Estate and Personal Records
(2) Financial Resources
(3) Movements during the War
(4) Opinions at the Outbreak of Hostilities
(5) Examination by the Gestapo
(6) Personalities
(7) Financial Support of the Nazi Party
(8) Defence of his Support of the Nazi Party
(9) The Famous Meeting in DUESSELDORF, 1932
(10) The Book I Paid HITLER
(11) Opposition to the Nazi Party
(12) Resistance in the Ruhr, 1923
(13) The YOUNG Plan
(14) The HERMANN GOERING WERKE

2. The report is based on interrogations of THYSSEN by Mr. CLIFFORD
HYNNING, U.S. Group Control Council (Germany), Finance Division, at DUSTBIN,
on 13, 20, and 23 July 1945.

For the Director of Intelligence:

WALTER K. SCHWINN
Chief, Economic and Financial Branch
FIAT (US)

PREPARED BY:

R. H. SUPER
Economic & Financial Br.
FIAT (US)

R E S T R I C T E D

— 165 —

I. WHERE DID THE NAZIS GET THEIR FUNDS FOR REVOLUTION?

In *Wall Street And The Rise of Hitler* we described several financial conduits between Wall Street and the Nazi Party. This was later supplemented by publication of a long suppressed book, *Hitler's Secret Backers*.[1] Still other books have emphasized the Fritz Thyssen financial connection to Hitler. After he split with Hitler, Thyssen himself wrote a book, *I Paid Hitler*. We are now in a position to merge the evidence in these books with other material and our documentation on The Order.

The records of the U.S. Control Council for Germany contain the post-war intelligence interviews with prominent Nazis. From these we have verification that the major conduit for funds to Hitler was Fritz Thyssen and his Bank fur Handel and Schiff, previously called von Heydt's Bank. This information coincides with evidence in *Wall Street And The Rise Of Hitler* and *Hitler's Secret Backers*, even to the names of the people and banks involved, i.e., Thyssen, Harriman, Guaranty Trust, von Heydt, Carter, and so on.

The document reproduced on page 167 slipped through U.S. censorship because the Office of Director of Intelligence did not know of the link between Fritz Thyssen and the Harriman interests in New York. Documents linking Wall Street to Hitler have for the most part been removed from U.S. Control Council records. In any event, we reproduce here the Intelligence report identifying Fritz Thyssen and his Bank fur Handel und Schiff (No. EF/Me/1 of September 4, 1945) and page 13 of the interrogation of Fritz Thyssen entitled "Financial Support of the Nazi Party."

II. WHO WAS THYSSEN?

Fritz Thyssen was the German steel magnate who associated himself with the Nazi movement in the early '20s. When interrogated in 1945 under Project Dustbin, Thyssen recalled that he was approached in 1923 by General Ludendorf at the time of French evacuation of the Ruhr. Shortly after this meeting Thyssen was introduced to Hitler and provided funds for the Nazis through General Ludendorf.

In 1930-31 Emil Kirdorf approached Thyssen and subsequently sent Rudolf Hess to negotiate further funding for the Nazi Party. This time Thyssen arranged a credit of 250,000 marks at the Bank Voor Handel en Scheepvaart N.V. (the Dutch name for the bank named by Thyssen in the attached document), at 18 Zuidblaak in Rotterdam, Holland.

Thyssen was former head of the Vereinigte Stahlwerke, The German

[1]*Wall Street And The Rise Of Hitler* and *Hitler's Secret Backers* are obtainable from Research Publications, P.O. Box 39850, Phoenix Arizona 85069. Some other aspects are covered in Charles Higham, *Trading With The Enemy* (Delacorte Press).

R-E-S-T-R-I-C-T-E-D

G. Financial Support of the Nazi Party.

My first connection with the Nazi party was through General LUDENDORF, following the evacuation of the Ruhr by the French troops. He told me about the Party and asked for my help. I agreed, but I did not want to give any money directly to the Party, so I gave it to LUDENDORF and he gave it to the Party. LUDENDORF introduced me to HITLER in 1923 before the Putsch. After the Putsch the two got separated, and I too got separated from the Nazis.

In 1930 or 1931, I think, EMIL KIRDORF asked me to obtain some foreign credits for the Nazi Party. I had known him for a long time, though not in connection with business. He was my neighbor. After the death of my father, he was the oldest industrialist in the Ruhr. KIRDORF sent HESS to me; HESS had gone first to KIRDORF and reported that he had purchased the Brown House in MUNICH and could not pay for it, and KIRDORF said he could not help him, but that he should apply to me. I told HESS that I could not do as he wished, but that in order to show my good will and because Mr. KIRDORF sent him I would arrange a credit for him with a Dutch bank in ROTTERDAM, the Bank für Handel und Schiff.

I arranged the credit by writing a letter in which I arranged that if the bank would give credit to HESS, he would pay it back in three years in equal rates. I was not officially guarantor of the loan, but because I had proposed it, I was really responsible. I chose a Dutch bank because I did not want to be mixed up with German banks in my position, and because I thought it was better to do business with a Dutch bank, and I thought I would have the Nazis a little more in my hands. HITLER pretended he never got any help. It was difficult to do nothing in those days when things were going, nobody knew where, and I always thought I would have some influence. It was for the same reason that I would not give up my position later as member of parliament, because I always thought perhaps I could prevent war.

The credit was about 250-300,000 marks—about the same sum I had given before. The loan has been repaid in part to the Dutch bank, but I think some money is still owing on it; it had not all been paid when I left Germany in 1939. I have had to make payments on it myself—perhaps 200,000-280,000 marks which the Nazi Party didn't pay; they did repay some.

The Nazis applied first to KIRDORF rather than direct to me because KIRDORF was a great friend of HITLER— he was fascinated by him. But KIRDORF told me that he was not himself in a position to give such an amount, and so I made this arrangement. But I certainly would not have done it if KIRDORF had not sent this man HESS to me.

I do not know of anyone else among the industrialists who was supporting the Party financially in 1926; I was then its principal supporter. Later TENGELMAN, KIRDORF, VOEGLER, KLEPPER all contributed; that was some sort of tax imposed on the whole industry. The reason for it was that HITLER would fight the communists: it was clear that the power would fall either to the communists or to the Nazis. When the Reichstag was burned, everyone was sure it had been done by the communists. I later learned in Switzerland that it was all a lie.

My contributions to the Party since that day have not been important—part of what the industry gave. I did help them in the riding school in my place. In 1932 I made two small contributions to Gauleiter TERBOVEN. He came and asked for the winter help and assistance: the winter contribution was made every year. At that time I gave him a pretty nice sum, something like 20,000 marks. This became an annual contribution; I am not sure whether the sum was increased. You see, we had a winter contribution of our own. When the unemployment began, my family undertook a winter help of our own, and gave poor people food, clothing, and shelter.

I joined the Party when they offered me membership in the Reichstag, I think in the election of 1931 or 1932. Before that time I was a German Nationalist. It is correct to say that my only contributions from my personal resources to the Party were the small annual dues, the subscription to various publications of the Party, and the winter help to the amount of 20-30 thousand marks. In other words the total amount I paid to the Nazi Party and its affiliates in any one year may have been a little over 50,000 marks; certainly not so much as

- 13 -

R-E-S-T-R-I-C-T-E-D

steel trust, financed by Dillon, Read (New York), and played a decisive role in the rise of Hitler to power by contributing liberally to the Nazi Party and by influencing his fellow industrialists to join him in support of the Fuehrer. In reward for his efforts, Thyssen was showered with political and economic favors by the Third Reich and enjoyed almost unlimited power and prestige under the Nazi regime until his break with Hitler in 1939 over the decision to invade Poland and precipitate the Second World War.

This incident and Thyssen's subsequent publication, *I Paid Hitler*, has a parallel wtih the history of his father, August Thyssen. Through a similar confession in 1918 the elder Thyssen, despite his record as a staunch backer of pan-Germanism, succeeded in convincing the Allies that sole responsibility for German aggression should be placed on the Kaiser and German industrialists should not be blamed for the support they had given to the Hohenzollerns. Apparently influenced by August Thyssen and his associates, the Allies made no effort to reform German industry after World War I. The result was that Thyssen was allowed to retain a vast industrial empire and pass it on intact to his heirs and successors.

It was against this background that Fritz Thyssen took over control of the family holdings following the death of his father in 1926. The new German steel baron had already achieved fame throughout the Reich by his defiance of the French during their occupation of the Ruhr in 1923. Like Hitler, Thyssen regarded the Treaty of Versailles as "a pact of shame" which must be overthrown if the Fatherland were to rise again This is the story in *Hitler's Secret Backers*.

Thyssen set out along the same road as his father, aided by ample Wall Street loans to build German industry. August Thyssen had combined with Hugenburg, Kirdorf, and the elder Krupp to promote the All-Deutscher Verband (the Pan-German League), which supplied the rationale for the Kaiser's expansionist policies.

His son became an active member of the Stahlhelm and later, through Goring, joined the Nazis. Finally, after the crash of 1931 had brought German industry to the verge of bankruptcy, he openly embraced national socialism.

During the next 2 years Thyssen dedicated his fortune and his influence to bring Hitler to power. In 1932 he arranged the famous meeting in the Dusseldorf Industrialists' Club, at which Hitler addressed the leading businessmen of the Ruhr and the Rhineland. At the close of Hitler's speech Thyssen cried, "Heil Herr Hitler," while the others applauded enthusiastically. By the time of the German Presidential elections later that year, Thyssen obtained contributions to Hitler's campaign fund from the industrial combines. He alone is reported to have spent 3,000,000 marks on the Nazis in the year 1932.

III. THE UNION BANKING CONNECTION

This flow of funds went through Thyssen banks. The Bank fur Handel and Schiff cited as the conduit in the U.S. Intelligence report was a subsidiary of the August Thyssen Bank, and founded in 1918 with H.J. Kouwenhoven and D.C. Schutte as managing partners. In brief, it was Thyssen's personal banking operation, and **affiliated with the W.A. Harriman financial interests in New York.** Thyssen reported to his Project Dustbin interrogators that:

> "I chose a Dutch bank because I did not want to be mixed up with German banks in my position, and because I thought it was better to do business with a Dutch bank, and I thought I would have the Nazis a little more in my hands."

Hitler's Secret Backers identifies the conduit from the U.S. as "von Heydt," and von Heydt's Bank was the early name for Thyssen's Bank. Furthermore, the Thyssen front bank in Holland — i.e., the Bank voor Handel en Scheepvaart N.V. — controlled the Union Banking Corporation in New York.

The Harrimans had a financial interest in, and E. Roland Harriman (The Order 1917), Averell's brother, was a director of this Union Banking Corporation. The Union Banking Corporation of New York City was a joint Thyssen-Harriman operation with the following directors in 1932:

E. Roland Harriman (The Order 1917)	Vice President of W.A. Harriman & Co., New York
H.J. Kouwenhoven (Nazi)	Nazi banker, managing partner of August Thyssen Bank and Bank voor Handel Scheepvaart N.V. (the transfer bank for Thyssen's funds)
Knight Woolley (The Order 1917)	Director of Guaranty Trust, New York and Director Federal Reserve Bank of N.Y.
Cornelius Lievense	President, Union Banking Corp. and Director of Holland-American Investment Corp.
Ellery Sedgewick James (The Order 1917)	Partner, Brown Brothers, & Co., New York
Johann Groninger (Nazi)	Director of Bank voor Handel en Scheepvaart and Vereinigte Stahlwerke (Thyssen's steel operations)
J.L. Guinter	Director Union Banking Corp.
Prescott Sheldon Bush (The Order 1917)	Partner, Brown Brothers. Harriman. Father of President G. H. W. Bush.

The eight directors of Union Banking Corporation are an interesting bunch indeed. Look at the following:

- Four directors of Union Banking are members of The Order: all initiated at Yale in 1917 — members of the same Yale class. All four were members of the same cell (club) D 115.
- E. Harriman was the brother of W. Averell Harriman and a Vice-President of W.A. Harriman Company.
- Guaranty Trust was represented by Knight Woolley.
- Two of the Union directors, Kouwenhoven and Groninger, were Nazi directors of Bank voor Handel en Scheepvaart, formerly the von Heydt Bank. Von Heydt was the intermediary between Guaranty Trust and Hitler named in *Hitler's Secret Backer.*
- Ellery S. James and Prescott S. Bush were partners in Brown Brothers, later Brown Brothers, Harriman.

Out of eight directors of Thyssen's bank in New York, we can therefore identify six who are either Nazis or members of The Order.

This private bank was formerly named Von Heydt Bank and von Heydt is named by Sharp in *Hitler's Secret Backers* as the intermediary from Guaranty Trust in New York to Hitler between 1930 and 1933. Above all, remember that Shoup was writing in **1933** when this information was still only known to those on the inside. Out of tens of thousands of banks and bankers, Shoup, in 1933, names those that evidence surfacing decades later confirms as financing Hitler.

In brief, when we merge the information in PROJECT DUSTBIN with Shoup's *Hitler's Secret Backers,* we find **the major overseas conduit for Nazi financing traces back to THE ORDER and specifically cell D 115.**

IV. PROFIT FROM CONFLICT

Out of war and revolution come opportunities for profit.

Conflict can be used for profit by corporations under control and influence of The Order. In World War II, the Korean War and the Vietnamese War we can cite examples of American corporations that traded with "the enemy" for profit.

This "blood trade" is by no means sporadic or limited to a few firms; it is general and reflects higher policy decisions and philosophies. Corporations — even large corporations — are dominated by banks and trust companies, and in turn these banks and trust companies are dominated by The Order and its allies. (This will be the topic of a forthcoming volume).

Although the U.S. did not officially go to war with Germany until 1941, legally, and certainly morally, the U.S. was at war with Nazi Germany after the Destroyer deal with Great Britain in December 1940, i.e., the exchange of 50 old U.S. destroyers for strategic bases in British territory. Even before December 1940 the MS "Frederick S. Fales" owned by Standard Vacuum Company was sunk by a German submarine on September 21, 1940. Yet in 1941 Standard Oil of New Jersey (now EXXON) had six Standard Oil tankers under Panamanian registry, manned by Nazi officers to carry fuel oil from Standard Oil refineries to the Canary Islands, a refueling base of Nazi submarines.

A report on this dated July 15, 1941 from Intelligence at Fifth Corps in Columbus, Ohio is reproduced on page 172. The report is in error recording that no Standard Oil ships had been sunk by the Nazis; Major Burrows apparently did not know "Frederick S. Fales" in 1940.

Another example of profit from war is recorded in the document on page 173. This records the association of RCA and the Nazis in World War II. RCA was essentially a Morgan-Rockefeller firm and so linked to The Order.

Yet another example is that of Chase Bank. Chase was linked to The Order through the Rockefeller family (Percy Rockefeller, The Order 1900) and Vice-President Reeve Schley (Yale, Scroll & Key). Directors of Chase in The Order included Frederick Allen (The Order 1900), W.E.S. Griswold (The Order 1899) and Cornelius Vanderbilt, whose brother Gwynne Vanderbilt (The Order 1899) represented the family before his death. President of Chase was Winthrop Aldrich. This was the Harvard branch of the Aldrich family, another branch is Yale and The Order.

Chase Manhattan Bank is not only a firm that plays both sides of the political fence, but with Ford Motor Company, was selected by Treasury Secretary Morgenthau for post-war investigation of pro-Nazi activities:

> These two situations [i.e., Ford and Chase Bank] convince us that it is imperative to investigate immediately on the spot the activities of subsidiaries of at least some of the larger American firms which were operating in France during German occupation . . .

The extent of Chase collaboration with Nazis is staggering — and this was at a time when Nelson Rockefeller had an intelligence job in Washington aimed AGAINST Nazi operations in Latin America.

In December 1944 Treasury Department officials examined the records of the Chase Bank in Paris. On December 20, 1944 the senior U.S. examiner sent a memorandum to Treasury Secretary Morgenthau with the **preliminary** results of the Paris examination. Here's an extract from that report:

HEADQUARTERS FIFTH CORPS AREA
OFFICE OF THE CORPS AREA COMMANDER
FORT HAYES, COLUMBUS, OHIO

G-2   July 15, 1941

SUBJECT: Standard Oil Company of New Jersey Ships Under Panamanian
          Registry.

TO: A. C. of S., G-2,
          War Department
          Washington, D. C.

    1. A report has been received from Cleveland, Ohio, in which it is
stated that the source of this information is unquestionable, to the
effect that the Standard Oil Company of New Jersey now ships under Panamanian registry, transporting oil (fuel) from Aruba, Dutch West Indies
to Teneriffe, Canary Islands, and is apparently diverting about 20% of
this fuel oil to the present German government.

    2. About six of the ships operating on this route are reputed to
be manned mainly by Nazi officers. Seamen have reported to the informant
that they have seen submarines in the immediate vicinity of the Canary
Islands and have learned that these submarines are refueling there. The
informant also stated that the Standard Oil Company has not lost any
ships to date by torpedoing as have other companies whose ships operate
to other ports.

                            For the A. C. of S., G-2,

                            CHAS. A. PERKINS,
                            Major, Military Intelligence,
                            Asst. A. C. of S., G-2

DEPARTMENT OF STATE

Memorandum of ~~Telephone~~ Conversation

DATE: May 24, 1943.

SUBJECT: Communications.

PARTICIPANTS: Colonel Sarnoff, RCA

Mr. Long.

COPIES TO: PA, IN.

I talked to Colonel Sarnoff on the telephone and explained to him that we had reason to believe that more messages than the agreed 700 code-groups a week were being sent from B. A. by the Axis powers to their Governments. I told him I could not disclose down there the source of our information. In an effort to obtain additional information our representatives down there had approached Hayes. Hayes had seemed to them noncooperative. There may have been very sound reasons why he refused to disclose the exact number of messages sent in code-groups by each of the Axis representatives to their Government. However, there didn't seem to be any reason why the managership should not request a report on all code-groups being sent over a period of time, day by day, and to include a report on all belligerents, and that if he would obtain that information through confidential channels we would be appreciative. I suggested it be not done by telegraph or telephone and suggested the mail, but offered to make the pouch available.

Colonel Sarnoff replied that he would talk to Mr. Winterbottom but he saw no reason why we should not do it and that he would communicate with us if they wanted to use the pouch.

After receipt of this information we will be in a better position to judge what our policy should be.

B. L.

A-L:BL:lag

— 173 —

a. Niederman, of Swiss nationality, manager of Chase, Paris, was unquestionably a collaborator;

b. The Chase Head Office in New York was informed of Niederman's collaborationist policy but took no steps to remove him. Indeed there is ample evidence to show that the Head Office in New York viewed Niederman's good relations with the Germans as an excellent means of preserving, unimpaired, the position of the Chase Bank in France.

c. The German authorities were anxious to keep the Chase open and indeed took exceptional measures to provide sources of revenue.

d. The German authorities desired "to be friends" with the important American banks because they expected that these banks would be useful after the war as an instrument of German policy in the United States.

e. The Chase, Paris showed itself most anxious to please the German authorities in every possible way. For example, the Chase zealously maintained the account of the German Embassy in Paris, "as every little thing helps" (to maintain the excellent relations between Chase and the German authorities).

f. The whole objective of the Chase policy and operation was to maintain the position of the bank at any cost.

In brief, Chase Bank was a Nazi collaborator, but the above preliminary report is as far as the investigation proceeded. The report was killed on orders from Washington, D.C.

On the other hand, Chase Bank, later Chase Manhattan Bank, has been a prime promoter of exporting U.S. technology to the Soviet Union. This goes all the way back to the early 1920s when Chase broke U.S. regulations in order to aid the Soviets. As early as 1922 Chase was trying to export military LIBERTY aircraft engines to the Soviet Union!

In conclusion, we have seen that the two arms of the dialectic described in Memoranda Three and Four clashed in World War II. Furthermore, the corporate segment of the elite profited from Lend Lease to the Soviets **and** by underground cooperation with Nazi interests. The political wing of The Order was at the same time preparing a new dialectic for the post World War II era.

Memorandum Number Five:
The New Dialectic - Angola And China

I. THE NECESSITY FOR A NEW DIALECTIC PROCESS

World War II was the culmination of the dialectic process created in the 1920s and 1930s. The clash between "left" and "right," i.e., the Soviet Union and Nazi Germany, led to creation of a synthesis — notably the United Nations, and a start towards regional groupings in the Common Market, COMECON, NATO, UNESCO, Warsaw Pact, SEATO, CENTO, and then the Trilateral Commission. A start towards New World Order.

World War II left The Order with the necessity to create a new dialectical situation to promote more conflict to achieve a higher level synthesis.

The source of the current process may be found in National Security Memorandum No. 68 of 1950, with its extraordinary omissions (analyzed in *The Phoenix Letter*, January 1984). NSC 68 opened up the road for Western technology to build a more advanced Soviet Union — which it did in the 1960s and 1970s with computerized space-age technology. At the same time NSC 68 presented the argument for massive expansion of U.S. defenses — on the grounds of a future Soviet threat. The omission in NSC 68 was quite elementary, i.e., that the Soviets could not progress without Western technology. NSC 68 allowed that technology transfer to go on. In other words, by allowing Western firms to expand the Soviet Union, NSC-68 also **pari passu** created the argument for a U.S. defense budget. We identified in our *Phoenix Letter* article the link between NSC-68 and The Order.

Unfortunately for The Order, but not surprisingly, given their limited perception of the world, the dialectic plan based on NSC-68 misfired. The principal devices used to control the dialectic process in the past two decades have been (a) information, (b) debt and (c) technology. These have become diluted over time. They just don't work as well today as they did in the 1950s.

By and large, control of information has been successful. The intellectual world is still locked into a phony verbal battle between "left" and "right," whereas the real struggle is the battle between individual freedom and the encroaching power of the absolute State. The Soviet Union, with its tight censorship, presents a strictly Marxist (i.e., "left") orientation to its citizens. The enemy is always the "fascist" United States. The West is a little more complicated but not much more so. Quigley's argument in *Tragedy And Hope*, that J.P. Morgan used financial power to control politics, has been extended to The Order's control of information. In the West the choice is basically between a controlled "left-oriented" information and a controlled "right-oriented" information.[1] The conflict between the two controlled groups keeps an apparent informational conflict alive. Unwelcome facts that fall into neither camp are conveniently forgotten. Books that fall into neither camp can be effectively neutralized because they will incur the wrath of both "right" **and** "left".

In brief, any publication which points up the fallacy of the Left-Right dichotomy is ignored . . . and citizens keep trooping down to the polling booths in the belief they have a "choice".

The second control mechanism is debt. If Marxist countries have to import technology, they need to earn or borrow Western currencies to pay for it. Loans have to be repaid. So to some extent, debtors are under control of creditors, unless they default. Default is the weakness.

The third control mechanism is technology. If technology to advance to more efficient production levels has to be imported, then the recipient is always kept away from the "state of the art". The weakness for The Order is that military technology does not require a market system.

The dialectic plan therefore misfired for several reasons. Firstly, the informational blackout has not been as successful as The Order expected. We shall describe later how control of *Time* and *Newsweek* gave The Order dominance over weekly news summaries. The TV networks have been able to orchestrate viewer reactions — to some extent. For example, the three ABC blockbusters in 1983 were *The Day After*, *Thornbirds*, and *Winds Of War*, all with a common propaganda theme. But The Order was unable to restrict individuals and relatively small non-academic groups, almost always outside Universities, from exploring obvious inconsistencies in establishment propaganda. These groups often mistakenly termed "left" or "right" are outside the generally manipulated left-right spectrum.

Secondly, the debt weapon was over-used. Communist countries are now saturated with debt to Western bankers.

Thirdly, while technology is still a useful weapon, there are distinct stirrings among independent analysts of the danger posed for the Western world by building enemies.

Consequently, in today's world we can identify two facts in construction of a new dialectic. First, **cautious** reinforcement of the Marxian arm (the thesis presented in Memorandum Three), i.e., Marxist Angola gets a green light, but a Marxist Grenada got a red light.

Second, the construction of a completely new arm, that of Communist China, itself Marxist, but with conflict potential for the Soviet Union. Major efforts by The Order are in progress, only partly revealed

---

[1]There are exceptions. Obviously *Review Of The News, American Opinion* and *Reason* are largely outside the controlled "right" frame. To some extent the U.S. Labor Party is outside the "left" frame, but includes so much spurious material that its publications are hardly worth reading. Henry George is a clear-cut "left" exception.

in the press, to create a new superpower in a conflict mode with the Soviet Union. This is the new antithesis, replacing Nazi Germany.

II. THE ORDER CREATES A MARXIST ANGOLA

Angola, a former Portuguese province on the southwest coast of Africa, is a contemporary example of continued, but more cautious, creation of the Marxist arm of the dialectic process.

The official establishment view of Angola is that Angola was a Portuguese colony and oppressive Portuguese rule led to an independence movement in which the Marxists won out over "democratic" forces.

This view cannot be supported. If the Portuguese were colonists in Angola, then so are the Boston Brahmins in Massachusetts. Luanda, the chief town in Angola, was settled by the Portuguese in 1575 — that's half a century before the Pilgrims landed in Massachusetts. The indigenous population of Angola in 1575 was less than the Indian population of Massachusetts. Over three centuries the Portuguese treated Angola more as a province than as a colony, in contrast to British, French and Belgian colonial rule in Africa. So if Angola belonged to non-existent indigenous natives, then so does Massachusetts logically belong to American Indians.

In the early 1960s the United States was actively aiding the Marxist cause in Angola. This is clear from former Secretary of State Dean Acheson. The following extracts are from a memorandum recording a conversation between Dean Acheson (Scroll & Key), McGeorge Bundy (The Order '40), and President Kennedy dated April 2, 1962:

"He [Kennedy] then turned to the negotiations with Portugal over the Azores base. He said that not much seemed to be happening and that he would be grateful to have me take the matter over and see if something could be done. I asked him for permission to talk about the situation for a few minutes and said about the following:

"The Portuguese were deeply offended at what they believed was the desertion of them by the United States, if not the actual alignment of the United States with their enemies. The problem, it seemed to me, lay not so much in negotiations with the Portuguese as in the determination of United States policy. The battle would be in Washington, rather than in Lisbon."

Then Dean Acheson comments on a topic apparently already known to President Kennedy, that the United States was supporting the revolutionary movements in Angola:

"The President then asked me why I was so sure that there was no room for negotiations under the present conditions. I said that, as he perhaps knew, we had in fact been subsidizing Portugal's enemies; and that they strongly suspected this, although they could not prove it. He said that the purpose of this was to try to keep the Angolan nationalist movement out of the hands of the communist Ghanians, etc., and keep it in the most moderate hands possible. I said that I quite understood this, but that it did not make what the Portuguese suspected any more palatable to them. We were also engaged in smuggling Angolese out of Angola and educating them in Lincoln College outside of Philadelphia in the most extreme nationalist views. Furthermore the head of this college had secretly and illegally entered Angola and on his return had engaged in violent anti-Portuguese propaganda. We voted in the United Nations for resolutions "condemning" Portugal for maintaining order in territory unquestionably under Portuguese sovereignty. I pointed out that the Portuguese were a proud people, especially sensitive because they had declined to such an impotent position after such a glorious history. They would rather proceed to the ruin of their empire in a dignified way, as they had in Goa, than be bought or wheedled into cooperating in their own destruction."

There is an extremely important, although seemingly minor, point in President Kennedy's comments. Kennedy apparently believed the U.S. was financing Nationalists, not Marxists, whereas the U.S. was actually aiding Marxists, as it was later to do in South Africa, following a pattern going back to the 1917 Bolshevik Revolution in Russia. There is a point well worth following up in the Kennedy files, i.e., just how much Kennedy knew about CIA and State Department operations, where The Order was in control.

The Marxists under Neto's MPLA obtained control of Angola. The Order with powerful allies among multinational corporations has exerted pressure on successive Administrations to keep Angola as a Cuban-Soviet base in Southern Africa.

Back in 1975 the U.S. in conjunction with South Africa did indeed make a military drive into Angola. At a crucial point, when South African forces could have reached Launda, the United States called off assistance. South Africa had no choice but to retreat. South Africa learned the hard way that the U.S. is only nominally anti-Marxist. In practice the U.S. did to South Africa what it had done many times before — the elite betrayed its anti-Marxist allies.

By the early 1980s The Order's multinational friends came out of the woodwork while carefully coordinating public actions with Vice President Bush (The Order 1948). For example, in March 27, 1981 *The Wall Street Journal* ran a revealing article, including some nuggets of reality mingled with the Establishment line. This front page article viewed U.S. multinational support for the Angolan Marxists under the headline "Friendly Foe: companies urge U.S. to stay out of Angola, decline aid to rebels" (these rebels being anti-Marxist Savimbi's UNITA forces aided by South Africa).

The leader of the pro-Marxist corporate forces in the U.S. is Melvin J. Hill, President of Gulf Oil Exploration & Production Company, a unit of Gulf Oil which operates Gulf Cabinda. This is a refinery complex in Angola, protected from Savimbi's pro-Western rebels by Cubans and Angolan Marxist troops. Hill told the WSJ "Angola is a knowledgeable, understanding and reliable business partner." Hill not only appeared before Congress with this pro-Marxist line, but met at least several times with then Vice President Bush.

PWJ Wood of Cities Service added more to the Gulf Oil mythology. Said Wood:

"The Angolans are more and more development oriented. They aren't interested in politicising central Africa on behalf of Cubans or the Soviet Union. Our people aren't persona non grata in Angola."

Hill and Wood, of course, are no more than public relations agents for Marxist Angola, although we understand they have not registered as foreign agents with the U.S. Department of Justice. Angola is very much a Cuban-Soviet base for the take-over of Southern Africa, yet 17 western oil companies and other firms are in Angola. They include Gulf, Texaco, Petrofina, Mobil, Cities Service, Marathon Oil and Union Texas Petroleum. Other firms include Allied Chemical, Boeing Aircraft, General Electric — and Bechtel Corporation. It should be remembered that both Secretary of State Schultz and Secretary of Defense Weinberger are on loan from Bechtel Corporation.

Gulf Oil Corporation is controlled by the Mellon interests. The largest single shareholder of the outstanding shares. The Mellon Bank is represented on the Board of Gulf Oil by James Higgins, a Yale graduate but not, so far as we can determine, a member of The Order.

The next largest shareholder is the Mellon Family comprising the Andrew W. Mellon Foundation, the Richard King Foundation, and the Sarah Scaife Foundation. This group, which thinks of itself as "conservative," holds about 7 percent of the outstanding shares. Morgan Guaranty Trust (a name we have encountered before) holds 1.8 million shares or about 1 percent of the outstanding shares.

To a great extent these corporations with Angolan interests have themselves out on a limb. It is surprising, for example, that South Africa has not moved to take counter action against Angolan based firms, especially General Electric, Boeing, Morgan Guaranty Trust, Gulf Oil and Cities Service. After all, the South Africans are directly losing men from the massive support given to the Angolan Marxists by these firms.

It would be cheaper in South African lives to direct retaliatory action against the corporations rather than against Cubans and Angolans.

After U.S. betrayal of South Africa in 1975, when South African forces could have reached Luanda, it is a tribute to South Africa's caution that it has not used this rather obvious counter weapon. After all, a South African surgical strike on Cabinda would neatly remove the Angolans' largest single source of foreign exchange, and give multinational Marxists a little food for thought. We are not, of course, recommending any such action, but it does remain an option open to South Africa. And the possible U.S. reaction? Well the State Department and CIA had best be ready with an explanation for the U.S. Embassy plane caught photographing South African military installations!

We cite the above only to demonstrate the dangerous nature of The Order's conflict management scenarios.

III. THE ORDER BUILDS A NEW DIALECTIC ARM IN CHINA

Just as we found the Bush family involved with the early development of the Soviet Union, then with financing the Nazis, and vaguely behind the scenes in Angola, so we find a Bush active in construction of the new dialectic arm: Communist China.

In 1971 Mr. Nixon appointed George "Poppy" Bush (The Order 1948) as U.S. Ambassador to the United Nations, irrespective of the fact that Bush had no previous experience in diplomacy. As chief U.S. delegate, Bush had responsibility for defense against the Communist Chinese attack on the Republic of China, an original free enterprise member of the United Nations. With the vast power of the United States at his disposal, Bush failed miserably: the Republic was expelled from United Nations and Communist China took its seat. Shortly after that fiasco, Bush left United Nations to take over as Chairman of the Republican National Committee.

This is not the place to tell the whole story of American involvement in China. It began with Wall Street intervention into the Sun Yat Sen revolution of 1911 — a story not yet publicly recorded.

During World War II the United States helped the Chinese Communists into power. As one Chinese authority, Chin-tung Liang, has written about General Joseph W. Stilwell, the key U.S. representative in China from 1942 to 1944: "From the viewpoint of the struggle against Communism . . . [Stilwell] did a great disservice to China."[1]

Yet Stilwell only reflected orders from Washington, from General George C. Marshall. And as Admiral Cooke stated to Congress, ". . . in

---

[1]Chin-Tun Liang, *General Stilwell In China, 1942-1944: The Full Story.* St. John's University, 1972, p. 12.

1946 General Marshall used the tactics of stoppage of ammunition to invisibly disarm the Chinese forces."[2]

But when we get to General Marshall we need to remember that in the U.S. the civilian branch has final authority in matters military and that gets us to then Secretary of War Henry L. Stimson, Marshall's superior and a member of The Order (1888). By an amazing coincidence, Stimson was also Secretary of War in 1911 — at the time of the Sun Yat Sen revolution.

The story of the betrayal of China and the role of The Order will have to await yet another volume. At this time we want only to record the decision to build Communist China as a new arm of the dialectic — a decision made under President Richard Nixon and placed into operation by Henry Kissinger (Chase Manhattan Bank) and George "Poppy" Bush (The Order).

As we go to press (early 1984) Bechtel Corporation has established a new company, Bechtel China, Inc., to handle development, engineering and construction contracts for the Chinese government. The new President of Bechtel China, Inc. is Sydney B. Ford, formerly marketing manager of Bechtel Civil & Minerals, Inc. Currently Bechtel is working on studies for the China National Coal Development Corporation and the China National Offshore Oil Corporation — both, of course, Chinese Communist organizations.

It appears that Bechtel is now to play a similar role to that of Detroit-based Albert Kahn, Inc., the firm that in 1928 undertook initial studies and planning for the First Five Year Plan in the Soviet Union.

By about the year 2000 Communist China will be a "superpower" built by American technology and skill. It is presumably the intention of The Order to place this power in a conflict mode with the Soviet Union.

There is no doubt Bechtel will do its job. Former CIA Director Richard Helms works for Bechtel, so did Secretary of State George Shultz and Defense Secretary Caspar Weinberger. That's a powerful, influential combination, if any Washington planner concerned with national security gets out of line sufficiently to protest.

Yet, The Order has probably again miscalculated. What will be Moscow's reaction to this dialectic challenge? Even without traditional Russian paranoia they can be excused for feeling more than a little uneasy. And who is to say that the Chinese Communists will not make their peace with Moscow after 2000 and join forces to eliminate the super-super-power — the United States?

[2]Ibid., p. 278.

The Secret Cult of
THE ORDER

322

Memorandum Number One:
An Introduction to the Secret Cult of the Order

Secret political organizations can be — and have been — extremely dangerous to the social health and constitutional vitality of a society. In a truly free society the exercise of political power must always be open and known.

Moreover, organizations devoted to violent overthrow of political structures have always, by necessity, been **secret** organizations. Communist revolutionary cells are an obvious example. In fact, such revolutionary organizations could only function if their existence was secret.

In brief, secrecy in matters political is historically associated with coercion. Furthermore, the existence of secrecy in organizations with **political** ambitions or with a history of political action is always suspect. Freedom is always associated with **open** political action and discussion while coercion is always associated with secrecy.

There are numerous historical examples to support this premise. Back in the late 17th century the Elector of Bavaria, the constitutional government of Bavaria, banned the Illuminati organization. Accidental discovery of Illuminati documents demonstrated that a secret organization was devoted to the overthrow of the Bavarian state and establishment of a world society run by elitist Illuminati.

More recently in England there have been startling discoveries involving use of the masonic movement by the Soviet KGB to subvert and infiltrate British intelligence. True freemasonry is an establishment conservative organization, but its organizational structure can be — and has been — used for revolutionary purposes. Masonic aims are publicly stated to be fraternity and charity, but it is also well known that masons help each other in areas supposedly based on talent.

In *The Brotherhood*[1] Stephen Knight comments that many have suffered because freemasonry has entered segments of society where it has no place:

". . . there can be no doubt that many . . . have suffered because of freemasonry entering into areas of life where, according to all its publicly proclaimed principles, it should never intrude. The abuse of freemasonry causes alarming miscarriages of justice" (p. 4).

In England at any rate freemasonry has become a self-serving organization always discriminating in favor of its own members when it

---

[1]Stephen Knight, *The Brotherhood: The Secret World of the Freemasons*, Granada, London, 1984.

comes to contracts, jobs, careers and promotions. Moreover, we now know that the masonic movement in England was used by the Russian KGB to infiltrate, take over and finally head British intelligence organizations.

In September 1984 Scotland Yard in London advised all its police officers not to join the freemasons lest its reputation for impartiality be lost.

Given this background, The Order, a secret society also known as Skull & Bones, is a clear and obvious threat to constitutional freedom in the United States. Its secrecy, power and use of influence is greater by far than the masons, or any other semi-secret mutual or fraternal organization.

How secret is Skull & Bones?

The most careful analysis of the society is by Lyman Bagg in *Four Years At Yale*[1] published in 1871, but still the only source of documented information on the cultic aspects of The Order.

According to Bagg, The Order is intensely secret:

- "They (the senior societies at Yale) are the only Yale societies whose transactions are truly secret."
- "Their members never mention their names, nor refer to them in any way in the presence of anyone not of their own number, and as they are all seniors, there are no old members in the class above them to tell tales out of school."

This intense secrecy even extends to documents printed for internal use.

On the next page we reprint an internal circular distributed among Patriarchs which has disguised references as follows:

"P" i.e., Patriarch

"P---s" Patriarchs

If The Order has this intense secrecy, then how are we able to reproduce its documents and memberships rolls?

Simply because secrecy attracts attention. Secrecy creates suspicion of intentions. This in turn generates action to break the secrecy.

This series of books is based on several sources, including contemporary "moles." However, information on the cultic aspects comes from a century-old Yale concern about the operations and intentions of Skull & Bones. This concern generated two pamphlets, one issue of a journal and a chapter in a book, as follows:

(1) An anonymous pamphlet entitled *Skull & Bones*. This is an account of the 1876 break-in at the "Bones" Temple on the Yale campus.

---

[1]Lyman Bagg, *Four Years at Yale*, Henry Holt & Co., New York, 1871. The chapter "Senior Societies" is reprinted in full as an appendix to this book.

The distribution of the accompanying pamphlets establishes the custom of mailing these and similar publications of the College authorities, annually, to every P—. The issues of previous years, and other College publications will also be sent upon application. Badges and catalogues can also be obtained.

———————

Within a few months the "old kitchen" will doubtless be transformed, through the generosity of some New Yorkers, into a library room, lighted from above, affording accommodations for the books, etc., which are over-crowding the present shelves.

The "Library" has three departments:

1. All books, pamphlets, etc., written or edited by P——s.
2. All printed matter having any reference to Yale.
3. Very old or curious volumes, or engravings.

Each of these departments is at present very defective. An effort is being made to fill up these deficiencies.

Of the first, little need be said. Every one will know whether he has anything to add thereto—and *many have*. It is hoped that these will take notice.

The scrap books, student publications, college histories and miscellaneous pamphlets relating to Yale, compose the second section. The scrap books have been well cared for during the past *few* years, but very little of the College memorabilia of previous years has been preserved. Such a collection, however, would be as interesting as valuable, and would become more so every year, forming in one sense a history of Yale, or at least of that side of it which seldom gets into history—the character and customs of student life. Very few who read this will probably have anything to furnish to such a complete collection of Yalensia as, it is hoped, will be gathered, and fewer still will be willing to part with what they may have. Therefore, let every one who has anything of this description, and has lost something of his interest in it, or who is willing to make this disposal of it, communicate at once with the undersigned. Anything which you may have, could not be deposited in a safer place surely, nor where it would be more permanently useful. If any duplicates should be obtained they will be returned, or given to a similar collection in the College Library.

The third department is yet in its infancy.

ADDRESS   "HENRY E. NEVINS."

An extremely rare document, it is reproduced in full as an appendix to this book.

The pamphlet begins:

"As long as Bones shall exist the night of September 29th (1876) will be to its members the anniversary of the occasion when their temple was invaded by neutrals, their rarest memorabilia confiscated and their most sacred secrets unveiled to the eyes of the uninitiated."

This is reference to a break-in by a group of Yale students, and the pamphlet describes in minute detail the contents of the Temple. For example, it describes the walls, e.g., ". . . the walls are adorned with pictures of the founders of Bones at Yale and of the members of the Society in Germany when the Chapter was established here in 1832."

This sentence becomes of interest when the Illuminati aspect is discussed in Memorandum Five below.

Here's another interesting paragraph from this pamphlet:

"Bones is a chapter of a corps in a German University. It should properly be called, not Skull & Bones Society but Skull & Bones Chapter. General R------ (Russell), its founder, was in Germany before Senior Year and formed a warm friendship with a leading member of a German society. He brought back with him to college, authority to found a chapter here. Thus was Bones founded."

Think about this: **Skull & Bones is not American at all. It is a branch of a FOREIGN secret society.**

Presumably this is one reason why intense secrecy is vital. It also raises the question of just who and what this foreign organization is and whether its objectives are compatible with those of the Constitution of the United States.

(2) The Order, *The Fall of Skull and Bones* (New Haven, 1876)

This is an anonymous satire published 1876 apparently in New Haven, Connecticut by a group calling itself The Order.

The subtitle reads "Compiled from the minutes of the 76th regular meeting of The Order of the File and Claw."

The opening paragraphs are as in *Skull & Bones* cited above (1), however, the text continues with considerably more detail and appears to have been written by another member of the break-in crew.

In particular, this book gives the identification of the owner of the human skull found in one of the rooms of the Temple:

"A light is always kept burning in the Jo (D) which is ornamented with a dilapidated human skull . . . here is also a tombstone marked SPERRY, seemingly taken from the same grave as the skull."

In brief, it appears this "respected" Order of Yale gentlemen is no more than a coven of grave robbers hoarding skulls, skeletons and tombstones.

Then further down is the following:

"In the Pantry (F) are large quantities of dishes, each piece of crockery ornamented with a picture of a skull and crossbones, each spoon and fork marked S.B.T." (Skull and Bones Trust).

This suggests a preoccupation with skulls and human bones is built into the cultic structure of The Order.

Then on page 4 we learn that each member of Skull & Bones (as well as Scroll & Key) has an "inside name" and these names bear a remarkable resemblance to those used by the Illuminati, e.g., Chilo, Eumenes, Glaucus, Prisaticus and Arbaces.

The conclusion of this pamphlet is:

". . . we will say that a thorough examination of every part of the Temple leads us to the conclusions that the most powerful of college societies is nothing more than a pleasant convivial club."

This conclusion ignores other evidence presented elsewhere. It is acceptable given **only** the findings of the break-in crew.

(3) *The Iconoclast*, New Haven 1873

Only one issue of this journal has been found, and only a single copy of that issue exists. It is reproduced as an appendix below. The editor of *The Iconoclast* considered Skull & Bones "a deadly evil" and emphasized their interest in political control. Moreover, the *Iconoclast* states that The Order obtained control of Yale, and its members care more for their society than for Yale:

Out of every class Skull and Bones takes its men. They have gone out into the world and have become, in many instances, leaders in society. They have obtained control of Yale. Its business is performed by them. Money paid to the college must pass into their hands, and be subject to their will.

(4) Chapter "Senior Societies" in Lyman Bagg, *Four Years at Yale*.

This is the reference cited above at the beginning of this chapter.

Other sources include an article in *Esquire* Magazine by Ron Rosenbaum entitled "The last secrets of Skull and Bones" (September 1977). From this article we learn such tidbits as:

"Supreme Court Justice Potter Stewart . . . dressed up in a skeleton suit, howled wildly at an initiate in a red velvet room inside the tomb . . ."

"McGeorge Bundy wrestled naked in a mud pile as part of his initiation."

According to a dossier obtained by Ron Rosenbaum, the 1940 initiation ceremony went like this:

— 189 —

New man placed in coffin — carried into central part of building. New man chanted over and reborn into society. Removed from coffin and given robes with symbols on it (sic). A bone with his name on it is tossed into bone heap at start of evening. Initiates plunged naked into mud pile.

Again, we have a sordid preoccupation with coffins, skeletons and death.

This about summarizes sources of information.

Strangely enough, the long-time proponent of conspiracy theories, the John Birch Society, has made little contribution to our knowledge of The Order. Apparently JBS recognizes its existence but considers it merely a "recruiting ground," which, of course, it is.

This "recruiting ground" interpretation suggests several points. Firstly, the documentary evidence is quite clear: Knights, i.e., the just recruited initiates, spend only one year as Knights. They become Patriarchs after leaving Yale and spend a lifetime as Patriarchs. Second, continual correspondence and meeting **as Patriarchs** continues after leaving Yale. In fact, the Deer Iland Club is specifically for annual meetings of Patriarchs and the Russell Trust Association is run entirely by Patriarchs.

In brief, the JBS "recruiting ground" theory just doesn't match **all** the facts.

Furthermore, The Order is the ONLY fully documented example we have of a secret society within the U.S. establishment. JBS has never produced membership lists of any other society and yet seems unwilling to recognize the existence of The Order.

Similarly, New Solidarity, i.e., the Lyndon LaRouche outfit, claims to have exposed The Order back in 1979. Unfortunately, neither Lyndon LaRouche nor anyone else can produce documents dated 1983 and 1984 in 1979. In any event, the degree of documentation in our volumes on The Order has not been matched elsewhere.

The answer is that this author does have — and fully admits to having — clandestine sources within The Order. We understand that for specific reasons these sources are not available to either JBS or Lyndon LaRouche. At that point we will leave our discussion of sources and move on to the ritual aspects of The Order.

Memorandum Number Two:
The Organization of The Order

The Yale Senior society system is unique to Yale University. There is nothing like it elsewhere in the United States or for that matter in the entire world. According to Lyman Bagg in *Four Years at Yale*, "the senior societies are such peculiarly Yale institutions that it will be difficult for an outsider fully to appreciate their significance" (Bagg, p. 142, see page following for full context). Nothing like them exists elsewhere and according to Bagg, "Harvard is the only college where, under similar conditions they possibly could exist."

There are three senior societies, Skull & Bones, Scroll & Key and Wolfs Head. Each year 15 male Yale juniors are tapped for admission. They spend only one year in the society, an entirely different procedure to fraternal organizations found on other campuses.

Skull & Bones was founded in 1933 and has initiated 15 members each year since 1933 (except for 1945 when only 10 were tapped). Every year during commencement week 15 Yale juniors receive an invitation "Skull & Bones. Accept or reject?" Those who accept, presumably the greater number, are invited to attend the Bones Temple on campus to undergo an initiation ceremony. (See next page)

Tap day in modern times is a private, almost concealed operation; it was not always that way.

Before 1953 juniors were herded into a yard and representatives from senior societies would circulate among assembled students, selecting those wanted for initiation.

In those days rejection by a senior society was considered social suicide, so Yale ordered tapping a private affair, to avoid the traumatic wait and fear of rejection by the assembled juniors.

For the ambitious, "tapping" is the magic password to a future career. Wherever he turns, the success of the Yale senior society system is obvious. Yale University President, A. Bartlett Giamatti, was a member of Scroll & Key, while George Bush, Vice President of the United States was a member of Skull & Bones.

The Yale campus student is well aware that the senior society system is geared to the affluent outside world, to the world after graduation. Money and connections flow from membership. Reportedly, Skull & Bones donates $15,000 and a grandfather clock to each initiate. Certainly alumni pay for everything associated with society meetings. In one case reported by *New York Times* (April 16, 1983), the alumni paid for a three-hour phone call from Colorado to Yale by two members of Scroll & Key unable to attend a meeting in the Scroll & Key tomb.

YALE UNIVERSITY
COMMENCEMENT AND REUNION CALENDAR 1984

FRIDAY, MAY 25

2:00 p.m.	President and Mrs. Giamatti's Reception for members of the Senior Class and their guests, 43 Hillhouse Avenue.
8:00 p.m.	Commencement Review by the Yale Dramatic Association, University Theater, 222 York Street.

SATURDAY MAY 26

8:00 p.m.	Commencement Review. (See notice for Friday.)
9:00 p.m.	Senior Dance, Branford College and Saybrook College Courtyards.

SUNDAY, MAY 27

10:00 a.m.	Baccalaureate Address by President Giamatti, Woolsey Hall for students in Berkeley, Branford, Davenport, Timothy Dwight, Morse, and Ezra Stiles Colleges.
11:30 a.m.	For students in Calhoun, Jonathan Edwards, Pierson, Saybrook, Silliman, and Trumbull Colleges. (Guest seating only at 11:10.)
3:00 p.m.	Class Day Exercises (in academic costume), Old Campus.
4:00 p.m.	Receptions in Masters' Houses for Seniors and guests.
7:00 p.m.	Concert by the Yale Band, Old Campus.
8:00 p.m.	Commencement Review (see notice for Friday).
8:30 p.m.	Concert by the Yale Glee Club and Whiffenpoofs of 1984, Woolsey Hall.

MONDAY, MAY 28

9:30 a.m.	Assembly of Seniors (in academic costume), College Courtyards.
10:30 a.m.	Commencement Exercises, Old Campus.
12:00 noon	Presentation of diplomas at the individual Colleges and Schools by the Masters and Deans. (Presentation of Ph.D. diplomas in Woolsey Hall.)

THURSDAY, MAY 31

☞ # 322 VIII S. B. T.

(Supper at 7:00 p.m.)

FRIDAY, JUNE 1

Reunions for the Classes of 1919, 1919S, 1924-24S, 1929, 1934, 1954, 1959, 1964, 1969, 1974, and 1979. (The Classes of 1939, 1944, and 1949 held Fall 1983 Reunions.)
Registration at Class headquarters. Rooms available Thursday, May 31.

SATURDAY, JUNE 2

9:00 a.m.	Panel discussion: "College Admissions and Financial Aid," William L. Harkness Hall, Room 201.
11:00 a.m.	Panel discussion: "Education at Yale College," Sprague Hall.

SUNDAY, JUNE 3

11:00 a.m.	Yale-Harvard Boat Race, New London.
11:30 a.m.	Interfaith Service of Remembrance, Sprague Hall.
12:30 p.m.	Picnic for All Reunion Classes on the Cross Campus.

Although the John Birch Society, the long time conservative promoter of conspiracy theory, emphasizes that these senior societies are merely recruiting grounds, in effect the societies are the source of a vast establishment network, a formalized "old boy" network that effectively shuts out the newcomers and the non-Yale talented from the halls of power. Because these are **senior** societies, the emphasis is not on campus activities but on post graduation ambitions. That is the fundamental difference to all other campus societies in the U.S.

As Bagg points out:

"The statement is therefore again repeated that Bones and Keys are peculiarly Yale institutions, genuine outgrowths of a system that flourishes nowhere else, the only organizations of the kind existing in the country" (p. 183) and the senior society "is an association with no weak members whatever and the history of the matter shows that unless this ideal is adhered to with reasonable closeness, such a society cannot live long at Yale" (p. 144).

CLUBS OF THE ORDER

Each annual class of new initiates forms a club consisting of 15 members. Initiates are called Knights in the first year and thereafter Patriarchs.

The annual announcement of new initiates has not varied over the years. We reproduce on page 194 the announcement of new members for 1917 and on pages 195-196 those for 1984 and 1985.

Each club has a number. This is located in the top right hand corner of the announcement sheet (i.e., D 115 for 1917 and D 183 for 1984). Further, one member is designated a "club chairman" or agent, with the function to act as liaison with the Secretary of the Russell Trust Association in New York.

p. 2115.   w. 113.

Alfred Raymond Bellinger,	Syracuse, N. Y.
Prescott Sheldon Bush,	Columbus, O.
Henry Sage Fenimore Cooper,	Albany, N. Y.
Oliver Baly Cunningham,	Evanston, Ill.
Samuel Sloan Duryee,	New York City
Edward Roland Noël Harriman,	Arden, N. Y.
Henry Porter Isham,	Chicago, Ill.
William Ellery Sedgwick James,	New York City
Harry William LeGore,	LeGore, Md.
Henry Neil Mallon,	Cincinnati, O.
Albert William Olsen,	Glenbrook, Conn.
John Williams Overton,	Nashville, Tenn.
Frank Parsons Shepard, Jr.,	St. Paul, Minn.
Kenneth Farrand Simpson,	New York City
Knight Woolley,	Brooklyn, N. Y.

P. 2183   D. 183

James Emanuel Boasberg   Washington, D.C.

William John Carr Carlin, Jr.   Brooklyn, New York

Ashok Jai Chandrasekhar   New York, New York

Scott David Frankel   Pepper Pike, Ohio

Jay Alan Grossman   Randolph, Massachusetts

Wei-Tai Kwok   Annandale, Virginia

Peter Barnes Lindy   Memphis, Tennessee

Timothy Charles Misner   Silver Spring, Maryland

Steven Terner Mnuchin   New York, New York

James Gerard Pletela   Branford, Connecticut

Richard Hart Powers   Niantic, Connecticut

Morgan Robert Smock   New Hope, Minnesota

Horace Dutton Taft   New Haven, Connecticut

Gregory Allan Thomson   Brooklyn, New York

Kevin Sanchez Walsh   Pelham Manor, New York

1985

BOASBERG, James Emanuel, 3136 Newark Street, NW, Washington, D.C. 20008

CARLIN, William John Carr, Jr., 21 Schermerhorn Street, Brooklyn, New York 11201.

CHANDRASEKHAR, Ashok Jai, 120 East 34th Street, New York, New York 10016.

FRANKEL, Scott David, 3290 Kersdale Road, Pepper Pike Ohio 44124.

GROSSMAN, Jay Alan, 48 Niles Road, Randolph, Massachusetts 02368.

KWOK, Wei-Tai, 5 109 Philip Road, Annandale, Virginia 22003.

LINDY, Peter Barnes, 105 South Perkins, Memphis, Tennessee 38117.

MISNER, Timothy Charles, 1009 Crest Park Drive, Silver Spring, Maryland 20903.

MNU CHIN, Steven Terner, 721 Fifth Avenue, New York, New York 10022.

PATELA, James Gerard, 47 Knollwood Drive, Branford, Connecticut 06405.

POWERS, Richard Hart, 21 Haigh Avenue, Niantic Connecticut 06357.

SMOCK, Morgan Robert, 4017 Louisiana Avenue North, New Hope, Minnesota 55427.

TAFT, Horace Dutton, 403 St. Ronan Street, New Haven, Connecticut 06511.

THOMPSON, Gregory Allan, 118 Whitman Drive, Brooklyn, New York 11234.

WALSH, Kevin Sanchez, 1030 Clay Avenue, Pelham Manor, New York 10803.

THE SECRET CATALOGS
Each member of The Order receives an updated annual catalog of members. At one time it was a single volume bound in black leather.

CATALOGUE
OCTOBER 1983
VOL. I
LIVING MEMBERS

The latest practice is to issue the catalog in two clothbound volumes: Volume One for Living Members and Volume Two for Deceased Members.

Preceding is the title page of the October 1983 catalog, the latest issued. Volume Two is the same with "Deceased Members" in place of "Living Members."

Inside the title page is the address of the Secretary of the Russell Trust Association responsible for administration of the current affairs of The Order:

"Please send any corrections or changes of address to:
The Secretary
RTA Incorporated
P. O. Box 2138 Yale Station
New Haven, Conn. 06520"

Then follows an alphabetical listing of members and brief information on the following:

Name and class year with awarded degrees.

A brief notation of occupation, i.e., law, education, finance, business.

Date of birth is followed by current business and private addresses.

Then follows a list of positions held starting with current position.

Military and civilian awards and honors follow, usually extensive because The Order "old boy" network can guarantee awards to each other — an excellent means of mutual support to build up collective power and prestige.

The final item is a listing of wives and children.

A

ABERG, 1952, DONLAN VINCENT, JR.—(Business)—Born Nov. 18, 1928, Cleveland, O.; bus. Pres., Nutrition Products of America, 8929 S. Sepulveda Blvd., Suite 312, Los Angeles, Calif. 90045; res. 15843 Tobin Way, Sherman Oaks, Calif. 91403; Republican Committeeman, N.Y. '64-'69; m. July 16, '55, Jean Helen Brose; s. Donlan Vincent III, Peter Christopher ('81); d. Gretchen Mane.

ABRAMS, 1983, PETER MARK—add. 456 Concord St., Lexington, Mass. 02173.

ACHESON, 1943, DAVID CAMPION, LL.B.—(Law)—Born Nov. 4, 1921, Washington, D.C.; Ptnr. Drinker, Biddle & Reath, 1815 H St., N.W., Suite 1200, Washington, D.C. 20006; res. 3101 Garfield St., N.W., Washington, D.C. 20008; Assoc. '50-'58 & Ptnr. '58-'61, Covington & Burling; U.S. Attorney for Dist. of Columbia, '61-'65; Special Asst. to Sec. of Treasury, '65-'67; Senior V.P. & Gen. Counsel, Communications Satellite Corp., (COMSTAT), '67-'74; Ptnr., Jones Day Reavis & Pogue, '74-'78; Lieut. U.S.N.R., '42-'46; Campaign Ribbons—Pacific Theatre, Southwest Pacific—2 battle stars; Philippines—2 battle stars; Chmn., Leadership Gifts, Campaign for Yale, Washington, D.C. Area; Trustee, Washington Cathedral, '76-'82; Pres., National Cathedral Assn., '77-'80; Mbr. Bd. of Regents, Smithsonian Institution; Dir., Committee on the Present Danger; m. May 1, '43, Patricia James Castles; s. David C. Jr. ('72), Peter W. ('76); d. Eleanor Dean.

ACKERMAN, 1957, STEPHEN H., M.B.A.—(Finance)—Born August 22, 1935, Rhinebeck, New York; Vice President, Finance & Administration, Caesars World, Inc., 1801 Century Park East, Suite 2600, Los Angeles, Calif. 90067; res. 4145 Via Marina, Apt. 310, Marina Del Rey, Calif. 90291; Major, USMCR Sept. '57-Dec. '60; m. July 8, '60, Kaye Tamblin (divorced); d. Lani Ackerman Tulin.

5

DEER ILAND CLUB

The Order's retreat is the Deer Iland (spelled Iland after the request of Patriarch G.D. Miller) Alexandria Bay on the St. Lawrence River, New York. The island was donated in 1906 by Patriarch Miller and renovated over the years, but particularly in the 1950s and 1980s.

Here's an extract from the latest February 29, 1984, report to Patriarchs:

> Deer Iland had another successful year in 1983, the 76th season of the Club since its establishment under the direction of George Douglas Miller, D. 68* in 1907. Was it the best year ever? Maybe. They're getting better and better. The results of the past five or six years have seen the Club become a much more viable enterprise from the years of the late '60s and early '70s when its future was much in doubt.

The positive response made by Patriarchs is seen in the following paragraph from the same annual report:

> Increased use of the island is not the only factor in its present sound financial footing. Your generosity through your contributions to our annual fund drives has kept the Club going through lean times and supports it today. Most recently, the splendid response to the special capital fund drive in 1981-82, commemorating the 75th anniversary of the Club, has enabled us to make major capital improvements to our facilities — a process which is still underway. I should add that those special contributions are not being used to meet current operating expenses but are specially designated for capital improvements. Current income from all sources — guest receipts, the G.D. Miller trust, and the annual appeal — has met or exceeded our expenses for seven years, giving us both welcome security and the means to improve further the island's classic river-style structures. (I don't want to use the word "modernize" except perhaps in reference to the plumbing. You may so inform your wives.)

In brief: the organization of The Order both as Russell Trust Association and Deer Iland Corporation is essentially geared towards the post graduation world, **the outside world.** It is a senior society. Knights spend only one year as Knights. The rest of their lives are spent as Patriarchs in an active influential organization able to guarantee wealth and ambition.

---

*D. 68 — It is a practice for members to place their Club identification after their name in writing each other.

Memorandum Number Three:
The Ritual of The Order

The ritual of The Order is a closely held secret. The most that anyone can do at this stage is piece together some elements of the ritual and their probable meaning.

The extraordinary secrecy is itself part of a ritual. Members are sworn not to discuss the organization, its procedures or its objectives. Presumably, only an FBI or Congressional investigation could break this code of "omerta" (Mafia = silence).

The secrecy is carried to extraordinary lengths. Members may not remain in the room if The Order is under discussion. Words spoken within The Order may not be placed on paper, even in letters to fellow members. For example, witness the following extract from a letter circulated to members by W. Iain Scott (D. 171), President of Deer Iland Club Corporation:

> But beyond these mere quantitative measures of success, it is the quality of the Deer Iland experience that commends the Club to your attention. There are few, if any, places where the B-n-s life thrives in such luxuriance outside the thick and tomblike walls in New Haven. Our Order is, to use an economic term, very much horizontally integrated. That is, our ties to it are strongest through a very narrow slice of time — one special year. Deer Iland, for me and I believe many others, has expanded these ties vertically through contact with younger and older members. Visitors to the island last summer ranged from D. 124 to D. 182, twelve of them. It serves as prelude to the music of the B-n-s for the "newly fledged exalted K----ts" and as an endlessly rising canon on that wonderful theme to the p-tr--rchs."

Notice three abbreviations to conceal internal use of words from any possible outsider who may stumble on a copy of the letter:

B-n-s   = Bones (cited twice)

k----ts   = Knights

p-tr--rchs = Patriarchs

The reader may consider this juvenile, and it may well be. On the other hand, these "juveniles" are the men today running the United States.

Chapter meetings of Patriarchs are announced using a format which has not changed since the early 19th century. An interesting and significant aspect of these announcements is the manner in which they reflect elements of the ritual: the skull and bones, the periods into which The Order has placed its history and the club numbers.

We reproduce below announcements for the following years:

— 200 —

1. July 28, 1859 — the earliest year for which we have a copy. Note the Roman letters VI in the center of the sheet.
2. July 23, 1868 — the last year for which we have a record of the VI appearing. We understand that 1869 was actually the last year with VI.
3. July 21, 1870 — the first year with VIII in the center. Note that VII appears to have been skipped completely.
4. June 17, 1936 — note that the format remains almost the same. This one was signed by Potter Stewart, later (1958-1981) Supreme Court Justice.
5. May 31, 1984 — the latest announcement notice. Note that the Club number D. 183 now appears, but in essence the sheet remains exactly as in 1859. It appears they even used the same skull and bones.

The initiation ceremony itself has been partially described in both the 1876 documents (reproduced below) and a century later by Ron Rosenbaum in "The Last Secrets of Skull & Bones" (*Esquire*, September 1977).

Each year 15 newly tapped members are put through what has been described as a "harrowing" ordeal — presumably to test their manhood in a manner traditional with fraternity hazing.

According to Rosenbaum, "one can hear strange cries and moans coming from the bowels of the tomb" during initiation.

Four elements of the initiation ceremony are recorded:

- that the initiate has to lie naked in a sarcophagus,
- that he is required to tell the "secrets" of his sex life to fellow initiates,
- that Patriarchs dressed as skeletons and acting as wild-eyed lunatics howl and screech at new initiates.
- that initiates are required to wrestle naked in a mud pile.

Undoubtedly there is more. However, the above is enough to warrant branding The Order as based on behavior more suited to juvenile delinquents.

Undoubtedly the more serious part of the initiation process is peer pressure, the conversion of juveniles into presumably responsible members of an unelected elite. As Rosenbaum comments, "the real purpose of the institution was . . . devoted to converting the idle progeny of the ruling class into morally serious leaders of the establishment."

What happens in the initiation process is essentially a variation of brain-washing or encounter group processes. Knights, through heavy peer pressure, become Patriarchs prepared for a life of the exercise of power and continuation of this process into future generations.

In brief, the ritual is designed to mold establishment zombies, to ensure continuation of power in the hands of a small select group from one generation to another. But beyond this ritual are aspects notably satanic.

322

Thursday Evening, July 28, 1859.

☞   VI   S. B. T.

———✦———

Cara tamen lacrymis ossa futura nostris.

Prop. I. 19 : 18.

———✦———

Edw. T. Boltwood. S. E. C.

Yale College,
Thursday Evening, July 7.

322

𝕿𝖍𝖚𝖗𝖘𝖉𝖆𝖞 𝕰𝖛𝖊𝖓𝖎𝖓𝖌, 𝕵𝖚𝖑𝖞 23𝖉, 1868.

☞   VI   𝕾. 𝕭. 𝕿.

Boni Bonos diligant, asciscantque sibi.

Cicero Laelius, XIV, 50.

John B. Ishaw S. E. C.

YALE COLLEGE,
Thursday Evening, July 9th. {

322

ℭhursday ℭvening July 21st, 1870.

     VIII.   S. B. C.

Hoc quidem constat, bonis inter bonos quasi necessariam benevolentiam.

Cicero de Amicitia, xiv. 50.

ABMason S. C. C.

YALE COLLEGE, }
Thursday, July 7th. }

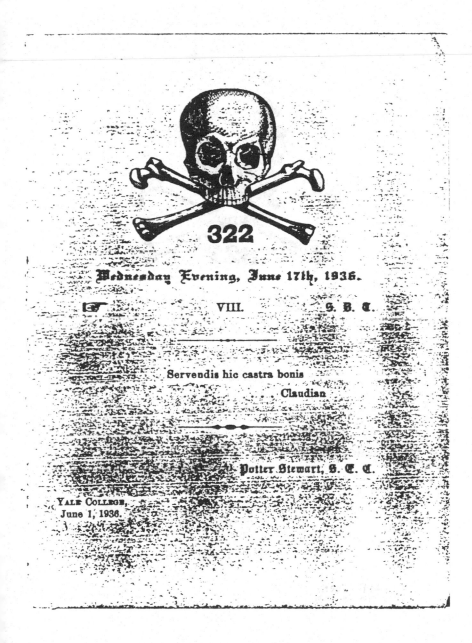

322

Wednesday Evening, June 17th, 1936.

☞   VIII.   S. B. C.

Servendis hic castra bonis
                    Claudian

Potter Stewart, S. E. C.

YALE COLLEGE,
June 1, 1936.

𝕿𝖍𝖚𝖗𝖘𝖉𝖆𝖞 𝕰𝖇𝖊𝖓𝖎𝖓𝖌, 𝕸𝖆𝖞 31, 1984

  VIII. 𝕾.𝕭.𝕿.

———

D. 183

Quamvis mors non sit bonum, bona tamen est bonis.
Holbein, Alphabetum Mortis. 14.

———

𝕯𝖔𝖚𝖌𝖑𝖆𝖘 𝕽. 𝕳𝖊𝖓𝖘𝖙𝖔𝖓, 𝕾.𝕰.𝕿.

YALE UNIVERSITY
APRIL 25, 1984

Memorandum Number Four:
Satanic Aspects of The Order

Even with our limited knowledge of the internal ritual of The Order we can make three definite statements about the links between The Order and satanic beliefs.

These observations should be seen as a start point for further research and consideration.

The first link is through photographic evidence of the association of Skull & Bones with satanic devices, i.e., the skull and crossed bones.

The second link is through satanic symbolism.

The third link is through the association of The Order with the New Age Movement, well documented in a remarkable new book by Constance Cumbey, *The Hidden Dangers of the Rainbow* (Huntington House, Inc., Suite G, 1200 North Market Street, Shreveport, LA 71107).

THE PHOTOGRAPHIC EVIDENCE

Photographic evidence exists of the use of the satanic devices of a skull and crossed bones in ceremonies of The Order.

We reproduce on the following page a photogrpah of the "Class of 1869." Fifteen members of the Club, thirteen standing and two seated, are grouped around crossed thigh bones and a skull. A handwritten list of these men is also reproduced.

In the background is a grandfather clock. From 1833 to the present time a grandfather clock is presented to each Knight upon initiation and stays with him throughout his life as a memento of what is called "the Bones experience."

We also reproduce two other photographs of other classes seated around a skull and bones. According to other evidence, at least three sets of skulls and assorted bones are kept within the Bones Temple on the Yale campus.

An obvious point is that these bones and skulls are former human beings. Instead of sacred treatment, they are exhibited and used for ceremonial purposes. Where the bones should be resting decently in a grave, they have become the center of a secret ceremony. In brief, the photographs reveal the men portrayed as grave robbers who reject human dignity and decency and use satanic devices.

Class of 1869 left to right.
Standing.
1 Heaton
2 Shirley
3 Lear
4 Foster
5 Hooker
6 Richardson
7 Raymond
8 Bissell
9 Bonnard
10 Perrin
11 Freeman
12 Isham
13 Eno
Seated
1. Beers
2 Brown

THE SATANIC SYMBOLISM OF THE SKULL

Artist Elizabeth Stucki[1] has commented on the mask and the skull in modern art and the symbolic meaning.

Says Stucki:

"The Skull — Mortality Unmasked

The opposite of the mask is the skull. The face of the person is a fleshy skin worn between the two. People who deny the person as made in the image of God directly, and individually created and loved by Him, will seek either of these exits to being truly human — the mask which covers the mortal man or the skull which is left after mortal man has departed. Primitive minds who have not yet found God and sophisticates who have rejected Him, desire the mask and the skull."

Collectivist artist Picasso, darling of New York establishment elitists, was also preoccupied with skulls in a manner very similar to members of Skull and Bones. The preoccupation is portrayed by Leo Steinberg in *Art News*, October 1971. Artist Stucki comments on Picasso's morbid interest in skulls as follows:

> In 1945, Picasso painted "Skull and Pitcher." Leo Steinberg states that in it "the light's character is consistently altered." The light is as hard as an axe-blade, not softly spiritual. Steinberg also gives the painting a Freudian interpretation of sexuality and interprets the pitcher to be the "receiving part in a Satanic annunciation." He refers to Morgenstern's poetry on sex and the skull. In this article he feels that Picasso projected himself into the skulls. He made eight skulls in one week as a method of mastering his fear of death. In 1930, Picasso was self-projecting into the Minotaur monsters he painted. He had painted skulls all along; an earlier one in 1907, is in a still-life now in Leningrad. In the same year, he discarded the idea of using a skull in his "Demoiselles d'Avignon." In the mid-1940s, he used it as a mask, on an owl, or on a horseface."

THE HIDDEN DANGERS OF THE RAINBOW

Constance Cumbey in *The Hidden Dangers of the Rainbow* identifies several organizations linked to The Order and the objectives of The Order.

Cumbey identifies Benjamin Creme and the Tara Center based in New York, Los Angeles, Amsterdam and London as a New Age phenomenon. To Creme are linked Unity and Unitarian Church leaders.

---

[1]Margaret Elizabeth Stucki, *War on Light: The Destruction of the Image of God in Man Through Modern Art* (Available from Freedom University Press), p. 7.

Unknown to Cumbey, The Order has long-standing and significant links to the relatively small Unitarian Church. In fact, former President William Taft, whose father co-founded The Order, was President of the Unitarian Association in his time.

Cumbey identifies the link between Hitler and the New Age movement and former research by this author linked The Order to the founding and growth of Naziism.

Most significantly, Cumbey states that the New Age movement plans to bring about a New World Order "which will be a synthesis between the U.S.S.R., Great Britain and the United States."

Finally, Cumbey points out that the anti-Christ and satanic aspects are woven into the cult of the New Age movement.

Memorandum Number Five:
Is The Order also the Illuminati?

The Illuminati was a group of Bavarian conspirators dedicated to the overthrow of government. The society was founded on May 1, 1776 by Adam Weishaupt, Professor of Canon Law at the University of Ingolstadt. The Order of the Illuminati presumably ceased to exist when it was raided by the Bavarian police in 1786 on orders from the Elector of Bavaria. The Order was dissolved and its seized papers published. Because the Bavarian state ordered the Illuminati papers published, we have authentic information about the organization and its methods of operation.

At this point we want to draw a comparison between The Order known as Skull and Bones and The Order known as the Illuminati in 18th century Bavaria. This is not the time or the place to draw final conclusions. These have to await more information. Here are some parallels worth considering.

1. THE GERMAN ORIGINS OF THE ORDER

The Illuminati had its origins at University of Ingolstadt and recruited mainly from the Student-encorpos, the student bodies common to German universities.

The Order had its origins at Yale in 1833, but Skull & Bones is a chapter of a German secret society. It was introduced into the United States by William Russell, later General William Russell, who brought a charter back from his student days in Germany.

The German origins have been denied on the Yale campus, but evidence exists to confirm German origins. When the Temple was raided in 1876 the entrants found a card on which was written: "From the German Chapter. Presented by Patriarch D.C. Gilman of D. 50."[1]

2. THE STRUCTURE OF THE ORGANIZATIONS

The Illuminati and Skull & Bones are both known **internally** as "The Order" or "Our Order." However, this terminology is not uncommon among secret societies and perhaps nothing can be read into this coincidence. Moreover, the structure is quite different. The Illuminati had a structure, apparently based on the Jesuits, where only two members were known to each superior member.

Skull & Bones has an entirely different structure, one designed to continue into perpetuity. Each Club has 15 members chosen by the Club immediately preceding. This has remained a consistent procedure from 1833 to 1985. Each club has an "Agent" who is in communication

---

[1]See Item 2 following page, *The Fall of Skull and Bones*, p. 5.

with the Secretary of RTA, the Russell Trust Association, the legal entity for The Order.

Obviously from the structural viewpoint, there is no similarity whatsoever between the Illuminati and Skull & Bones.

3. SECRECY IN BOTH ORDERS

On the other hand, both are intensively secretive organizations. We have already commented that Bonesmen are supposed to refuse to discuss even membership in The Order, and this unquestionably applied to the Illuminati. Secrecy can be used to conceal illegal activities. **Obviously secrecy is only needed if there is something to conceal.** Secrecy is superfluous if there is nothing to conceal.

Initiates are sworn to secrecy. They are required to leave the room if The Order comes into discussion. They cannot — under oath — answer questions on The Order and its organizations. In correspondence between members concealment even involves spelling Patriarch as P------ch and Knight as K----t, etc. The membership lists are secret. The only information to be surfaced has been obtained by illegal means. This poses a moral problem for research and writing. Are we justified in publishing secret information?

The Illuminati is also secret.

The following is from a private letter between members of the Illuminati and published by the Elector of Bavaria: "The great strength of our Order lies in its concealment; let it never appear in any place in its own name, but always covered by another name and another occupation."

Members of both Orders use their power and influence to help fellow members. This is a longstanding arrangement well known inside and outside The Order. In Volume One, *Introduction To The Order* we analyzed what we termed the Chain of Influence in the Whitney-Stimson and Bundy families. How these three families, all with members in The Order, working closely together to maintain a hold over U.S. foreign affairs for almost a century.

Now here's an extract from an Illuminati letter:

> The power of the Order must surely be turned to the advantage of its members. All must be assisted. They must be preferred to all persons otherwise of equal merit.

There is also an interesting piece of circumstantial evidence that points to an Illuminati connection. The membership catalogs are intended for internal use by members so it is reasonable to assume that any markings or information is authentic and has some meaning within The Order. The catalogs have always printed in one form or another, usually at the head of the page, the letters "P and D." Thus, the 1833 list has "Period 2 Decade 3."

The period is constant at "2" while the Decade increases by one each ten years, i.e., decade 3, 4, 5, etc. The "D" number is always less than the class number. Up to 1970 by 2 and after 1970 by 1. In other words the first list of members — the class of 1833 was designated "P. 231—D.31."

In brief, the organization started in the United States **was in the third decade of the second period**. So a sensible question is — where does that place the start? Presumably in Germany. The first decade of the second period would then begin in 1800 and the first period would have ended in the decade 1790 to 1800. **That places us in the time frame of the elimination of Illuminati by the Bavarian Elector.**

Reprints of
Rare materials on
THE ORDER

322

Anonymous

SKULL AND BONES

No date

An account of the break-in "Bones Temple" 1876.

Let it be stated in advance that this pamphlet is published solely with a view to clear away the "poppy-cock" which surrounds the greatest society in college. It has no malicious intent. The sole design of the publishers and those who made the investigations, is to cause this Society to stand before the college world free from the profound mystery in which it has hitherto been enshrouded and to lessen, at least in some degree, the arrogant pretensions of superiority.

Table of Contents:

APPENDIX

Plan of the Building

PART I. — METHODS OF INVESTIGATION

Any one who was noticing the Bones men of '77, on the morning of Sunday, Oct. 1st, 1876, was probably struck by the crestfallen air which characterized them all. As long as Bones shall exist, the night of September 29th will be to its members the anniversary of the occasion when their temple was invaded by neutrals, their rarest memorabilia confiscated and their most sacred secrets unveiled to the eyes of the uninitiated. We have thought a description of how this was done might be of interest to the collegeworld. The back cellar windows of the eulogian temple were fortified as follows: First, to one seeking entrance from the outside was a row of one inch iron bars; behind them was a strong iron netting fastened to a wooden frame; behind this another row of iron bars 1¼ inches thick; and still behind this a heavy wooden shutter. Formidable as these defences appear, we determined to effect an entrance. The work proceeded slowly and it was only after many hours of patient work that one of the outside iron bars was cut into. Next, by means of a powerful claw, the long nails that fastened the iron netting to the wooden frame were drawn out. Then the bar was refastened in its place by means of a little putty, and we retired to wait a favourable night for completing the undertaking; 8 o'clock, Friday evening, Sept. 29, was the time selected. First, one of our number proceeded to remove the iron bar and netting; and then, for the sake of more room, he, with considerable difficulty, got out the strong wooden frame to which the latter had been fastened. Pushing head and shoulders into the opening thus made, there still remained a strong row of 1¼ inch iron bars. Fortunately, there was no need to file these through. They were fastened above in a thick joist, but below, ran into a brick "damp-wall" that was built up inside and two inches from the stone foundation of the building. By the aid of a hatchet, it was the work of but a very few moments to dig away about twenty inches of this wall and thus loosen an iron plate through which the lower ends of the bars ran. Upon pushing this plate inward, the bars all fell out of their own weight; the flimsy wooden shutter was then wrenched from its position, and, at just half-past ten, an entrance was effected. Passing in through the window, we broke open the wooden door at the top of the cellar stairs, opened the two iron shutters which close the back windows of the main hall and proceeded to examine the temple at our leisure.

A WARM SUMMER'S NIGHT

witnessed the other entrance and the fuller investigation which enables us to enlighten the hitherto mystified college world about the interior of the recent addition. It also supplied the missing links in the history of the society and the mode of working it, which the previous investigators neglected to secure.

One day in the Spring, a young man happened to be passing Bones hall, late Thursday night, and noticed a gleam of light from the skylight in the roof. Reasoning that where that ray appeared there must be some entrance, sometime afterwards several public spirited under-graduates made the exploration we chronicle.

They got a ladder, which the painters who were rejuvenating the old brick row were using, some stout rope, a dark lantern, a small crow bar, a hatchet, cold chisel and jimmy. One Sunday night, about eleven o'clock, they carried the ladder across the campus and placed it against the rear of the building. One man was stationed across High Street to act as watchman. The others ascended the ladder; previously, however, they took the precaution to remove their shoes and went up in their stocking feet, to avoid all noise. Going over the roof to the skylight, they easily pried it open with the crow bar. The opening would admit them, one at a time. The rope was tied to the skylight. Separately, with joy and trembling, the investigators slide down. They were now in the mystic recesses of Bones.

As the result of their investigations is summarized with the result of prior research, we need not go into it more at length here. Suffice to say that shortly before dawn they climbed the rope, refastened the skylight, descended to the ground and put the ladder back where they had got it. It may be safely said that no hearts in the whole college were more joyful and no sincerer thanks went up in chapel that morning, than from those daring men, who had taken such great risks to disclose the inner parts of our Yalensian Juggernaut.

PART II — INTERIOR OF SKULL AND BONES HALL

Besides the cellar the temple is divided into two stories Fig. 1 is a rough plan of the cellar:

a a a a — Windows.
A — Entrance.
B — Furnace.
c c — Stairways to first floor.
D — Jo.
E — Kitchen.
F — Storeroom

There is always kept burning in the Jo a lamp which is ornamented with a dilapidated human skull and a framed set of "Directions to new Eulogians." The kitchen is well appointed, and the furnace a new one. Each dish on the kitchen shelves is ornamented with the skull and bones. Each spoon and fork is marked S.B.T.

On ascending the stairs from the cellar, you find yourself, after bursting open the door C, in a entry, from which a winding staircase (K) leads to the upper floor. The door C is of wood, but broken open easily.

H is the outside iron door covered on the inside with a pair of light frame doors. *B* is a small toilet room. *D* opens into the lodge called **324**, is fitted up in black velvet, even the walls being covered with that material. A glass case here holds quite a quantity of memorabilia — among which may be seen a hat said to belong to Pret. Pierson, a number of base balls and several textbooks. *G* contains two side-boards of mahogany and one large table in the centre. Besides these the walls are adorned with pictures of the founders of Bones at Yale, and of the members of the Society in Germany, when the Chapter was established here in 1832. There are also two smaller tables. The glassware, decanters; &c., on the side-board, all have the skull and the bones blown into the glass.

Ascending to the next floor, we come into a long hall (*F*). Entering room *A* immediately on the left is seen a book-case which contains the Bones library and which is very complete, containing about every book of note ever published at Yale. Hanging on the wall toward High street was a handsomely-framed cushion of velvet on which were fastened the pins of every society ever in Yale University. On the south side of the room is a handsome open fireplace and above this a marble mantel and a mirror. On the mantel were two casts of the pin; one in silver and the other in bronze — the first about two inches in diameter, the second, about three. Several mystical engravings hung on the walls. The room is handsomely furnished. Tobacco, pipes and cards are abundant.

Room B, called **322,** is the "sanctum sanctorum" of the temple. Its distinguishing feature is a fac-simile of the Bones pin, handsomely inlaid in the black marble hearth, just below the mantel, and also inlaid in marble is the motto: "Rari Quippe Boni," in old English text. This room is furnished in red velvet, and is very luxurious. On the wall is a star with a finger pointed towards it. On the walls of the long hall *F* are hung groups of pictures of each Bones' crowd. *H* is an old plain lock safe, but contained nothing save a knife covered with blood stains. *C* is the memorabilia room, and contains the old college bell, old boating flags, old mss.,&c. *D* contains two Brunswick & Balke combination tables (billiard) and a 'bouffe', beside cue racks &c. *E* is a Jo and toilet room.

PART III — HISTOLOGY OF THE SOCIETY

Bones has no constitution. Its grip &c., are handed down from fifteen to fifteen. The records though, which are made at each meeting, show all anybody could want to know. These records are profusely illustrated, making an interesting memorial to future Eulogians. Some well-skilled amateur has evidently spent much time illustrating them. The motto "Boni bonis adpacunt" constantly appears.

Bones is a chapter of a corps in a German University. It should properly be called, not Skull and Bones Society, but Skull and Bones Chapter. General R——, its founder, was in Germany before Senior Year and formed a warm friendship with a leading member of a German society. He brought back with him to college authority to found a chapter here. Thus was Bones founded. The 322 on the pin has been commonly supposed to mean, founded in '32 and 2nd chapter. But the Bones man has a pleasing fiction that his fraternity is the descendant of an old Greek patriotic society, dating back to Demosthenes 322, B.C. the Bones records, 1881 for example, with huge pride, are headed Anno-Demostheni 2203. A secondary date is from the time of the fire in the hall or annoconflagrationis, as the records style it.

Immediately on entering Bones, the neophyte's name is changed. He is no longer known by his name as it appears in the college catalogue, but, like a monk or knight of Malta or St. John, becomes Knight so and so. The old Knights are then known as Patriarch so and so. The outside world are known as Gentiles and vandals.

We have tried to prepare this brief sketch without injuring the feelings or susceptibilities of any PERSON. It has been done through an earnest belief that Bones, as at present conducted, is a blight on Yale College. It makes bitter the time when all should be pleasing. It forms emities and creates discussions when all should be harmony. But, above all, it lowers our standard of honor and detracts from that manliness which is our pride.

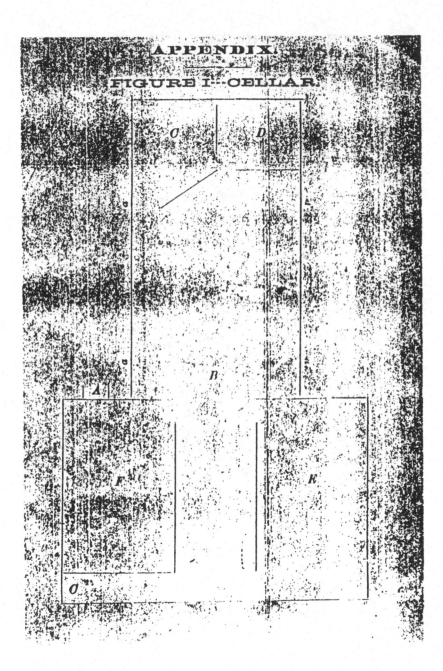

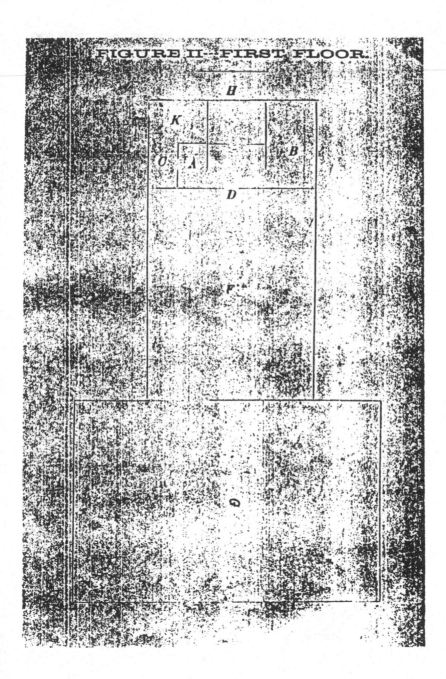

FIGURE II.—FIRST FLOOR.

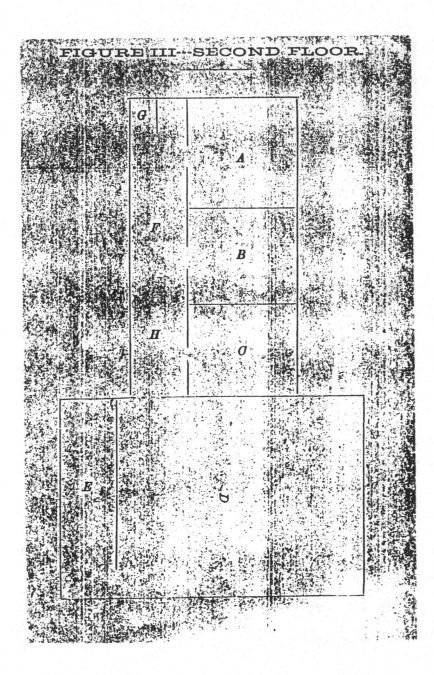

FIGURE III--SECOND FLOOR.

Anonymous

THE FALL OF SKULL AND BONES

Published by The Order, New Haven 1876.

Satirical essay.

BABYLON IS FALLEN

Anyone who was noticing the Bones men of '77 on the morning of Sunday October 1st, 1876, was probably struck by the crest-fallen air which characterized all of them. At any rate there were those who observed that during the church services their eyes suspiciously scanned the faces of one neutral after another, and invariably dropped if their glance was returned. The reason for this is a simple one. As long as Skull and Bon̈es Society shall exist, the night of September 29th will be to its members the anniversary of the occasion when their Temple was invaded by neutrals, some of their rarest memorabilia confiscated, and their most sacred secrets unveiled to the vulgar eyes of the uninitiated.

We have thought that a description of how this was done might be of interest to the college world. The back-cellar windows of the Eulogian Temple were fortified as follows:

First, to one seeking entrance from the outside, was a row of one-inch iron bars; behind them a strong iron netting fastened to a wooden frame; behind this another row of iron bars, one and one quarter inches thick; and still behind this a heavy wooden shutter. Formidable as these defenses appear, the Order of the File and Claw, having procured a supply of files, skeleton keys, etc., determined to attempt to effect an entrance. For reasons that need not be rehearsed here, the work proceeded slowly, and it was only after many hours of patient and cautious labor that one of the outside bars was cut in two. Next, by means of a powerful claw, the long nails that fastened the iron netting to the wooden frame were drawn out. Then the bar was re-fastened in its place by means of a little putty, and we retired to await a favorable night for finishing the job. Eight o'clock Friday evening, September 29th, was the hour selected.

First, one of our number proceeded to remove the iron bar and the netting, and then, for the sake of more room, he, with considerable difficulty, got out the strong wooden frame to which the latter had been fastened. Pushing head and shoulders into the opening thus made, there still remained a strong row of one and one quarter inch iron bars. Fortunately there was no need to file through these. It was found that they were fastened above in a thick joist, but below ran into a brick "damp-wall" that was built up inside, and two inches from the stone foundation-wall of the building. By the aid of a claw and a hatchet, it was the work of but a few moments to dig away about twenty inches of this wall, and thus loosen an iron plate through which the lower ends of the bars ran. Upon pushing this plate inward, the bars all fell out with their own weight; the flimsy wooden shutter was then easily wrenched from its position, and at just half past ten o'clock an entrance into the cellar was obtained. Passing in through the window, we broke open the wooden door at the top of the cellar stairs, opened the two iron shutters which close the back windows of the main hall, and proceeded to examine the Temple at our leisure. For the benefit of future explorers, and as a directory for new-fledged Bones men for all time, we will now give a brief description of

THE INTERIOR OF SKULL AND BONES HALL

Besides the cellar, the Temple is divided into two stories. Fig. 1 is a rough plan of the cellar:

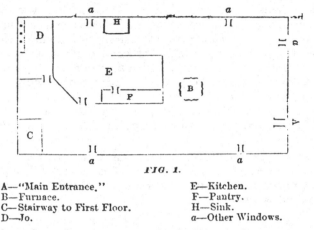

FIG. 1.

A—"Main Entrance."	E—Kitchen.
B—Furnace.	F—Pantry.
C—Stairway to First Floor.	H—Sink.
D—Jo.	a—Other Windows.

A light is always kept burning in the Jo (D), which is ornamented with a dilapidated human skull and a framed set of "Directions to Freshmen," signed Thomas Clap, and dated *Yale College, 1752.* Here is also a tombstone marked Sperry, seemingly taken from the same grave as the skull. On the west wall of the kitchen (E), which contained the ordinary conveniences, hangs a picture of Napoleon Bonaparte. In the Pantry (F) are large quantities of dishes, each piece of crockery ornamented with a picture of a skull and crossbone and each spoon and fork marked. S.B.T.

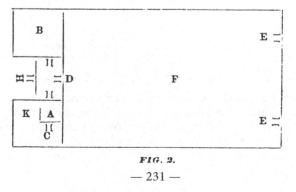

FIG. 2.

On ascending the stairs from the cellar, you find yourself, after bursting open the door C, Fig. 2, in an entry (A), from which a winding staircase (K) leads to the next floor. The door C, which is of wood, we found locked, but broke open without difficulty. H is the outside iron door, covered on the inside with a pair of light frame doors. B is a small toilet room. The door D, which is without a lock, opens into the main hall (F), called by the initiated "324". The floor is of coloured tiles; the walls are rather gaudily frescoed, mainly in red and black, somewhat like those of D K hall. A few settees, resembling those in Linonia Hall, and a table, make up the furniture of the room. The wood work is painted white, and, like the walls, is in many places scratched and dirty. EE are two narrow windows, guarded by strong iron shutters. The latter are concealed from view by some light wooden blinds stained to look like walnut. The only objects of interest in the room were a glass case in the southeast corner containing a large number of gilded base-balls, each inscribed with the date, score, etc., of a university game, and a well-thumbed text-book, either a Physics or a Human Intellect, on the fly-leaf of which was inscribed the autograph of Bones' irrepresible an-noyer, Arjayjay of '76.

Thus far we had found little to compensate us for our trouble, but on ascending to the next floor, and passing, on our right a little store-room and draw-bridge which extend over the front entrance from High Street, our pains was rewarded.

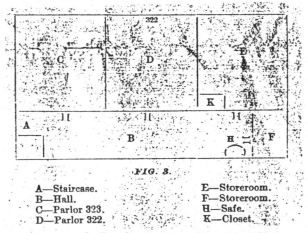

FIG. 3.

A—Staircase.
B—Hall.
C—Parlor 323.
D—Parlor 322.

E—Storeroom.
F—Storeroom.
H—Safe.
K—Closet.

Entering the room C, Fig. 3, immediately on the left is seen a book-case, which contains the Skull and Bones library, including a complete set of the Yale Lit., handsomely bound college catalogues and books published by Bones men. Here, too, was the Constitution of the Phi Beta Kappa and a catalogue of Scroll and Key Society, containing a list of members down to 1868. It was bound in black, and had on the front cover the letters C.S.P. and on the back C.C.J. In Old English text. For the year LI only eleven names are given, and for XLII only twelve. It contains several typographical errors, as for instance; D. Cady Eaton's first name is printed Samuel. Opposite the names of the first two Keys men for LXII, some one has written, in a bold hand, the mystic symbol "Ass". And at the top of the page which give the men of LII, is written, "Croud packed by Boies," and Boies is the name of a Keys man of that year. From the catalogues we learn that the President and Secretary of Scroll and Key are known "inside" as Chilo and Eumenes, and that, as in Bones, each member has a nickname given him. Some of these are handed down from class to class, of these Glaucus, Prisaticus and Arbaces appear to be the favourites.

Hanging on the wall towards High street was a handsomely-framed cushion of dark velvet, on which were fastened the pins of all the societies which have existed in college, including Spade and Grave, Bull and Stones, and the like. On the south side of the room is a fire-place, and above this a mantel and mirror. Upon the mantel were a Skull and Bones of silver, the skull about two inches in diameter, and engraved "32 from the S.E.C. of 1858;" another of bronze, a little larger than the silver one, and various other insignia relating to Skull and Bones. On the west wall hung, among other pictures, an old engraving representing an open burial vault, in which, on a stone slab, rest four human skulls, grouped about a fool's-cap and bells, an open book, several mathematical instruments, a beggar's scrip, and a royal crown. On the arched wall above the vault are the explanatory words, in Roman letters, "We War Der Thor, Wer Weiser, Wer Bettler Oder Kaiser?" and below the vault is engraved, in German characters, the sentence;

"Ob Arm, Ob Beich, im Tode gleich,"

The picture is accompanied by a card, on which is written, "From the German Chapter. Presented by Patriarch D.C. Gilman of D. 50" The room is handsomely furnished; tobacco and pipes were abundant, and packs of wellworn cards served to indicate how the society manages to kill five or six hours every Thursday evening. The pipe-bowls, which are representations of skulls, and bear the stamp of M. Gambier, Paris, have the Eulogian name of the owner and his decade written upon them with red ink; for instance the one belonging to the present "Member from Bath" was marked "Trim, D. 75."

Room D, the Bones name of which is "322," is the *sanctum sanctorum* of the Temple. Its disinguishing feature is a lifesize *fac simile* of the Bones pin handsomely inlaid in the black marble hearth. Just below the mantel, and also inlaid in marble, is the motto:

Bari Quippe Boui

in old English text. This room is even more richly furnished than "323", but contains no book-case, and no pictures of special significance.

On the walls of the long hall B are hung a couple of score of photographs, about 12x20 inches, each representing fifteen Bonesmen grouped around a table, on which rest a human skull and crossbones. As the finish of these pictures is poor and of an antiquated style, it is probable that they are taken each year with the apparatus belonging to the society. H is an old-fashioned plain-lock safe, size about 20x26 inches, and 15 inches deep, set in the wall. It is probably used as a place of deposit for money and valuables, but on the night of the 29th contained only a bunch of keys and a small gold-mounted flask half filled with brandy.

K is a small closet in which are kept unbound sheets of the Bones Society catalogues and a set of handsome memorabil books, one for each year. Some of the old memorabil is quite curious, and the collections relating to recent years are very complete.

The Bones catalogue is essentially as described in *Four Years at Yale.*

The doors to E and F, which are used as general storerooms, are protected by plates of sheet-tin, but the locks were not "what we may call" proof against skeleton keys. The memorabilia in these rooms was noteworthy for amount rather than quality. However, in the midst of a good deal of rubbish we found four or five boating flags, and a number of old Greek, Latin and German works in MS. None of these were society records, but works of well-known authors; into the genuine antiquity of the MSS. We have not as yet been able to examine.

In conclusion, we will say that a thorough examination of every part of the Temple leads us to the conclusion that "the most powerful of college societies" is nothing more than a pleasant convivial club. The kitchen contains the materials for serving refreshments for the inner man; there are neither billiard tables nor any kind of musical instrument in the building; there is a total absence of all the "machinery" which we had been led to expect; the bell heard on initiation nights is not "the old college bell;" Skull and Bones has no secrets beyond a few that may be handed down annually by word of mouth, and no written constitution beyond a few directions similar to the suggestions appended to the Delta Kappa by-laws.

Before leaving the hall, it was asked whether we should inform other members of the college of what we had done, and throw open the hall to the public. We think no one will deny that we had it in our power at one stroke not only to take away forever all the prestige which her supposed secrecy has given this society, but to make her the laughing-stock of all college, and render her future existence extremely doubtful. But while we had no consideration for the mysterious poppiecock of Skull and Bones Society, we nevertheless remembered that some of the Bones men of '77 are our warm personal friends, and therefore we preferred a less radical course. To Bones as a pleasant convivial club, we have no objections. Let her live on as long as men enjoy good suppers and quiet whist. But her mystery and her secrecy are at an end, and we hope her absurd pretensions and her poppiecock are dead also.

The burglary was not discovered until the following evening, at about eight o'clock. All day Saturday the great Skull and Bones lay at the mercy of any one who might notice the back window.

How thoroughly the society was frightened can be seen by the way they have sealed up the window through which we entered, as well as more recently all of the other five basement openings. We have no idea that Skull and Bones will deny that their hall has been entered, for we are not without proofs that our tale is true. We have above spoken of different manuscripts, trinkets and memorabilia as existing in the Temple. In several cases we should have written "*existed*" for the place that knew them shall know them no more forever. In short, while robbery was not our errand, on the principle that the second thief is the best owner we helped ourselves to a few pieces of memorabil, which can be put on exhibition, and a few documents which can be printed, should any authoritative denial be made to any essential point in this statement. Nor will Bones usual policy of silence avail to throw discredit upon our story. Part of our memorabil has been seen by Senior neutrals, and the remainder will be put where it will do the most good, as soon as the protection of a sheepskin has been placed between us and the Faculty and the law.

YALE COLLEGE, 1877.

SKULL AND BONES TEMPLE.
35 x 44 x 39 ft.

Anonymous

THE ICONOCLAST

New Haven, October 13, 1873

Volume 1 Number 1 (All published)

Strong Yale campus criticism of the Brotherhood of Death.

THE
ICONOCLAST.

Vol. I. NEW HAVEN, OCTOBER 13, 1873. No. 1.

THE
ICONOCLAST.

Vol. I.   NEW HAVEN, OCTOBER 13, 1873.   No. 1.

SALUTATORY.

"YOUR object and your reason for thrusting yourself so obtrusively upon us?" is the question with which every one greets a new publication. A few words in our case will be sufficient to answer this query.

Our object is to ventilate a few facts concerning "Skull and Bones," to dissipate the awe and reverence which has of late years enshrouded this order of Poppy Cock, and to enable its character and influence to be fully and rightly comprehended.

Our reason for doing this is, because we believe that false impressions are current concerning this society; because we believe that a society badge does not make a man, or entitle him to extra respect and consideration; because we believe the majority of the students are hoodwinked and deluded by a few outward signs and symbols, and because we believe that Skull and Bones, directly and indirectly, is the bane of Yale College.

We speak of the institution, not of its members personally, although if all were revealed that we know concerning members of Skull and Bones, how some of them wormed their way there, and how others felt after they had entered that tomb to be closeted six hours every Thursday night with those whom they could not respect, we believe that scales would fall from the eyes of many.

We ask our readers to weigh and consider what we have presented on this subject, rejecting what is false, if any, and maintaining what they find to be true.

We speak through a new publication, because the college press is closed to those who dare to openly mention "*Bones.*"

TO WHOM IT MAY CONCERN.

We come before the college now on Justice's side arrayed,
To claim redress for open wrongs that Vandal hands have made,
To give to college sentiment expression bold and free,
Asserting each man's native right, if such a thing there be.

We represent no clique or clan, but honest men and true,
Who never will submit to that which *fifteen* men may do,
Who feel the shameful yoke that long has on the college lain,
And who propose to do their best to break that yoke in twain.

We are not "soreheads." God forbid that we should cherish strong
Desires to be identified with principles that long
Have been a blight upon the life and politics of Yale,—
Before whose unjust aims the glow of "Boss Tweed's" brass
    would pale.

We represent the neutral men, whose voices must be heard,
And never can be silenced by a haughty look or word—
Of those whose influence here at Yale would be but void and null
Did they not wear upon their breasts *two crossed bones and*
    a skull.

We hold no grudge 'gainst any man, but wish that all may be
United by the common bond of peace and harmony;
Yet, when a *few* do to themselves most proudly arrogate
The running of affairs, there can be no such happy state.

What right, forsooth, have *fifteen* men to lord it over all?
What right to say the college world shall on their faces Fall
When they approach? Have they, indeed, to "sickly greatness
    grown,"
And must each one with servile speech them his "superior" own?

If they have grounds on which they base their claim as just and
    true,
We challenge them to set them forth exposed to public view,
That all may know the reasons why this oligarchy proud
Elect themselves as lords supreme o'er us, the "vulgar crowd."

We offer no objections to their existing clan,—
No one disputes with them this right, we question but the plan
On which they act,—*That only he who wears upon his breast*
Their emblem, he for every post shall be considered best.

We wish this understood by all. Let none who read this say
That we are moved by petty wrongs or private spite obey;
It is for principles of right that we with them contend,
For principles which they've ignored, but which we here defend.

O fellow students, who with us revere these classic halls,
O ye across whose pathway bright their sacred glory falls,—
Ye men of every class who feel our Alma Mater's care,
Shall college life beneath these elms this loathsome aspect wear?

Shall none assert the right to act as to each seemeth best,
But cringe and fawn to him who wears a *death's head* on his
    breast?
Nay, let all rise and break the spell whose sickly glamour falls
About all that originates within those brown stone walls.

And if they will not hear our claims, or grant the justice due,
But still persist in tarnishing the glory of the blue,
Ruling this little college world with proud, imperious tones,
Be then the watchword of our ranks—Down, DOWN WITH
    SKULL AND BONES!

THE ICONOCLAST.

BONES AND THE ALUMNI.

It is a world-wide law that a bad institution should either be changed to a good, or wholly removed. We have nothing to do with the fact that evil will work itself out in some way. If a thing be bad, the rule laid down should be applied. The case of changing for the worse we notice, but need not consider here.

Whether an established society deserves toleration, two questions, well answered, will decide. First, is it useful? Second, is it harmful? If the first seems to cover the second, we say that, in a mixture of good and evil, the former may preponderate and warrant our bearing with the evil. But if there be no good, and, beside this lack, real harm, then is the case doubly strong against that institution.

For more than forty years a secret society, called Skull and Bones, has existed in Yale College. It receives a certain number of men from each class. These are chosen nominally by the members of the class next previous, although it is understood that a prominent man's influence avails for his friends and relatives through several years after his graduation. By observing the men elected from year to year, we find that they are chosen with a distinct end in view, namely, that of obtaining for the society the most honors. Some of these honors are given to literary, some to wealthy men. This, then, is the case. Men receive marks of distinction from Yale College or from their entire class, because of which they are taken into this secret society. Since Yale honors men, this fraternity professes to honor them also. There is something in this double action that calls our attention. With respect to the first method, there are several ways in which distinguishing marks are given by the college. Prizes are distributed for excellence in composition or in scholarship. They are small, but are considered well worth striving for. Why? Because to receive honors at the hands of so venerable and respected an institution as Yale College is justly thought a mark of genuine ability. Then, after the college has given what it holds to be a proper degree of attention to worth and effort, this society steps in and by its action says: "Yale College cannot do these men justice. We will receive them into our sacred circle. To wear our gaunt badge is alone honor."

Again, an able man is not unnoticed by his classmates. There are many places of trust to be filled by men of means and executive ability. There are literary distinctions, too, which men receive at the hands of their fellows. One need only attend a few class-meetings to believe that these distinctions are eagerly sought. We often, in Junior year, hear the remark that "such a man's being on such a Committee will take him to Bones." So we are again called to listen to this assertion: "Your class cannot honor you aright. To be a member of our august body is alone true honor."

But what is this high power that thus assumes a place above class and college? It is just what we have said—a series of fifteens. It is made up of men—*mortal men,*—who, whatever their intrinsic worth, can, in the name of the society they form, lay no claim to the power they assume. The men whom they choose have, for the most part, been honored as they deserved. Every year, when Skull and Bones makes up its quota, it offers a direct insult to the succeeding class and to Yale College. Yet intense self-feeling blinds it to its own arrogance.

This, then, is the place which the fraternity fills, in regard to usefulness. In answering our second question, we pass over the many minor evils springing from the existence of Skull and Bones. The influence of continued stress upon members themselves, the discord among classmates, the favoritism shown to Bones men by members of the Faculty, the objections to it as a secret society, all give way before a graver charge. When Skull and Bones was founded, the evil which we are about to unfold did not exist. It is an evil which has grown up—

THE ICONOCLAST.

which is growing to-day. Why is it that Yale College is so lamentably poor?—so poor, indeed, that an officer said : " We do not feel able to have our magazines bound for use." Her powers are cramped in every direction for want of money. Many of her buildings are old and inconvenient. But three classes can find room in her dormitories. Her officers are poorly paid. She cannot furnish the instructors or aid the students she would. Let us not be understood to say that she does not do much. But she is poor, considering her aims and opportunities.

We are told that Yale's Alumni have not wealth to compare with that of the Alumni of other colleges. This idea has prevailed to such an extent that the saying, " Rich men go to Harvard," has become trite among us. Is it, then, true that our Alumni cannot support the University? *No! it is false.* Her graduates have the power to place her before any college in America, so far as money is concerned. Then why have they not done so? We will show why.

Out of every class Skull and Bones takes its men. They have gone out into the world and have become, in many instances, leaders in so-

shut themselves off from others, and assume to be their superiors. But what return do they give? Let facts answer. They leave their Mother University in want, while they complain bitterly of her calls to them for help. Whether the refusal of the many to give is right, does not affect the matter. The reason stated avails for them. Moreover, no one but a Yale graduate can fully understand the case, just as none but slaves could appreciate the curse of slavery.

To tell the good which Yale College has done would be well nigh impossible. To tell the good she might do would be yet more difficult. The question, then, is reduced to this— on the one hand lies a source of incalculable good,—on the other a society guilty of serious and far-reaching crimes. *It is Yale College aganist Skull and Bones ! !* We ask all men, as a question of right, which should be allowed to live ?

BONES INITIATION.

WHEN the Faculty prohibited Freshman society initiation in Yale College for this and all succeeding years, because those engaged in it made too much noise and acted in too barbarous a manner, we cannot see why they did not ex-

4 THE ICONOCLAST.

tend their decree so as to include the initiation in Skull and Bones. On the evening of May 27, 1873, when that ceremony took place in Bones Hall, the noise made by blowing fish-horns, stamping of feet, singing, yelling and howling, by those engaged in celebrating the solemn mysteries of the 322 order, was so loud that it could be heard over in the college yard. A view through the grating in the rear into the basement showed a number of '72 and '73 men stripped to their undershirts and washing off the dust and perspiration caused by their violent exercise. The writer recognized also a Congregational clergyman of this city, stripped to his shirt, who has several times preached to the unregenerate students in Yale College. What was *he* doing there? Is this Bones Hall a place where preachers, professors, tutors and students, such as have been thought worthy to enter the solemn precincts, congregate and have a jolly good time, pulling each other up and down stairs with bladders* on their heads, blowing fish-horns and stamping like the gallery gods in a Western-theatre on Saturday night? With what consistency did those members of the Faculty, who are in the habit of visiting the old stone jug, vote to abolish Freshman initiations, while they knew that the society whose badge they wear on their vests, and at times display with pride, is accustomed to practice the same barbarities which by their vote they condemn? Appropriate pastime, is it not, for men of high scholarship, fine literary ability and gentlemanly qualities? stamping and yelling, blowing tin horns and howling, until an unprejudiced passer-by in the street would think that the door to the infernal regions had just been opened and that Davy Satan and all his demons were holding high carnival within. "*Fiat justitia, ruat cœlum;*" and if society initiations are to be prohibited on account of their "barbarity," why should Skull and Bones escape?

* The heads of the neophytes are kept covered with bladders until the initiation ceremonies are over.

CAPT. COOK AND THE SENIORS.

In order to remove the false impressions which pervade not only the college but also the outer world, with regard to the late boating difficulty, we here, though with much reluctance, revive the subject. "Let bygones be bygones," is the well-known maxim, but justice demands a somewhat clearer statement of the matter than has hitherto been made. It is evidently the prevailing idea that a certain portion of the neutrals of the Senior class were influenced in their late action merely by a prejudice against Senior societies, and, therefore, against any of their representatives. This idea is far from the truth. The Senior class will not allow personal prejudices to be a stumbling-block to the interests of the whole college, in proof of which witness their conduct in the choice of the President of the Ball Club. Not a murmur of disapprobation was uttered in this case, for the man chosen is best fitted to further the interests of this branch of athletic sports and to lift it up to a higher level than it now rests upon. In their action in regard to boating matters, the persons mentioned had the common interests at heart. The gentleman whom they desired to see President of the Navy seemed to them the more able of the two candidates proposed, and hence their unselfish, unprejudiced motives in acting as they did.

An impression also exists that the conduct of the Senior class was the result of animosity felt toward the Captain of our last University crew. This we strenuously deny. No one had fewer enemies or was more liked at the beginning of the term than Capt. Cook. To him, as has been said before, belongs the credit of our last and greatest achievement in boating, and to him we ascribe all possible honor and praise. The gentleman whom he proposed, however, did not meet with our honest approbation, and hence the contest,—not against Capt. Cook, but against his candidate, on the part of those who, from three years experience, were better qualified than himself to judge of

THE ICONOCLAST. 5

the abilities of Mr. Monroe and Mr. Dunning. We are heartily glad that the matter has been so amicably settled and that peace once more reigns.

THE INFLUENCE OF BONES UPON BASE BALL.

AT the close of the first boating meeting of the term, an enthusiast requested the assembly to remain and listen to a few words from him upon the subject of base ball. The speaker deprecated our lack of interest in that matter, and endeavored to raise our spirits in regard to future prospects. During his speech he asked, " Why have men lost their enthusiasm in matters pertaining to base ball?" but could not himself explain the cause, and, as it appeared to many of us, for the reason that, as he himself is a member of the so-called society of Skull and Bones, he was unconsciously blinded in regard to the injurious influences which that fraternity exerts upon ball.

Any one, who has been in college three weeks, knows that a Bones man is not at liberty to speak of his society or pin in the presence of other human beings, and that if reference is made to them he feels deeply wounded and insulted (poppy-cock!). Consequently, those of us who felt that we knew the secret of the lack of enthusiasm, deemed it imprudent to reply to the question, inasmuch as it would have placed the speaker in a somewhat unpleasant situation and have cast a damper on a most enthusiastic meeting. Since, then, that was not the place to express our opinion on the subject, and since we feel assured that our views are not without foundation, we now set forth in these pages the real cause of this universal apathy. Our ideas might have been sent to the college papers, had we not been certain that they would never have been allowed to appear in those publications. A delicate theme like this would not have met with the sanction of the Bones men on the *Record* or *Courant* boards, and, consequently, our piece would have lain in a waste basket. Our only resort, then, is this publication.

In the first place, we would state that the enthusiasm of one Bones man, though it be extraordinarily intense, cannot compensate for the pernicious influences which his society exerts.. It may diminish them to a small extent, but it can by no means counterbalance them. His energy would be put to much better use, if he attempted to eradicate the evils of the fraternity and cause it to countenance base ball. Bones prefers to give her elections to the high-stand man and the literary man, as well as to the political toady, while she looks coldly on superior ball men and passes them by in disdain. If it were understood that the best base ball player in every class was as sure of an election to Bones as he who takes 1st prize compositions, would it not call out a great amount of latent talent? When a Freshman enters college, his head is turned in less than a week. He conceives that an election to Bones would be the crowning success of his course. He bethinks himself of the best means of attracting the attention of upper classmen. He lays his plans. According to the characters of the men, these plans are noble and honorable, or base and despicable. Thrice happy are those under classmen whose brains are not crazed by the sight of some haughty and conceited wearer of the Bones pin. But such men are few in every class. Freshmen will stare ; Sophomores will not whisper in the presence of a Bones man, lest they should spoil their " chances ;" and Juniors will stoop to any servility, if by that servility they can attract the attention of a superior being. Unaccountable as such a state of things may seem, every upper classman will bear testimony to the fact that most collegians are the personification of obsequiousness. Now, it is certain that if under classmen are striving to enter Bones, they will follow in the footsteps of previous successful men. They will study their methods and conform themselves to those methods. It is evi-

6   THE ICONOCLAST.

dent to all who witnessed the disappointment of '74 when her best ball player—we might add, one of the best players that has ever entered college,—failed to receive an election to Bones, and when men of no merit whatever supplanted him, that that society does not make it a point to encourage base ball. Here, then, lies the evil ; all men want to go to Skull and Bones ; playing ball will not take them ; hence, men will not play base ball to get there.

Their energies will be applied elsewhere. Some play for the amusement they get ; others take their exercise in this way ; many enter the ranks for the honor of being on the University nine and the notoriety which such a position affords. But not a single soul takes up base ball as a means of helping him to Bones. If there were no such institution as Bones in existence, we might look for more proficiency with the bat. But as it is, the honor of being on the nine is thought far inferior to the glory of strutting round the college yard with a ghastly badge upon one's bosom. Under these circumstances, men in every class who are or would develop into superior players, are led to turn their abilities into other channels. Some seek the retirement of a study and work up high stands ; others spend their spare moments in composing essays which tickle the judges and are rewarded with prizes ; and some individuals, whose independence is reduced to zero and whose obsequiousness is only exceeded by their capacity for wire-pulling, slide into Bones as a bad oyster down the throat of a fastidious epicure, causing, only after it is too late, a sickening and highly uneasy sensation. Men come to college for the purpose of improving their literary abilities, and when they occupy their spare time in writing, the labor expended benefits them personally ; that is to say, they improve themselves by the exercise and receive in addition a reward in the shape of an election to Skull and Bones. The base ball player, on the other hand, who equally needs literary culture, foregoes the benefit he might gain by writing,

and spends the three hours a day which he could devote to self-improvement in exercising at Hamilton Park. At the expense of his own mental development, he works for the honor of the whole college, and is magnanimously rewarded with—nothing. Consequently, only those will take up base ball who care little for Bones, and who prefer to spend their leisure time in a pleasant and healthy game rather than in sitting on the fence or card-playing. One of the reasons why Harvard is victorious year after year is that she offers great attractions to ball men to join her classes. More than once has she induced an excellent player, who fitted for Yale, to enter her walls. Our Freshman classes have ceased to bring in fine players, and those who could be developed into prime men by practice, give little attention to the game. To the society of Skull and Bones, then, is this lack of enthusiasm attributable. These opinions are not from one who is unacquainted with the subject in hand, but, on the contrary, are the honest and heartfelt sentiments of a zealous and earnest adherent of base ball.   †

THE ICONOCLAST. 7

"" A sound of revelry by night,"
A sound that seems to tell
That demons wild instead of men
Within its portals dwell.

And often at the dark midnight,
When earth is draped in gloom,
The beings weird are seen emerge
From out their living tomb.

They step so proud, they look so loud,
Their bearing is so high,
That common folk are fain to shrink,
Whenever they pass nigh.

Like spirits from another world,
Down, deeper down than ours,
They seem to come all furnished
With dark and deadly powers.

And on their breasts they wear a sign
That tells their race and name;
It is the ghastly badge of death,
And from his kingdom came.

The son of Satan, son of Sin,
The enemy of man,
Still claims these worthies as his own
And counts them in his clan.

The sign they bear, in former days
The pirates of the seas,
The foes of God and scourge of man,
Unfolded to the breeze.

Where'er they steered their bloody barks,
Their pennon stained the air;
They flung aloft the Skull and Bones
And bade the world beware.

Are these the pirates of our day?
Have they with petty crime
Together joined in evil league
In this, our later time?

Strive they to emulate the deeds
Whose fierce and fiendish thought
Upon the outlaws of the main
The curse of man has brought?

Whate'er they be, from whence they come,
Where'er they seek to go,
Their badge defies an honest world
And brands it as their foe.

O! may our Yale so fondly loved,
The Skull and Bones beware;
Avoid it like a faithless friend,
A serpent in his lair.

being a neutral, the other a Bones man, returned at the beginning of the college year laden with several conditions, some of which, upon examination, they failed to pass. Up to this point the cases were parallel, and the leniency, if there was to be leniency, should have been shown to the neutral, who has done all that lay in his power to further the interests of the college, rather than to the Bones man, who has, during his three years at Yale, accomplished nothing that we wot of. But, strange to say, the former has been suspended until the end of the term and obliged to leave town, not being permitted to pass another examination until he returns. The Bones man, on the contrary, is allowed to remain in New Haven, attends recitation daily, is called upon to recite, and will have a second examination in less than six weeks. Why is this distinction made? "O, Mr. So-and-so's is a *special* case," said a professor (a Bones man),—the specialty, we presume, being the fact that Mr. So-and-so wears a death's head and cross bones upon his bosom. We understand that Mr. So-and-so claims to have been ill during vacation and offers the illness as an excuse for not passing the examination; but the neutral gentleman was also ill, as the Faculty were expressly informed in a letter from his father.

The circumstance has caused a very lively indignation throughout the Senior class. It is certainly time for a radical reform when the gentlemen who superintend our destinies, and who should be just if nothing else, can allow themselves to be influenced by so petty a thing as society connections.

THE FAVORITISM SHOWN TO BONES MEN.

ARE not we coming to a sad state when open injustice can be done by the Faculty, and when the fact that a man is a member of Skull and Bones can prejudice them in his favor? Briefly, the case which calls forth this question is this: Two members of the Senior class, the one

WHAT KILLED BROTHERS AND LINONIA?

WE put this question to the Corporation and Alumni for consideration. No one doubts that these societies were useful and necessary institutions in connection with the college. No satisfactory explanation as to the cause of their suspension has been offered in the *Record, Cour-*

8 THE ICONOCLAST.

ant, or *Lit.* In No. 2 of the *Record* an editorial consoles the lamentations of the Alumni over the death of Brothers and Linonia, by saying: "As to the causes of that loss of interest various opinions are entertained. But none seems to us so satisfactory as that which finds this cause in the lack of interest in mere speechmaking and the rigidly observed class distinctions of these later days." It immediately adds: "We of course know nothing about the case." But what were these "lamentations" at the Alumni dinner? We quote from the *Palladium* of June 27: "J. Wayne McVeagh made a very brilliant speech, which we are sorry we cannot print in full. He made an irresistible plea for the resuscitation of Brothers and Linonia, attributing their death to the lack of fire and enthusiasm which he noticed here. THESE ARE NOT THE DAYS FOR SECRET METHODS. He was followed by Homer B. Sprague, who also asked for the revival of the two open societies." Those who know anything in regard to the history of the college will pronounce the *Record's* reasons groundless, after a moment's reflection. Since the other departments have grown so large, class feeling has been pretty much ignored. In our boating and ball meetings, any one who has anything to offer is listened to respectfully. Since the war, nearly all those customs which depended upon class feeling have been abolished. The *Record* by its "buncombe" stigmatizes one of the most laudable ambitions which an American student can cherish. When we remember under whose management the *Record* is, we know that said empty editorial could only have been written as a sweet morsel to the Alumni. Why does not this exponent of college feeling and opinion give respect to the judgment of many of the undergraduates, perhaps a large majority, and lay the charge where it justly belongs, upon the present society system, and more especially that of Senior year? What has been the deceitful opiate which has put to rest all literary "fire and enthusiasm" in college for the past

fifteen or twenty years? Is it not high time that the whole college, Corporation, Faculty, Alumni, students and friends should rise up as a strong man and shake off these shackles which surround us in the form of "Trust Associations?" What necessary part do these independent and obtrusive Trust Companies play in the growth and development of intellectual culture in our midst? If they are an indispensable factor, why not advertise them as such in the college catalogue? We ask then that the Alumni who expect to attend next Commencement will come prepared to make this the topic of the occasion, that they will discuss thoroughly the merits and faults of the new and old systems—that if their verdict is against the former, they will petition the Legislature to recall the charters of these Senior societies as college Trust Associations.

BONESICULA.

Our publication is printed of its present size in order that it may be bound in with the *Record*.

A Bones man of '74 is said to have obtained his election by "knowing how to get drunk at the right time." A most laudable method, truly.

In its issue of Sept. 24, the *Record* states that the *Banner* was adorned with eight new cuts. But, if we are not mistaken, there was a *ninth* cut—"the most unkindest cut of all"—to the Bones men.

Is it not strange, to say the least, that on *Friday* the *Bones* men are invariably called up on the *review* by our Bones professor? Yesterday morning the first *five* men asked to recite were nearest the "crab." The remaining three Bones men in the division were allowed to escape entirely.

A Bones man of '74 is said to have asserted (before he received his election) that he wouldn't give ten cents to be in Bones. We assure him that he might have sold his "chances" for far more than that. He may still be open to offers. Any who care to apply may obtain the gentleman's name by speaking to the editors of this publication.

A gladiatorial contest between a certain dog haunting the north entry of Farnam, and a black cat dwelling in the north entry of South, and belonging to one of the mystic fifteen, will take place, if the weather be favorable, next Thursday evening at eight o'clock, in front of the premises known as 322 High street. Freshmen are advised not to attend, inasmuch as it might spoil their "chances." Immediately after the contest refreshments will be served within the "Old Brown Jug." Admission, free.

Anonymous (Lyman H Bagg)

FOUR YEARS AT YALE

1871 Henry Holt & Company New York

An excellent account of the senior society system at Yale.

Out of copyright. Can be reproduced freely.

FOUR YEARS AT YALE

By a Graduate of '69

Lyman H Bagg

NEW YORK
HENRY HOLT AND COMPANY

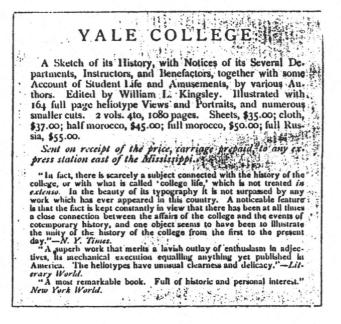

YALE COLLEGE

A Sketch of its History, with Notices of its Several Departments, Instructors, and Benefactors, together with some Account of Student Life and Amusements, by various Authors. Edited by William L. Kingsley. Illustrated with 164 full page heliotype Views and Portraits, and numerous smaller cuts. 2 vols. 4to, 1080 pages. Sheets, $35.00; cloth, $37.00; half morocco, $45.00; full morocco, $50.00; full Russia, $55.00.

Sent on receipt of the price, carriage prepaid to any express station east of the Mississippi.

"In fact, there is scarcely a subject connected with the history of the college, or with what is called 'college life,' which is not treated *in extenso*. In the beauty of its typography it is not surpassed by any work which has ever appeared in this country. A noticeable feature is that the fact is kept constantly in view that there has been at all times a close connection between the affairs of the college and the events of cotemporary history, and one object seems to have been to illustrate the unity of the history of the college from the first to the present day."—*N. Y. Times.*

"A superb work that merits a lavish outlay of enthusiasm in adjectives, its mechanical execution equalling anything yet published in America. The heliotypes have unusual clearness and delicacy."—*Literary World.*

"A most remarkable book. Full of historic and personal interest." *New York World.*

CHAPTER IV.

SENIOR SOCIETIES

Peculiarities of these Societies — Skull and Bones — Its Badge Pin and Numeral — Hall and Corporate Title — Origin — Catalogue — Mode of Giving out Elections — Initiations — Mode of Summoning Members to the Annual Convention — Attendance upon the Regular and Special Meetings — Peculiar Customs and Traditions — Scroll and Key — Its Badge Pin and Vignette — Hall and Corporate Title — Origin and Growth — Customs and Traditions — Spade and Grave — Its Origin, Precarious Existence, Change of Name, and Final Catastrophe — the Societies and the Neutrals — Bull and Stones — The Coffin of '69 — The Tea-Kettle of '53 — Crown and Scepter — Star and Dart — Notable Members of the Existing Societies — Mode of Packing and Making up a Crowd — Comparison of the Societies — Their "Policies," Actual and Possible — Failure of their Imitators in Other Colleges — General Facts about all the Class Societies — Comparison of their Importance in Each Year — General Result of the System.

The societies of the first three years, though possessed of special characteristics, have yet such a general resemblance to one another and to those of other colleges, that their position in the system can be readily comprehended by any reader of these pages, — at least, if he be college-bred. But the senior societies are such peculiarly Yale institutions, that it will be difficult for an outsider fully to appreciate their significance. Nothing like them exists in other colleges; and Harvard is the only college where, under similar conditions, they possibly could exist. In the first place, they are the only Yale societies whose transactions are really secret. Their members never even mention their names, nor refer to them in any way, in the presence of anyone not of their own number; and, as they are all Seniors, there are no "old members in the class above them" to tell tales out of school. There is no electioneering nor pledging for these societies, and no Junior is approached upon the subject in any way until an election is actually offered him. The number of elections given out to each class is small and never varies, and no class nor honorary elections are ever allowed. Both societies combined comprise but little more than one fourth the members of an average class, and the part played by them in politics is simply a negative one. A man's chances for office are never bettered because he belongs to a senior society, but are frequently, for that simple reason, injured or destroyed altogether. The societies do not take their names from the initials of a Greek motto, but from the peculiar emblems adopted as a badge. This badge is constantly worn by active members; by day upon the shirt bosom or neck-tie, by night upon the night dress. A gymnast or boating man will be sure to have his senior badge attached to what little clothing he may be encumbered with while in practice; and a swimmer, divested of all garments whatever, will often hold it in his mouth or hand, or attach it to his body in some way, while in the water. Only graduate members wear the badge upon the vest, where for the first few years they display it quite regularly. Old graduates seldom "swing out" except on special occasions, or while visiting New Haven; and members of the faculty, except may be young freshman tutors, never display a society badge when engaged in their official duties. Members who have ceased to show the badge openly, nevertheless may wear it about them pretty constantly, perhaps by night as well as day, for quite a number of years. The senior societies, in theory, are composed exclusively of "big men"; of those who, for whatever reason, have become preeminent above their fellows in college repute. In this they differ from those of the two preceding years, which of necessity are half made up of comparitively second-rate men. There are a certain number — say twenty — in each class, who, at the end of the third year, may be picked out as the confessed superiors of the others in popular esteem. Were it possible to do this a year or more earlier, and were one junior society preeminently "the best", it is doubtful if the twenty could all be persuaded to join it, or the society to elect them all; for it is plain that their individual political influence would be greater in separate societies, partly made up of less important men. The senior-society type, on the other hand, is an association with no weak members whatever; and the history of the matter shows that unless this ideal is adhered to with reasonable closeness such a society cannot live long at Yale.

There are two of these societies, but as one takes its tone from the other it may be well to describe them separately, and treat first of the oldest and most famous member of the modern system. Its name is "Skull and Bones," — formerly printed "Scull and Bone," — and its badge, of solid gold, consists of the face of a skull, supported by the crossed thigh bones, with a band, bearing the number "322," in place of the lower jaw. Its original badge was a rectangular gold plate, about the size and shape of the present Beta Xi pin, whereon the skull-and-bones design and the numeral were simply engraved. Its wood-cut vignette merely represents the emblems, and is identical with that employed for general purposes in college papers elsewhere. The number "322" is always printed below it, though the size of the type is not invariable. In the cut formally used, the design was smaller than that now than in vogue, but there never has been added to the simple emblems anything in the way of ornament or embellishment. Popularly the society is known as "Bones," and its members as "bones men". The pin is sometimes called a "crab" from its supposed resemblance to that animal. The hall, erected in 1856, is situated on High street, near the corner of Chapel, about opposite the Yale Art Building. It is a grim-looking, windowless, tomb-like structure, of brown sandstone, rectangular in shape, showing a front of about 35 and a length of 44 feet, and is, at a guess 35 feet in height. The entrance in front is guarded by a pair of massive iron doors, a dozen feet high, finished off in panels, and of a dark green color; while heavy clasps of brass close over the key-holes and are secured by padlocks, beneath one of which the bell-pull is concealed. Previous to 1864, when these doors were put in position, their places were occupied by commoner ones of iron, upon which the society emblems were displayed. The roof is nearly flat, and is covered with half-inch plates of iron, which in 1867 took the place of the tin before employed. There is a skylight, similarly protected, and the chimneys and ventilators are ranged along the edges of the roof. Behind, are a pair of small windows barred with iron, and close to the ground are two or three scuttle holes, communicating with the cellar. The building is rapidly becoming covered with the "Virginia creeper," first planted there in 1864, and stands back a rod or more from the street, being separated from it by a post-and-chain fence. The dimensions of the lot upon which it stands are about 40 feet (front) by 70 (deep); and total value of the premises must be upwards of $30,000. Before taking possession of its present quarters, the society for many years, — perhaps from its original organization, — occupied a low-studded back room in the third story of what is now the *Courant* building, opposite the college yard. At the May, 1856, session of the State Legislature the society was incorporated as the "Russell Trust Association," with the same legal formulas as those quoted in the case of Psi U. The names mentioned in the act were William H. Russell of '33, John S. Beach of '39, Henry B. Harrison of '46, Henry T. Blake of '48, Henry D. White of '51, and Daniel C. Gilman of '52; — the first of whom has since acted as president, the one next to the last as treasurer, of the association. All are residents of new Haven.

The society was originated in 1832 by fifteen members of the class which graduated the following year. General Russell, the valedictorian of that class, is its reputed founder, and the best known of his associates is Judge Alphonso Taft of Cincinnati. Some injustice in the conferring of Phi Beta Kappa elections seems to have led to its establishment, and apparently it was for some time regarded throughout college as a sort of burlesque convivial club. It is said that the faculty once broke in upon one of its meetings, and from what they saw determined upon its abolishment, but by the intercessions and explanations of its founder, then serving as tutor among them, were finally induced to spare it. The popular college tradition, that it was transplanted from a German university, is scouted by old neutral graduates as absurd. But, whatever be the facts as to its origin, the mystery now attending its existence is genuine, and forms the one great enigma which college gossip never tires of discussing. Its catalogue is a unique affair, having a page six inches by four, printed upon one side only. Each right-hand page contains the members of a year — fifteen names indicated in full and alphabetically arranged — with the residences, printed in old-English text, and surrounded by a heavy border of black. A title page, bearing the society cut and the words "Period 2. Decade 3," precedes the list of the founders, and a similar one, "Period 2. Decade 4," stands before the class of '43, and so on for every successive ten years, the "Period" being always "2", but the "Decade" increasing each time by one. At the top of the first list of names — the class of '33 — and separated from them by a broad line of black, are the characters, "P.231.—D.31," which regularly increase by one with each succeeding class, and are therefore, for the class of '71, "P.269—D.69." The first page of the book displays, in full-faced old-English capitals, the letters, "Otirunbeditf," arranged in a semi-oval, between two black lines. The catalogue is black-edged, and is bound in black leather, with the owner's name and "D.", stamped in gilt upon the cover, — though of late the "D." is less often indicated. It will be observed that the "D." is always two less than the class; thus, a catalogue labeled "John Smith, D.62", would belong to a member of the class of '64, and so on. What these "Periods" and "Decades" and "P.'s" and "D.'s" may signify is known only to the initiated; but, as the catalogue is never shown to outsiders, they were probably not put there for mystification solely. That the founders are put down as belonging to the "third decade of the second period" may seem to make in favour of the German university theory, in the minds of many; and the blank space in place of the eleventh man's name in the list of the founders, may perhaps be thought a straw in the same direction. The last edition of the catalogue was prepared in December, 1870, and was as usual sent out in unbound sheets to each surviving member of the society. The total membership of the 39 classes represented was of course 585.

The elections to this society are always given out on the Thursday evening which precedes Presentation Day. Since no Junior is ever pledged or spoken to in advance, the excitement which prevails among the "likely men" is intense, though suppressed, as the hour of fate draws nigh. All college, too, is on the alert, to find what the result may be. It is said that formerly the fifteen Bones men, at midnight, silently moved from their hall to the rooms of the chosen ones, when the leader, in each case displaying a human skull and bone, said simply, "Do you accept?" and, whatever was the reply, the procession as silently departed. As the neutrals got into the way of tagging about, insulting and annoying the society on its march, this plan was abandoned in favour of the less formal one now in vogue. According to this, at an early hour of the appointed evening, a Bones Senior quietly calls at the room of a Junior, and having been assured that "we are alone," says: "I offer you an election to the so-called Skull and Bones. Do you accept?" If the answer is affirmative the Senior — and perhaps the graduate member who sometimes accompanies him — shakes hands with the neophyte, and bidding him to keep to his room for the present, hurries back to the hall to report the result. If the election is refused, the result is likewise reported to headquarters, and influential members are sometimes sent back to argue the case; but, as a rule, the few men who refuse elections are not offered a chance to repent. Bones will not be dictated to, and when a man says, "I accept, in case So-and-So is elected with me," or "in case Such-a-One is kept out," he is never allowed to carry his point; Yes or No is the only answer recognized. Suppose the elections begin to be given out about seven, in case there are no refusals the whole number will be made up before nine o'clock; if there are refusals it may take an hour longer. In anticipation of this possibility, a half-dozen extra men are chosen in Bones, in addition to the regular fifteen, and in case any of the latter fail to say Yes, elections are offered to a corresponding number of these "second choices," in the order in which they were elected. By going quickly and quietly about their business the Bones men manage to elude in great part the attentions of the rabble, which ranges about the college yard on the night in question, — barring up the entry doors, raising false alarms, and otherwise disporting itself. The names of the chosen men, however, are known about as quickly as the elections are conferred, and many in the crowd make out complete lists of them, for circulation at the breakfast table or in the division-room upon the following morning, when they form the sole topic of discussion throughout the college. Usually, the names are first printed in the *Courant* of the Wednesday following; though for a year or two past some of the city dailies have had the tact to secure them for their next morning's issue. The initiation begins, after the close of the Wooden Spoon Exhibition, at midnight of the following Tuesday, and lasts till about daybreak. The candidates for the ceremony are assembled in a room of the college Laboratory, which is guarded by Bones men, and are singly escorted thence, by two of the latter, to the hall. As the grim doors open for each new member, there are sounds of a fish horn, as of many feet hurrying up an uncarpeted stairway, as of a muffled drum and tolling bell, — all mingling in a sort of confused uproar, like that from a freshman initiation a good many miles away. Perhaps, while being led to the hall, a candidate may pass between rows of neutral Juniors or other college men, some of whom may "bid him good bye," with expressions of congratulation and good will, if they think his election deserved, or insult and revile him, if their belief goes in the contrary direction. There is usually someone to flash a dark lantern upon each approaching candidate, and, if he makes no other personal comments, to at least shout forth his name, for the edification of the rest. To all this the Bones men of course pay no attention. It perhaps takes an hour or more thus to initiate the fifteen candidates; and when the self-constituted leader of the outside hangers on announces that "the last man's in", his followers agree that the fun is over, and sullenly disperse. If they stayed longer perhaps they might hear songs sung to strange old tunes, and the tones of the orator's voice, and the applause which follows it, and the prolonged cheers for "the Skull and the Bones". And of course there is a supper. Every resident graduate attends the initiation, as well as many from New York and elsewhere, some of whom come to town as early as election night; and the initiation itself, at least the outside part of it, is conducted by graduates alone. Long ago, it is said, the initiation took place on the evening of Presentation Day.

"The annual convention of the Order" is held on the evening of Commencement. Three weeks previous to this, — which, of late years, is therefore at the time of the first regular meeting, two nights after initiation, — a printed invitation is sent to every living member of "the Club" whose whereabouts are known. This invitation is upon the first page of a sheet of note paper. Below the society cut is the date — for example, "Thursday evening, July 22, 1869" — of Commencement night; followed by VI. S.B.T.;" a Latin quotation, playing upon the word "Bones"; the signature of the secretary, and the date. Upon the third page is the list of new members, printed alphabetically in old-English text, and surrounded by the black borders, exactly as in the catalogue, of which it in fact constitutes a new "P." and "D." Each one who receives it, by fitting the new leaf to his catalogue, thus keeps the same perfect from year to year. These pages are doubtless stereotyped, and preserved by the society, whose entire catalogue is thus always kept in readiness for the printer. With this invitation and catalogue-page, is also sent a printed slip specifying the exercises of Commencement week. A card-size photograph of the new members, grouped — in front of an antique clock whose hands point to the hour of eight — about a table on which lies a skull, is also sent to graduates, at this time or afterwards. In the picture, the thigh bones are held by certain members, — sometimes the tablecloth has the emblems embroidered upon it, and the whole arrangement of the group is apparently significant. Official notes to old members are written upon black bordered paper of the catalogue size, with or without the society cut at the head; and society communications sent through the mails are often enclosed in black-edged envelopes, — bearing at the end a printed request to the postmaster to return them to the society's post-office box if not delivered within a certain time, — sealed with a skull and bones and the letters "S.C.B.," impressed upon black wax. Bones men never display in their college rooms any posters or other reminders of their society, — though it is rumoured that actual skulls were formerly used for this purpose, — but graduates often keep on the walls before them a richly-framed photographic group of the classmates who made up their own special "D.", — the picture being simply an enlargement of the card photograph before noted. As specimen jokes from the convention invitations the following may be quoted: "Nisi in bonis amicitia esse non potest" (Cic. de Am. 5.1); "Grandiaque effossis mirabitur ossa sepulchris" (Virg. Georgs. I 497); "Quid dicam de ossibus? Nil nisi bonum"; and, in 1856, at the time of erecting the hall, "Quid dicam de ossibus? (Cir. de Nat. Deorum. II. 55.) O fortunati, quorum jam moenia surgunt!" (Virg. A.En. I. 430). At the head of the editorial column of the city dailies, on Commencement morning, was usually displayed the "322 VI. S.B.T." notice, between parallel black rules, but for the past few years the practice has been abandoned. Up to about the same time printed announcements of the place and time of the Commencement meeting, headed by the cut, were posted about college, and upon the notice-boards of the different churches, a few days in advance. Formerly, too, similar warnings were printed, in connection with the society cut, among the advertisement of the city papers. As their hall is called "the Temple" by Bones men, a current guess — and a wrong one — interprets "S.B.T." as "Skull and Bones Temple". A more likely reading makes "T." stand for "time", and so interprets the notice, "Six minutes before eight", — the hour eight being "Bones time".

The meetings are held on Thursday evening, commencing exactly at eight o'clock, and every acting member is obliged to be in attendance from that time until the adjournment, at two or three in the morning. The society formerly had a way of marching from its hall in dead silence, — tramp, tramp, tramp, — to the north entry of North College, where it might leave a man or two, and so on, silently, in front of the row, growing smaller as it passed the different buildings, until at the south entry of South the few who were left disbanded. Formerly, too, it was customary, before breaking up, to sing a college song whose refrain was, "And I shall be his dad"; but this practice, for lack of voices perhaps, was abandoned some years ago. A Bones Senior is never seen about New Haven after eight o'clock of a Thursday evening. Nothing but actual sickness ever keeps him from his society, except it be absence from town, — and those who have been absent are apt to appear for the first time at Friday morning chapel. A good share of the fresh graduates who are residents, and many of the older ones, are also ordinarily in attendance at the regular weekly meetings. Aside from the annual convention on Commencement night, there are two other "bums" held during the year, — one each at about the middle of the first and second terms — which bring many graduates from out of town. These usually reach the city just before the meeting, and leave it on the midnight trains, so that their coming and going is not known to outsiders, except from the hotel registers or a chance contact upon the street.

Each Bones man has a nick-name by which he is known to his in-itiated classmates. One or two of these names, probably official titles, are retained from year to year, but most of them change with the classes, and are apparently conferred according to individual peculiarity or caprice. All members of the society are also spoken of among themselves by a certain general title; another is conferred upon members of the other senior society, and a third is bestowed upon the neutrals. As these titles, especially the latter, might convey a wrong im-pression if generally known, they are not mentioned here. The society itself, among its members, is known as "Eulogia," or the "Eulogian Club". It is believed to have little or no regard to any formal, written constitution, but to be governed chiefly by tradition in its customs and usages. The hall is reputed to be a sort of repository for old college mementos; like the "first college bell", the original "bully-club", the con-stitutions of defunct societies, etc., which are all said to be preserved there; and when anything of the kind disappears, this is surmised to be its final destination. Though Thursday night is the regular time of meeting, when attendance is compulsory, the hall is generally fre-quented on Saturday and other nights also, and is often visited in the day time besides. An old member often goes there as soon as he reaches town, especially, if in quest of information in regard to classmates who were formerly associated there with him. At convention time, the members who cannot in person attend, send to the society such facts as to their whereabouts and occupations for the year, as may interest old classmates and friends; and their letters are filed away for future reference. Every book or pamphlet written by a member is also preserved in the society archives; and its collection of printed and manuscript "Yalensia" is said to be very complete.

To discover the exact meaning of the inevitable numeral "322," has long been a problem for college mathematicians. According to some, it signifies "1832," or the year the society was founded; others make it "3 + 2 + 2" or "7," which is said to be the number of "founders" in the class of '33, who persuaded the other eight to join them in making up the original fifteen; still another surmise sets it at "3X2X2", or "12," which might refer to the midnight hour of breaking up, or something equally mysterious; while a fourth guess interprets it to mean "the year 322 B.C.", and connects it with the names of Alexander or Demosthenes. What these heroes may have in common with the Skull and Bones society, aside from departing this life on or just before the year in question, is not very plain; but it is pretty well established that Bones "322" refers to that year B.C., whatever may be its additional significance. While the class of '69 were in college the hall, according to report, was twice broken into by neutrals, and strange stories were cir-culated of the wonderful mysteries there discovered by the interlopers.

It is probably a fact that these men did really enter the hall, through the skylight in the roof; but there is no reason for trusting their own account of their exploits any further than this, since, if, as is not unlikely, the arrangement of things inside prevented their making any important discoveries, they would of course invent a sufficient number of suppositious mysteries, to clear themselves of the reproach of having ventured upon a fool's errand. None of their statements, therefore, have been thought worth repeating here. A surreptitious visit, real or pretended, was hardly necessary as a preliminary to assuring the college that "Bones keeps its most valuable documents locked up in an iron safe," since the same fact holds good for every society after sophomore year.

"Scroll and Key" is the name of the other senior society, which was founded nine years later than its more famous rival, that is to say, in 1841, by a dozen members of the class of '42. Popularly it is known as "Keys," though this abbreviation has only come into general use within the last half-dozen years. Its pin, of plain gold, represents a key lying across a scroll, and its wood-cut simply copies it. The design is such that it is difficult to tell the right side from the wrong, and the cut, when printed bottom upwards, as it often is, is rarely noticed as possessing other than its ordinary look. The original badge was a rectangular gold plate, of the same size and shape as the old Bones pin, whereon were engraved an eagle, poised above, suspending a scroll, and a right hand below, grasping a key. This is still worn, by a single member at a time, in place of the usual scroll and key, presumably as a mark of office, like society president or something of the sort. The letters "C.S.P.," "C.C.J.," are always printed with the society cut, — the former above, the latter below it, — and with it usually serve as the only introduction to the lists of members printed in the *Banner* and elsewhere, though the name "Scroll and Key" is sometimes prefixed. The Bones lists, on the other hand, are always headed with the full name of the society. The posters which, until within a few years, were put up about the college yard and elsewhere at Commencement season, for the benefit of graduates, displayed an eagle poised above the ordinary emblems, with no print — in addition to the inevitable letters — except the day and hour of the meeting, — "9 P.M.," perhaps, — or the numeral "142." A small, seal-like wood-cut of the society, displays the clasped hands upon an open scroll, with "Adelphoi" in Green capitals at the top, "1852" below, and at the bottom two hieroglyphic characters, the one like a Gothic "T," the other like an old style Greek "T," while the only trace of the key is its head, which projects from the top of the scroll. Another, steel-engraved, seal, represents the eagle, looking down from above upon the central scroll and key, upon which the letters are indicated, while an open right hand reaches up from below. The framework of the device is made up of fifteen oblong links, and its shape cannot be better described than by saying that if there were sixteen links it would be an eight-pointed star; as it is, the ten lower links make up five points, but the upper five — in place of the six, which would make the remaining three — are simply rounded together. This, too, was the shape of the inner frame-work of the old gold plate badge. The present pin has been said to be plain, because the eagle and hand, faintly outlined upon it, do not change this general appearance. Neither of the senior badges have their owners' names or anything of the sort engraved upon their backs. The invitations to the "Z.S." — or; "bum" held at the middle of the first and second terms — are printed within a scroll-like design from which the key is absent; or else with the ordinary cut at the head of the note. The company of the "brother" is simply requested upon the appointed evening, and he is directed to answer the secretary, which officer is designated by the letter "G," and is his "in truth." Aside from these initial letters, there is no mystery about the affair, which is either printed in gilt, or, if in black, has mourning bands about the edges of the page. All society communications are also forwarded in black-edged "return" envelopes, as in the case of Bones, sealed in black wax with the society emblems and letters. There have been several editions of the society catalogue; and it is probable that a printed list of the elections is forwarded each year to every old member, in connection with the invitation to the celebration of Commencement night. A card-size photograph of each new group of fifteen is doubtless similarly distributed, either then or afterwards. In this picture, the central figure holds a large gilt model of the society badge, — the six letters being indicated on the scroll, — and each of the end men grasps a large key, pointed towards the centre of the group. Eight are seated, including the three mentioned, and the remainder are standing, but the position of each individual is probably not significant. Enlarged photographs of the same sort are handsomely framed and hung in the rooms of graduates. The anniversary of Commencement night used to be announced among the ordinary advertisements of the city papers, in connection with the society cut. More recently, at the head of their editorial columns of Commencement morning, "C.S.P. — P.V.S.$_9$P.M. — C.C.J.," or something of the sort, appeared, between double rules of black. But this practice has now been abandoned.

The hall hitherto (since 1847, when the house where it stayed was destroyed by fire) occupied by the society is in the fourth story of the Leffingwell Building, corner of Church and Court streets, across from the Tontine Hotel. The headquarters of the Yale "law department" are upon a lower floor of the same building, and a Masonic lodge-room divides the upper story with Keys. Judged from the outside, this hall must at the most be limited to two not very large rooms, and the Keys men, when assembled in force, be cribbed, cabined and confined together in uncomfortably close proximity. This old order of things, however, has recently come to an end, and Keys is now in possession of a hall, far superior in costliness and architectural beauty, not only to Bones hall, but to any college-society hall in America. It stands on the north-west corner of College and Wall streets, and its erection had been planned and talked about for a dozen years or more. At midnight of Thursday, Nov. 25, 1869, — the date of the fall "Z.S.," — the society, graduates and all, marched to the vacant lot, round which they formed a ring, while prayer was offered, and a society-song sung, after which, a graduate with a silver spade formally broke ground for the new edifice. Then came the singing of the "Troubadour" song, and the procession, dangling its keys, silently moved back to the old quarters on Church street. Only the foundation of the building was laid before the setting in of winter; but the work was resumed the following May, and rapidly pushed to completion; and it is presumed that the formal ceremonies of entering and taking possesison will be celebrated at the next Commencement. The structure has a front of 36 feet on College street, with 6 feet of ground each side, and is 55 feet long, with an open space of about 20 feet before and behind, in other words, it stands in the centre of a lot 48 by 92. Its height is perhaps 35 feet. The light yellow Cleveland stone is the chief material of which it is composed. This is set off by thin layers of dark blue marble, while four pillars of Aberdeen granite, with marble cappings, sustain the three projecting arches in front. Each arch surrounds a narrow opening, provided with three bull's eyes for the admission of air. Below the central arch are a pair of paneled, massive iron doors, to which entrance a flight of half-a-dozen stone steps leads up from either side. Five similar arches, though without projections or supports, serve to adorn and ventilate each side, and a corresponding number of closely protected scuttle-windows communicate with the cellar below. Rows of short pillars — four at each end, six at each side — surround the top, — the central two at the rear end serving to hide the chimneys, — and a couple of stars are cut out in the stone between every pair of them. The architect was Richard M. Hunt of New York, and the builders were Perkins & Chatfield of New Haven. The value of the entire property cannot be much less than $50,000, and it is to be presumed that a good share of that amount has already been raised by the society. The "Kingsley Trust Association," which is the legal style thereof, was incorporated at the May, 1860, session of the State Legislature, in the names of John A. Porter, of '42, William L. Kingsley of '43, Samuel C. Perkins of '48, Enos N. Taft of '51, Lebeus C. Chapin, George E. Jackson, and Homer B. Sprague of '52, Charlton T. Lewis of '53, Calvin G. Child and Josiah W. Harmar of '55, and Edward G. Mason and Mason Young of '60. These comprise its best known names, and were perhaps chosen on that account, since only the president, Mr. Kingsley, is a resident of the city.

In the Yale *Banger* of 1845, published by the Sigma Theta Sophomores, is a burlesque of the Keys cut, representing the Scroll as a "Declaration of Independence from the Scull and Bone," signed by the "great seal", which consists of a view of the historical fox reaching after the equally celebrated sour grapes. This probably represents, with substantial accuracy, the motive which originated Keys. Its founder, not being lucky enough to secure elections to Bones, determined to start in business upon their own account, and hence the society. Its ceremonies, customs, hours of meeting, etc., have all been patterned after those of Bones, and the nearer it approaches to its model the more of a success it is judged to be, both by its own members and by the college at large. Its existence for the first dozen years was apparently a precarious one. In only three classes before 1852 did it obtain the regular number of members (15), which Bones has never varied in electing, but ranged from nine — the lowest, in '51 — to fourteen. Since that time exactly fifteen names for each class have always been printed in its public lists, and since 1860 exactly fifteen men and no more have joined the society from each class. Previous to the latter date, it was a common thing to give out one or two or more class or secret elections, so that in some classes there have been seventeen or eighteen members, and almost all the classes which at first fell below the regular number, now appear in the catalogue with their full complement of fifteen names apiece. The men who accepted these after-elections to the society usually displayed their badge like the others, though sometimes the fact of their membership was kept a secret and they were not allowed to wear them about the college, not until after graduation. Hence in every class to the present day there are almost always one or two men, who are believed by many to be "secret members" of Keys, because, being friends of the "crowd," they naturally associate with it, as they would were there no such society in existence. It is also rumoured, with less probability, that notable men are sometimes chosen as honorary members. George Vanderhoff, the reader, is one of them, according to the authority of the *Banger*, — which, however, may have meant the statement for a joke. Similar rumours are also sometimes started in regard to Bones, but are far less generally credited, and are probably altogether groundless. Certain it is that the fact of there being a secret or honorary member, of there being more or less than fifteen members from each and every class since 1833, has never been in a single case authenticated. Up to as recent a date as 1860, Keys had great difficulty in making up its crowd, rarely being able to secure the full fifteen upon the night of giving out elections, but, by dint of electioneering and "packing" in the interval between that time and initiation night, managed — after 1851 — to swing out the orthodox number of new badges upon Presentation morning. Probably it would have given pledges in advance, like the lower-class societies, save that in those days any one standing the slightest chance for Bones preferred it to a "sure thing on" the other society. The true Caesar-or-no-one sentiment seems to have had full sway, and the best men of the class who did not secure Bones elections apparently preferred to go through senior year as neutrals rather than as members of a confessedly inferior society. The proportion of "big men" among the neutral Seniors was consequently much greater then than in these latter days. Keys, in fact, up to the time when it attained its twenty-first birthday, occupied a position in college regard very much analagous to that more recently held by the Diggers' society, to be described hereafter. It is only within the last lustrum that it has come to be a rival of Bones, and that the half-loaf sentiment has grown common, which prompts a man when his chances for the latter are spoiled, to "lay" diligently for the former.

The Keys mode of giving out elections — as well as the rest of its customs — corresponds as nearly as possible to the practice of Bones. Formerly the fifteen members, each carrying a key some two feet in length, in a body silently marched to the rooms of the men who had been chosen; and then the leader — possibly displaying the large gilt scroll-and-key model before mentioned — may have said simply, "Do you accept?" Of late, however, the practice is for two members, — one a Senior, the other a graduate, — each carrying one of the exaggerated keys, to proceed together to the room of each chosen man. The Senior raps sharply with his key upon the door, and, both stepping in, says, "I offer you an election to the so-called Scroll and Key. Do you accept?" If the answer is Yes, both Keys men shake the Junior by the hand, and tramp back to their hall, where the result of the first election is received before the party start out to confer the second, and so on for the others. On this account the elections progress much more slowly than in the case of Bones, and more opportunities are given to the rabble in the yard to yell "Keys! Keys! Keys!" and surge about the bearers of those implements, whose approach is usually announced, by self-stationed outposts, in the neighborhood of the State House steps. In 1868, all the Bones elections had been given out for more than an hour, and the "packed Keys crowd" of '69; had begun to feel a trifle nervous, when the first key-bearers appeared in the yard. There seems to be no very great significance in the order in which the elections are conferred, except that the one first received is perhaps to be interpreted as especially honorable; but on the other hand this is sometimes offered to a man, who is by no means the society's first choice, in order if possible to anticipate Bones in securing him.

The initiation takes place at the same time as the other one, and like it lasts till morning. The rendezvous for the candidates is probably some room in the neighborhood of the hall, at all events is outside the college yard, and as the hall is not so convenient to the colleges as that of Bones the neutrals pay less attention to what takes place there on initiation night. Visitors who may be stopping at the Tontine Hotel on the night of Wooden Spoon, however, seldom sleep very soundly, if their rooms chance to be situated upon the north side of the building. Resident and other graduates attend the initiations, and the regular meetings also, — though to a less extent than in Bones, — and the rule requiring the presence of active members on Thursday nights from eight o'clock till two, is also strictly enforced. An absent member of '68, suspected of make-believe sickness, was one time forcibly hurried off to the meeting by two classmates, who rushed up from the hall for that purpose, with a great display of crossed keys; and the procedure may be gone through with in other instances which excite less attention than did that, — though the cases where it is necessary to enforce discipline are of course uncommon. At the close of its meetings, the society was in the habit of marching up through the green, past the State House, to the college yard, singing on the way, or just before disbanding, the well-known song, "Gaily the Troubadour touched his Guitar." Though this was always finely done, and very acceptable to all who heard it, the faculty — induced, it is said, by the discordant howlings of the "Stones men" — included Keys in the general edict promulgated last year against society singing, and ordered its discontinuance. The current traditions in regard to Keys are not very numerous, nor is the belief in its mysterious origin wide-spread, as in the case of Bones. Its letters are supposed to signify: "*Collegium Sanctum Pontificum; Collegium Conservat Jupiter.*" Bones having set up Demosthenes as its patron saint, Keys seemed determined to "go one better" and claim the recognition of great Zeus himself. "Zenome" is one the society words supposed to possess mysterious significance. According to rumour, a magnificent stuffed eagle forms one of the chief decorations of its hall; though as this report originated with a '66 neutral who profesed to have "been there," not much reliance should be placed upon it. Keys, like Bones, also keeps the photographs of its members, a library, paintings, pictures, obsolete society badges, old college mementos, and general memorabilia.

A third senior society also existed during the time that the class of '69 was in college. Its name, taken from its badge, was "Spade and Grave." The spade, partly thrust into the grave, rested upon the footstone of the same, and upon the headstone was represented a crown, — gold of course being the material of the entire pin. The grave was perhaps a little more than an inch in length, and the badge had one or two variations in size and shape. The "Bed and Broom," it was at first called by outsiders; and, by the more respectful ones, the society was known as "Graves," and its members as "Graves men." None of these names were ever popular, however, and "Diggers" soon came to be the only title by which the society or its members were referred to. Bones men, among themselves, also adopted this name for them. "To give community and sweetness to the eating of sour grapes" was, even more notoriously than in the case of the original Keys men, the object for which the Diggers started their society. The immediate cause which banded them together in the scheme was a quarrel in the class of '64. Of the five Yale, *Lit.* editors in that class, three had been chosen to Bones and two were neutrals. One of these two published, as a leading article in the magazine for February of that year, a piece called "Collegial Ingenuity," reflecting on the mode by which men may worm their way into Bones, and, it was claimed, making personal insinuations against a particular member of that society; and·on this latter ground the Bones editors, who formed a majority of the five, voted to suppress the article, and requested its writer to produce another to take the place of it, — themselves meanwhile seizing upon all the printed copies. The neutral editor refused to obey, and called a class meeting which voted to sustain him, and commanded the Bones editors to surrender the magazines with a certain time, or be expelled from office. As they paid no attention to the order, the class elected three neutrals in their places, and these, with the two original neutral editors, duly brought out a new edition of the February number, "Collegial Ingenuity" and all, and edited the two following numbers, — with the latter of which their term of office expired by limitation. The Bones editors meanwhile issued the February number, — with an explanation of their action printed in place of the obnoxious "leader," but otherwise unchanged, — and duly published the two remaining numbers of their term, still keeping the five original names at the head of the title-page, as if nothing had happened. Thus, for three months, there were two issues of the *Lit.* each of which claimed to be the "regular" one. The Bones editors were really in the right, as the class had no legal power to interfere in the matter, and the three magazines issued by the other editors have been known as the "second issue." The five members of that second editorial board of '64 have the credit of founding Diggers,' and they with ten other classmates first swung out the Spade and Grave badge at the beginning of the summer term of that year. On the Thursday before Presentation Day, elections were given out to fifteen members of '65, who were the first Diggers to have their names in print (in the *Banner* of the following autumn). The grave scene in "Hamlet," wherein the digger tosses up the skull and bones with his spade, is said to have suggested the badge as a fit emblem to typify the hostility of the new society to the old one and its power ultimately to work the overthrow of the haughty Skull and Bones itself. Its hall was in the Lyon Building, on Chapel street, on the same floor with that of Gamma Nu; was supplied with common iron doors without and a billiard table within; and was reputed to be elegantly furnished, and among other things to have one of its rooms entirely covered with black velvet. In February, 1870, as already stated, its premises were taken possession of and have since been occupied by the sophomore society of Theta Psi. Its wood cut was simply a copy of its badge; and the same design, enlarged, carved in black-walnut and mounted in a frame of the same wood, was displayed in the rooms of members, as a sort of poster; though the practice was not much in vogue after the first year or two.

The society started under a cloud, and never emerged from it, but rather seemed to fall deeper and deeper into its shade the older it grew. It was always despised and looked down upon. Even those who joined it, in many cases cursed and ridiculed it by turns, up to the very moment of accepting their elections. In spite of careful packing and electioneering in advance, it always had difficulty in making up its crowd on the same night with the other societies and it always had elections refused. No one standing the least chance for Bones or Keys could be got to go to it, and the best of those left out by these societies preferred to remain neutrals altogether. Psi U men used to boast that no member of their society ever became a Digger; and the four classes between the first and last were certainly composed exclusively of Delta Phi and DKE men. There was, however, one member of Psi U among the founders, and four in '69 accepted elections, — much to the chagrin of their comrades. Everyone sneered at the society, including many of course who would gladly have joined it had they been able; but the scrubbiest neutral of them all would affect to take offense were such an idea hinted at, and stoutly assert that, "had the Diggers ventured to offer him an election, he would have indignantly hurled back the insult in their faces!" This show of independence after election time is past is quite a common thing; but the men of '69, even as Juniors, used to shout a sort of chorus, "Todtengraber ist gut," to the tune of "Truncadillo;" they equipped a burlesque 'spade and grave" in the college yard one day; and in other ways so defied the powers above them that it became a problem whether the Diggers of '68 could secure any successors. There was the usual amount of electioneering and packing, but on election night only three men could by the most entreaties be secured, from the indefinite number to whom elections were offered; so these three were released and no new Digger pins were swung forth upon the morning of Presentation Day. The next public appearance of the society was on the first Friday morning of the following October, when fifteen senioric shirt-bosoms were adorned by as many new badges, the design being a crown from within which projected the ends of a crossed sword and scepter. This was superseded the following term by a larger sized pin of the same pattern. By a pretty thorough canvassing of the class, in the three months' interval, these new members had been raked together, and induced to "run" the society for a year, in the hope that under a changed name the same old story could not be told concerning them. At least half of them were secretly pledged and initiated before Commencement, and wore the old Grave badge during vacation, in localities where they would be unlikely to meet with Yale undergraduates. From the headstone of this old badge, it will be observed, the crown itself was taken. Above the old cut, in the *Banner*, the name "Spade and Grave" was printed in full; while above the new crown design were simply the letters, "S.L.M." (popularly translated "Slim" or "Slimy"), which had not before been made public, though reckoned among the original mysteries of Diggers'. Freshmen spoke of the society as "Crown and Scepter," or "Sword and Crown," but upper-class men clung relentlessly to the old title, and the doom of Diggers' was sealed. Its usual arts were wasted upon the class of '70 not one of them would pledge, either before, on, or after, election night; and so, after a precarious existence of five years, it was forced to give up the hopeless fight and the ghost.

Like Keys', its customs were all modeled as closely as possible after those of Bones, which it was to spade out of existence so quickly. Three men always came up from the hall to give out each election, two of the trio walking abreast in front, and the third following close upon their rear. A dark lantern or a club was often carried by one of them. The yell and outcries with which the rabble greeted the approach of Digger election carriers were far more prolonged and uproarious than in the case of the other societies. The Juniors upon whom they called would be invoked with such cries as "Kick 'em out, Jim!" "Oh Tom! *dont'* be a Digger!" "Shut your door on 'em Jack! Don't let 'em fool you!" and so on; while the Diggers themselves would be treated to all manner of compliments and personal attentions, such as were never bestowed upon the other election carriers. "How can I leave Thee," was the song sometimes sung outside at the close of the meetings, either while marching, or on arriving at the college yard; otherwise the procession silently tramped up Chapel street to South College, and so on in front of the row, dropping its men at each entry until none were left. It was believed to have had a good many secret members, — even including some from the Scientific School, — and several '63 men are known to have belonged to it. After the change of base in 1868, the graduate members ceased to wear the old Grave badge. The society was unincorporated, and had never printed any catalogue. Its letters were supposed to represent the motto, *Sceptrum Ligonibus Mors.*

Not only do senior-society men never mention their own society in the presence of others, but then never even refer to the existence of a rival society, and when an outsider mentions this in their presence, even to a third party, they appear to take offense, and perhaps withdraw. So, too, they are offended if a man sings, or even hums the air, of the songs which they sometimes sing in public; though these are familiar melodies, and have long been procurable in the form of sheet music.

This same fact holds true, to a lesser extent, in the case of the junior and sophomore societies. A certain air gets in a measure identified with a particular society song; and as members of the society never use it except in singing together, they dislike to hear it whistled by an outsider. A Sophomore, for instance, a few years ago, by persistently whistling, "All on a summer's day," would probably have injured his chances of a DKE election; and, in the case of Psi U, perhaps the same would still be true of one who should be constantly humming, "In a few days." Senior-society men may also refuse to speak when passing in front of their hall, and in some cases to notice a neutral classmate whom they may chance to meet after eight o'clock of a Thursday evening. An instance is related in the class of '67 of two Bones men who brought from their meeting a sick classmate and put him to bed in his room, without paying any attention to his neutral chum who was there present, though he was also a classmate with whom they were on friendly terms. This exaggerated display of secrecy is quite a modern outgrowth, however, being altogether unknown to the old members of fifteen or twenty years ago, and it attained its highest pitch in the class just mentioned, — since when, senior-society men have conducted themselves much more sensibly. For many evident reasons, the costs of membership in a senior society are much greater than in any other, though most of their money is raised by voluntary contributions, and a man eligible in other respects is not kept out on account of his poverty. On the other hand, a man's wealth of course adds to his chances of election in senior years more than in any other. The annual running expenses of a society, in which graduates take so prominent a part, cannot and ought not to be borne by fifteen men alone, and there are doubtless permanent funds whose income is available for such purposes, — at least in Bones, whose property is fully paid for. To increase this fund, almost every old member sends in an annual contribution, according to his means, for five or ten years after graduation day.

It is in senior year alone that the neutrals largely outnumber the society men, that they have nothing to hope for in the way of class elections, and that they are not overawed by the presence of upper-class men. These three circumstances combine to foster in some of them a sort of reckless hostility towards these societies, such as is not felt towards those of the earlier years. This displays itself in a variety of ways. The conduct of the neutrals when the senior elections are given out has been already described, and the fact notice, at least by implication, that they never in the least interfere with the similar ceremonies of the other societies. Nor yet do they ever attempt to break into the halls of the latter. It was in the class of '66 that this hostility-first definitely displayed itself, in the institution of a sort of a mock "society" called "Bowl and Stones," — the name being a take-off on that of Bones, and the duties of its members being simply to range about the colleges at a late hour on Thursday night, or early on Friday morning when the senior societies disbanded, singing songs in ridicule of the latter, blocking up the entries, and making a general uproar. The refrain of one song, to the tune of "Bonnie Blue Flag" was "Hurrah! Hurrah! for jolly Bowl and Stones;" of another, to the tune of "Babylon," "Haughty Bones is fallen, and we gwine down to occupy the Skull." Another function of the 'Stones men" was to offer bogus elections to simple minded classmates, or even to under-class men, — whom they were sometimes able to "sell." In the class of '67 they were at their worst, and wantonly smashed bottles of ink upon the front of Bones hall, and tore the chains from its fence. On the Thursday morning which preceded the Presentation Day of 1868, the Stones men of that class posted up a comic handbill, purporting to show the "order of exercises" which would be observed by the senior societies in giving out their elections that evening. There was some little wit employed in the composition of this notice, and it was the only thing emanating from the "society" that was not at once weak and discreditable. The modified name, "Bull and Stones," then first appeared; which form has since been retained. Some members of the class of '70 even went so far as to procure a small gilt representation of "a bull" standing upon "stones," which was worn as a burlesque badge pin, even in public, and in some cases quite regularly, during the first term of their senior year. Of course there is nothing to this "society" except what has been told; its "members" are few or many according to the state of the weather; and any neutral senior who is ready to join a crowd for making an uproar on Thursday night is, from that fact only, a good and regular "Stones man." Indeed, the name has of late come to be accepted as a synonym for any senior-society neutral whatever; and every one not elected to either of the two societies is said to "belong to Stones." At the time of the last initiation, the Stones men seized upon and confiscated for their own use the ice-cream and other good things which the confectioner was engaged in taking into Bones hall. Since then, one or two projected "raids" of the same sort have been frustrated by the presence of a policeman. Now-a-days, Thursday night is the favourite time for the more depraved Stones men to "go off on a bum" together, and afterwards wake the echoes of the college yard with their discordant howlings.

That this "society" showed no signs of existence in the class of '69 was perhaps due in great measure to the existence of another more creditable organization, some of whose members would probably, save for it, have been leading "Stones men." On the morning of Presentation Day, 1868, fourteen men, who had been neutrals since freshman year, were noticed to wear upon their shirt bosoms, gilt coffin lids, about an inch in length. Their names were printed in the annuals of the next term, under the "senior-society" heading, beneath a wood-cut of the badge, above which appeared the letters "E.T.L.," but no name. They were spoken of as 'Coffin men," or "ETL's," when mentioned at all; and, so far as known, met quite regularly on Thursday nights, perhaps in some room rented for the purpose. They said nothing in regard to themselves or the regular senior societies, and they attempted to give no elections in the class of '70. The society passed in the class for a joke; but, for the negative benefit it effected in restraining some who would otherwise have been uproarious, as well as for the positive advantages it may have conferred upon all its members, it deserves to be held in grateful recollection. Perhaps somewhat similar to this was the "Tea-Kettle" society, established in the class of '53, which has left nothing behind it save the announcement of its birth in the *Lit.* Another short-lived association was the "Sword and Crown" which was existing in 1843 with fifteen members. Its badge was a rectangular gold plate, upon which, within an ornamental border, the appropriate emblems were engraved. These did not much resemble the last badge of the Diggers, as the crown was a much more elaborate and highly ornamented affair, and the sword and scepter were crossed behind rather than within it. An existing poster showing a wood-cut of the simple emblems bears the direct, "S.T.G. 8.30 a.m." Another poster, which perhaps had no connection with this or any other society, shows the three letters "Iota Kappa Sigma," printed in heavy black type, with "24 D" appended. Still another, represents a naked figure just trundling over a precipice a wheelbarrow in which are loaded a skull and some bones and a scroll and a key and a star and a dart. The "Star and Dart" society was established in 1843, and apparently occupied a position somewhat analogous to the present one of Bull and Stones, though it really had an organization of some sort. The frame-work of its rectangular gold-plate badge was an exact copy of that of the Bones pin, and the emblems of the two societies now existing formed the chief part of the engraved central design. The eagle of Keys, that is to say, was represented as fiercely picking to pieces the Skull and Bones at its feet, while a Dart, appearing in the right upper corner, was about to destroy the eagle, and a Star in the left upper corner was supposed to denote "the prosperity and final success of the society over its rivals." A woodcut copy of this design surmounted the following notice printed among the advertisements of a New Haven newspaper: "*Nos in vita fratres sumus.* C. 2954a F. 8 dd Z DL. There will be a general meeting in New Haven on Thursday evening, Aug. 15, 1944. Yale College, Aug. 10." Possibly there were other Commencement times at which a similar notice was printed, and doubtless posters to the same effect used also to be displayed about the college buildings at such seasons. After a period of suspended animation, the society was revived in the class of '49, and the members belonging to it in the classes of '50 and '51 (fifteen in one case, eleven in the other) had their names published in the *Banner*, in connection with the society cut and the numeral "2954." From this publicity, as well as the character of many of the members, it is to be inferred that there was really a little something to the society, and that its existence was not altogether contemptible. Whether it had a hall of its own, and regular weekly meetings and exercises; whether it made any pretensions to equality with the two reputable societies; whether it was so hostile to them as its badge would imply; whether its crowd was made up before, at the same time, of after the other elections were given out; and whether it died by choice or by necessity, — all these things, on the other hand, must remain uncertainties, until some traitorous ex-member thereof shall reveal to an anxiously expectant world the real history and mystery of the late Star and Dart.

Among the many Bones men worthy of mention are: Henry C. Kingsley of '34, treasurer of the college; Prof. Thomas A. Thacker of '35; Col. Henry C. Deming of '36; Attorney General William M. Evarts, Profs. Chester S. Lyman and Benjamin Silliman, of '37; Rev. Dr. Joseph P. Thompson of '38; Provost Charles J. Stille of '39; Prof. James M. Hopping of '40; Gen. William T.S. Barry and Donald G. Mitchell, of '41; Henry Stevens, F.R.S., of '43; Senator Orris S. Ferry of '44; Ge. Dick Taylor of '45; Henry B. Harrison of '46; Henry T. Blake and Dwight Foster, of '48; Charles G. Came, Profs. William B. Clark and Timothy Dwight, of '49; President Andrew D. White of '53; Dr. John W. Hooker of '54; Rev. Elisha Mulford of '55; William H.W. Campbell, editor of the Norwich *Bulletin*, Chauncy M. Depew, N.Y. secretary of State, and Prof. Lewis R. Packard, of '56; Gen. John T. Croxton and Prof. Cyrus Northrop, of '57; Addison Van Name of '58, librarian of the college; Eugene Schuyler of '59, U.S. consul at Moscow; Edward R. Sill of '61; and Prof. Edward B. Coe of '62. The most prominent Keys men have already been mentioned in naming its twelve incorporators, but additional names to be noticed are: Gen. Theodore Runyon of '42; Rev. Dr. Gordon Hall of '43; Robert P. Farris of '47, editor of the Missouri *Republican*; Rev. John E. Todd of '55; son of Rev. Dr. Todd, the opponent of college secret societies; Sidney E. Morse of '56, publisher of the N.Y. *Observer;* Gen. John W. Swayne of '56; Dr. Daniel G. Brinton of '58; Prof. Daniel C. Eaton of '60; and Joseph L. Shipley of '61 editor of the Scranton *Republican*. Five Keys men and one Digger make up the famous "Wilbur Bacon crew" of 1865.

Formerly, when Seniors took a more active part than now in the junior societies, men who did not belong to these were often chosen to the senior societies, but of late a membership in the former is a necessary stepping stone for admission to the latter; not confessedly, of course, but by the rule which is sure to force a junior society into electing

— 271 —

every man eligible for election a year later, and to compel every such man to accept such election. It has been noticed of late years that Psi U generally has a majority in Bones, and DKE in Keys, though in '71 Psi U had six men in Bones and nine in Keys, to DKE's nine and six. It should not be inferred from this that senior-society men allow their junior year or earlier society connections to prejudice them in electing their successors. They apparently have regard for the interest of their senior society simply, and choose those whom they think will most benefit it, without much regard to outside considerations. Much of the excitement over the election of Cochs and *Lit.* Editors turns upon the question of senior societies. Each one of these officers is supposed to "stand a chance," and shortly after their election the two "crowds" begin definitely to be made up. There are always some "sure men" to form a nucleus, — the Spoon Man for instance, is always certain of receiving a Bone selection, — and about these the "Likely" ones who are not quite so "sure" try to "pack" themselves. Thus a "crowd" is made up in the interest of each society. Its members "run" together constantly, call one another by their first names, and make a great display of familiarity, — especially in the presence of "their" Seniors, — as much as to say, "We can't be separated. Take all of us or none." This sort of thing is practised chiefly by prospective Keys men, who can make up their crowd with a tolerable certainty that their evident wishes will be respected by the society. It is seldom that Keys ventures to keep out more than a single man from a well defined pack, and substitute one of their own choosing in his place. Such a pack really has the power in its own hands, and should the members of it agree to "stand by one another" they could of course carry their point; but the refusal of a senior-society election, even conditionally, seems so terrible a thing, that they have rarely the courage to make a direct demand. Keys, however, has in some instances been obliged to submit to such dictation. The society undoubtedly winks at "packing," and indirectly gives it on occasions its official aid, — though not as frequently nor as extensively as is sometimes reported. There are so many conflicting elements in the Bones crowd that it is never organized into a regular pack, and there is always more doubt as to the way its elections will turn. The nearest approach to a pack is when two or three "sure men" take it upon themselves to persistently "run" another, and make such a display of their fondness for him as to secure his election also. However Bones may allow its action to be affected indirectly, it will not be dictated to when once its elections have been made up, and it is useless for a man to attempt to alter the result by conditionally refusing his election, in favour of or against some particular classmate. Though the Bones crowd may be pretty accurately guessed at for some days before the elections are issued, it is the chance of its individuals which are estimated, not of the crowd as such, as in the case of Keys. There is no such general collusion of all the members of the Bones crowd; it is rather made up of separate cliques of two and threes, and single individuals, who hope for Bones elections, but have not much else in common. The fact that elections to this latter society have been refused in favour of Keys is hence not very difficult of explanation. A man whose chances for Bones are rather doubtful may be willing to throw them away altogether for the sake of the comparatively "sure thing" which he gains by joining a pack for Keys. So, receiving an election to Bones, he is in honor bound to decline it, and cling to the men with whom he had joined his fortunes. It will be found that all the Bones refusals in '67 and '70, over which so much ado was made, came in every case from men previously packed for Keys. Thus, Bones' greater independence and ceremoniousness sometimes work to its own disadvantage. A man may go to Keys for the sake of taking a friend or two with him whose companionship he could not be sure of were he to become a Bones man; and in general one has less uncertainty as to whom he will have to fraternize with when he packs for the former society.

In a direct comparison of the societies, it is seen that Bones in reputation, influence and prestige is altogether superior to its rival; and it seems almost as certain that it must always retain this preeminence. It is, in its main features, essentially unique. No other college society can show so large a proportion of distinguished and successful members. It is probably not too much to add that of the Yale graduates of the past generation who have attained a fair degree of worldly eminence, nearly half will be found to have been included within the mystic fifteens of this organization. Its apparent aim is to secure at once the best of the good scholars, good literary men, and good fellows; the former to bring it dignity and "tone," the latter to preserve its social and convivial character; and its success in equalizing these three elements — one of which is apt to predominate in a society — has been remarkable. It develops in its members, too, a genuine pride and affection, such as they feel in or towards no other society. Men who are careless and frivolous and selfish as to everything else, manifest an earnestness and a generosity where Bones is concerned, that is really surprising. And this, too, in a way not calculated to attract attention, nor suggest an appearance of exaggeration or make-believe. Keys men, on the other hand, are rather given to displaying their society zeal as much as possible. Old members who come from abroad to attend the "bums" are apt to make their presence generally known, and take pains to exhibit the extent of their "interest." Their affection for the society is no doubt genuine enough, but their carefulness in displaying it suggests the idea that its inspiration comes quite as much from an oppressive selfconsciousness of the need of "going one better" than Bones, as from the simple force of pleasant associations. Since the time, say about

1860, when Keys came to be recognized as a reputable society, settled upon an invariable membership of fifteen, and ceased to give out any class, secret, or honorary elections, its policy has seemed to be the making prominent of the social elements, the choosing of good, jolly fellows, — men of ability if possible, but at all events congenial and in the college sense of the word gentlemanly. Ability in the absolute, that is to say, has been accounted of secondary importance as a qualification for membership. Upon a strict and more rigourous adherence to this policy in the future — if it be worth while to express a prevalent college opinion — the success of the society will in great measure depend. In the latter's own chosen field, it can never hope to seriously rival Bones. To the "solid," thoughtful men of the class — the big scholars and writers — Bones will always be the more attractive, and if Keys enters into competition for them it will as inevitably have to take up with second-rate representatives of the "heavy," "respectable" element, at the same time that, by this very action, it renders itself less alluring to the "popular men," who are and should be its "best hold." If, on the other hand, it has the tact to depart for once from its Bones model, and set up an independent standard of qualifications of its own, it may in time gain in its own particular field a recognized pre-eminence. Keys' real "mission," as it seems to an outsider, is to draw together a genial, gentlemanly crowd, rather than an "able" one. If a pleasant, agreeable fellow chances to be possessed of something more substantial than popularity, — if besides being a gentleman, he be also a scholar, a writer, and energetic worker, — he should of course be all the more desirable; yet the first mentioned, more trivial, qualities should be regarded as the essential ones, after all, which recommend him for election. Ability, real or reputed, should never of itself elect a man to Keys. The prestige the society may gain by taking a man simply for his reputation cannot make up for what it thereby loses in attractiveness for "popular men." Keys' great opportunity is, by excluding all others, to make itself the most desirable society for the agreeable, jolly fellow in every senior class. If it resolutely adopts this "lay," it may, with the help of its hall, ere many years, leave bones in the lurch, so far as "popular" men are concerned; and, by occupying an independent field, prevent the possibility of direct comparisons which must always be to its own disadvantage. This seems so manifest that nothing but a foolish over-confidence in its own strength can induce it to engage in a "straight fight" on Bones' own chosen field, where, with all the odds against it, it must ever suffer defeat. Bones, on the other hand, would do well to consider whether it will be worth its while much longer to take in men for their popularity and agreeableness simply. It is just here that it has met with its most humiliating rebuffs hitherto, and that it is likely to meet with worse ones hereafter, unless it changes its policy. Four of the five

'70 men who rejected; Bones in favour of Keys, were simply "good fellows," who would have been somewhat out of their element in the crowd of the former society; and the case in the class of '67 was very similar. If Bones should insist more strongly than now upon ability as a prime essential in all its members, and upon this basis, modified by a reasonable regard for social qualities and harmoniousness, elect them, it would secure itself almost absolutely from having an election rejected, as well as add to its own lasting reputation, — even at the sacrifice of one of its cherished traditions, which it has managed to perpetuate thus far on the whole with a fair share of success. Whether Bones makes this concession with good grace at the outset, or waits to be forced into it by the success of Keys, when the latter shall turn all its energies upon this one point, remains to be seen. But appearances certainly point to the coming, at no distant day, of what may be termed a senior society millennium, when Bones and Keys shall each occupy an undisputed field of its own, and each be recognized as in its own sphere pre-eminent; and when the only question in a man's mind shall be, "In which field, on the whole, is supremacy the more desirable?" Then shall the Death's head be, even more certainly than now, the badge of intellectual superiority in college repute, and the unfolded Scroll be, even more invariably, the emblem of gentlemenly good fellowship and social popularity.

It was remarked at the beginning of the chapter that societies like Bones and Keys would be possible only at one other college than Yale, and that as a matter of fact they are peculiar to the latter institution. They are not, however, without imitators. At Columbia College is an "Axe and Coffin;" at Michigan University an "Owl and Padlock;" and at Wesleyan University are a "Skull and Serpent" and an "Owl and Wand." None of them are of any importance, and with the possible exception of the second, are in every way inferior to the Greek-letter societies connected with their respective institutions. There is no special difficulty in imitating the peculair names and mummeries of the Yale senior societies; but the gaining of a similar prestige and influence is quite another matter. It is the high character of their members, not their names and forms and ceremonies, which give the Yale societies their fame. It was a belief in the power of these latter non-essentials that induced the Diggers to persist so long in a worse than hopeless fight. At Yale, the strictly class societies of the first three years supply the machinery by which every class is carefully sifted and its best men are "brought out" in readiness for the senior societies. Yet even here, with from one hundred to one hundred and twenty men to pick from, and the three years' sifting process reduced almost to an exact science, it has been absolutely demonstrated that no more than two societies, of fifteen men each, can exist. Indeed, it was for a long time a problem whether more than one could live, and even now the two, to be at their best, must occupy somewhat different fields. But at other colleges, where no such class system prevails, where the numbers to select from are much smaller, where the competing societies are more numerous, the attempt to ape Bones and Keys can succeed in nothing save in making the would-be societies ridiculous. In view of their real worth, people may be willing to overlook the silly practices of the Yale senior societies; but when mock mystery and cheap cermonials are the only things which a society has to boast of, it cannot well help falling into contempt. The statement is therefore again repeated that Bones and Keys are peculiarly Yale institutions, genuine out-growths of a system that flourishes nowhere else, the only organizations of the kind existing in the country.

In concluding this account of the class societies, it may be well to add a few additional facts that are true alike of many or all of them, and to compare directly their general character in the different years. Each society, save Gamma Nu, has a "grip" of its own, but society men, in either of the four years, do not generally employ it in greeting one another. It is not a popular device with them, and comparatively few would be able, a year or two after graduation, to give the four different grips correctly, were they to try. Many of the active members, even, of these societies cannot remember their grips without an effort, and in junior year, when visitors from other chapters are expected, there is need of some preliminary practice before the guests can be welcomed in true mysterious fashion. At other colleges the society grips are constantly made use of, and when a Yale man who has forgotten his grip meets an outside brother he extends his hand with all the fingers separated, and returns the grip that he receives, in full faith that he has given "the right one" and concealed his ignorance. It is easy enough for an outsider to find out from someone or other the reputed grips of the dozen or less societies, and it is more than likely that these are really the true ones in many cases. But the whole matter is made so little of by Yale men that none of these peculiar hand shakings are worth describing. In the published report of a recent DKE convention, that society announced that it had adopted a new grip and motto, — presumably on account of the discovery of its old ones, and probably at the instance of the outside chapters. Whether the changes were really made, or the announcement offered simply as a "blind," the result was of course the same. The only two Yale society mottoes that seem to be unknown to outsiders are, oddly enough, those of Delta Kap and Theta Psi. That of the former used to be, $\Delta \epsilon \sigma \mu \acute{o} \varsigma \ K \rho \acute{v} \varphi \iota o \varsigma$, and was as well known as Sigma Eps' is at present, but the one which superseded it and is now in vogue has been by some miracle prevented from leaking out. Every junior society man can find out without much difficulty the mottoes and "secrets" of the other societies in his class, but he feels in duty bound not to make public his knowledge, and the neutrals are generally in ignorance of these matters. At Yale, one society never thinks of breaking into the hall of another, and making public all its mysteries, as is the practice at some of the smaller colleges. It is through these that some of the Yale junior-society secrets are divulged. Chapters which think it a fine thing to steal the constitution and documents of as many rival societies as possible, when they chance to gain those of societies which are also rivals at Yale, may forward to their brothers at the latter place their illgotten knowledge: knowledge which the latter are usually honorable enough to keep to themselves. It is only in the songs of the first two years that the societies mention the names of their rivals — to ridicule them, of course, but in a good natured way. A secret ballot, upon each candidate separately, in which a single blackball rejects, is the mode of election in all these societies. Every society has a janitor whom it allows to wear its badge. While '69 was in college the same individual was at once janitor of Delta Kap, Theta Psi and Psi U, and wore either one of the badges indifferently, though never displaying two at a time. A senior-society janitor is not allowed to serve for under-class organizations. The present Bones janitor is a negro named Robert, who assists the professors in the experiments at the philosophical lectures, and is a sort of college supernumerary. His predecessor, also a black man, died in the service, and was followed to his grave by the whole Bones society, resident graduate, solemn professors, and all. The societies of the two upper years have boxes at the post office wherein is placed all mail matter directed either to their popular or official, trust-association, titles. A letter directed to either of the lower-class societies is exposed to view beside the general-delivery window, until discovered and called for by one of the members. Society men as a rule preserve all their badges, — sometimes, in senior year, mounting their previously gained insignia in a velvet-lined, ornamental frame or case. Quite a number of freshman pins are disposed of, however, when the time for wearing them is past, and some sophomore and a very few junior badges go the same way, but a senior-society pin is kept by its owner until death doth them part. By other college men their junior-society badge, usually the only one they ever possess, is as a rule always preserved, and is in many cases steadily worn for some years after graduation. Yale men, who were senior neutrals, sometimes display their junior badge, on special occasions, after graduation, but never the pin of lower society. When a Freshman leaves college he usually takes off his society pin, but a Sophomore, if a society man, is likely to wear his badge for some time after his withdrawal.

In taking a general look at the societies of the four years, the first seems a working ground where Freshmen may display their abilities, and induce the Juniors to pledge them; the second, a place where these

pledged men as Sophomores may be kept quiet until they are further in-
spected, and the poor ones got rid of; the third, another working
ground of narrower limits, where the select Juniors who have passed
safely through two sifting processes may, by making the most of their
talents before the Seniors, prevail upon the latter to spare them in the
last grand turn of the sieve, and elect them into the fourth, beyond
which there is nothing higher. It is a fault of the system that each society
save the last is only a stepping stone to the next, and when the last is
reached the time left to enjoy it in is short indeed. The size of the
classes, and the class feeling thereby engendered, makes any other
system impossible, while the system in turn tends to strengthen and
perpetrate the class feeling. From his freshman society, a man usually
gains considerable solid advantage, and a fair amount of pleasure. The
direct benefit of a sophomore-society experience is not very great, and a
man loses less by being a neutral this year than any other, —
sophomore neutrals being often elected to senior societies, — but still,
he does lose something, both in a peculiar sort of "fun," and in general
social position. In a third-year society the advantages are many, and are
of a general as well as local character. The occasions thus afforded for
members of different colleges to fraternize together, the opportunities
given for making pleasant acquaintances at unexpected places, are
evidently of considerable value. A man's interest in his junior society is
not as intense or as lasting at Yale as at other colleges, yet it is altogether
greater than that which he feels toward any lower-class society. One
Yale graduate would not be apt to claim introduction to another on the
score of belonging to the same junior society, yet, once acquainted for
some other reason, this fact would form a sort of bond between them.
The attempt to make an outsider realize the overwhelming fasination,
which a senior society exerts upon the mind of the average Yale
undergraduate, would probably be useless. An election thereto is
valued more highly than any other college prize of honor; and in fact
these honors derive a good part of their attractiveness from their supposed efficacy in helping to procure the coveted election. There is
nothing in the wide world that seems to him half as desirable. It is the
one thing needful for his perfect happiness. And if he fails in gaining it,
the chances are that he becomes a temporary misanthropist, that is to
say, an ardent "Stones man." Though the advantages of membership
are no doubt exaggerated in anticipation, the real benefit gained in
belonging to a senior society is certainly considerable, — far more
valuable in fact, than that which accrues from membership in any other.
Quite aside from the enjoyment of the senior year itself, the facts that in
after life a man is thus introduced to the best graduates of the college,
wherever he may meet them, and that, whenever he visits New Haven,
he is sure of being entertained by the best of the oldest undergraduates,
and instructed as to the doings and whereabouts of the best of his

former classmates, — these facts, other things being equal, of themselves make membership in a senior society especially desirable.

College friendships do not at Yale run very closely in society lines. A pair of friends may be brought together or separated by almost numberless society combinations. They may belong to the same society in each of the four years, or in the first and last, or in the second and third, or in none at all, or one may be a society man and another a neutral for all the course, and so on through all the possible permutations. Still, it is pleasant for friends to keep in the same societies, and a general tendency of certain crowds to go together, year after year, has been already remarked upon. No neutral as such is looked down upon or avoided by society men. If the latter usually "run" together, it is because of similar tastes and proclivities, which would induce them to do so, were no societies in existence. In senior year there is hardly a society man without one or two special friends who are neutrals, and with whom he has quite as much to do as with his own regular associates. Such pairs often chum together than do two from rival societies; though this sometimes happens and previous to senior year is not at all uncommon. Aside from a man's real or reputed ability, good nature, and popularity, a thing which often helps to elect him is his relationship to a former or active member of the society. If a father or an uncle or a brother has preceded him, the fact helps him to follow in their footsteps, especially if they were in any way famous. An older brother in the class above, or even one or two classes removed, is almost certain to secure the election of a younger one, unless the latter is peculiarly unqualified or obnoxious. This species of favouritism attracts the most attention in the case of the senior societies, into which nearly every year, by his relationship with an older and worthier member, is dragged one man at least who is without other qualifications sufficient to recommend him. The cases of poor men taken in are, by the bye, a good deal more common and noticeable than those of desirable men left out. Every year almost there is a great show of indignation over the injustice in the senior-society elections which bring several big men to grief, yet it rarely happens that the good policy of the society in leaving them out is not vindicated within a twelve month. When fifteen men are to be shut up together for six successive hours, every week, and be thrown in with each other constantly, it is essential that thay should be reasonably harmonious if not congenial; and an organization whose members should be chosen for their reputation and ability simply, could not be in the right sense of the word a society.

Without now discussing whether college opinion always awards men the positions they deserve, it may be said, in conclusion, that the society system, viewed as a means for separating those who, for whatever reason, are high in college esteem, from those who, for whatever reason, are not, must be admitted to be in the main a fair and successful one. No one can reasonably deny that it has this effect, and that the society men of every year are as a class superior in college repute to the neutrals. It would of course be foolish to judge an individual solely by his society connections, but it would be far less foolish than to judge him solely by the number of prizes, or scholarships, or honors he could lay claim to, as is not infrequently the practice. To set up any one arbitrary standards whereby to judge character is manifestly unfair, yet, if it is to be done, there is no single test which embraces so many, in making an estimate of a Yale man's importance, as his share in the society system. Blockheads and simpletons certainly find their way into the senior societies, yet there are few generalities of the sort deserving of more confidence than these, that in a Bones man you will find ability and force of character, in a Keys man politeness and geniality, and in both the most favourable samples of the Yale graduate of the period.

The Order of
Skull & Bones
Yale Catalogue

322

This section compiled by Kris Millegan

FOUNDERS

William Huntington Russell

Alphonso Taft

322

The Order of Skull and Bones
1832

1833

Bates, Samuel Henshaw
Beach, John Campell
Bishop, Noah
Crump, John
Davis, Benjamin Franklin
Hart, Rufus Erastus
Lewis, Asahel Hooker
Marshall, Samuel Davies
Mather, Frederick Ellsworth
Miller, Phineas Timothy

Robertson, Robert
Russell, William Huntington
Taft, Alphonso
Wood, George Ingersoll

1834

Beaumont, George A. O.
Burr, William Shedden
Coffing, Churchill
Emerson, Alfred
Foster, Eleazar Kingsbury
Gordon, Alexander Blucher
Hall, Daniel Emerson
Houston, John Wallace
Kendall, John Newton
Kingsley, Henry Coit
Lea, James Neilson
Southmayd, Samuel Gray
Spencer, George Gilman
Tweedy, John Hubbard
Washington, William Henry

1835

Anderson, Edwin Alexander
Davis, John
Howard, Oran Reed
Johnston, Frank
McLellan, William
Mills, Ethelbert Smith
Rafferty, John Chandler
Seeley, John Edward
Seymour, John Forman
Sheffey, Hugh White
Strong, Caleb
Stubbs, Alfred
Sturges, Thomas Benedict
Thacher, Thomas Anthony
Walsh, Hugh

1836

Darling, Thomas
Deming, Henry Champion
Dent, Henry Hatch
Dunwody, James Bulloch
Harris, Henry Reeder
Hurd, John Codman
Martin, John Griffith
Marvin, George Lockwood
Pierson, William Seward
Preston, Henry Kirk
Rowland, William Sherman
Sherman, Frederick Roger
Swift, John Morton
Tyler, George Palmer
Wray, James McAlpin

1837

Carter, Edwin Osgood
Coit, William
Day, Thomas Mills
Evarts, William Maxwell
Hatch, Walter Tilden
Hyatt, Robert Underwood
Law, William Fabian
Lyman, Chester Smith
Owen, Allen Ferdinand
Robeson, Abel Bellows
Scarborough, William Smith
Silliman, Benjamin Jr.
Waite, Morris Remmick
Williams, Henry
Yerkes, Stephen

1838

Bartlett, John Knowlton
Cooper, William Frierson
Dodd, Albert
Fleming, William Stuart
Jones, Seaborn Augustus
Key, Thomas Marshall
Law, William Lyon
Lynde, Charles James
Ribeiro, Carlos Fernando
Rich, Charles
Spaulding, Ebenezer
Talcott, Thomas Grosvenor
Thompson, Joseph Parrish
Varnum, Joseph Bradley
Williams, Thomas Scott

1839

Beach, John Sheldon
Biddle, Thomas Bradish
Chandler, William Henry
Eldridge, Charles St. John
Faulkner, Endress
Hubbard, Richard Dudley
Jackson, Henry Rootes
Norris, William Herbert
Putnam, James Osborne
Stille, Charles Janeway
Trotter, Silas Flournoy
Washington, George
Watson, John Marsh
Williams, William Perkins
Wolcott, Elizer

1840

Beirne, Christopher James
Benedict, Theodore Hudson
Burnham, Curtis Field
Chauvenet, William
Fisk, Stuart Wilkins
Hoppin, James Mason
Hoyt, Joseph Gibson
Hudson, Ward Woodridge
Jesup, James Riley
March, Daniel
McCall, Henry
Perkins, John
Perkins, William
Richards, George
Tiffany, William Henry

1841

Barry, William Taylor Sullivan
DeSa, Pompeo Ascenco
Emerson, Joseph
Eustis, William Tappan
Field, David Irvine
Gillette, Augustus Canfield
Helfenstein, Charles Philip
Leaf, Edmund
Learned, William Law
Mitchell, Donald Grant
Raymond, Henry Hunter
Sturges, Hezekiah
Willis, Richard Storrs
Woolfolk, William Grey
Yarnall, Thomas Coffin

1842

Benton, Joseph Augustine
Brown, Joseph Venen
Buttles, Albert Barnes
Edwards, Newton
Gready, William Postell
Halsey, Jacob
Henen, William Davison
Huggins, William Sidney
Lewis, Henry
MacWhorter, Alexander
Mathews, Albert
Miller, Francis William
Perkins, Nathaniel Shaw
Peters, John Andrew
Pratt, Julius Howard

1843

Baratte, Julius Adolphus
Chambers, William Lyon
Eames, Benjamin Tucker
Gachet, Charles Nicholas
Grammar, Christopher
Granger, Gideon
Hart, Roswell
Havens, Daniel William
Lambert, Alfred
Lane, William Griswold
Lent, John Abram
Moody, Thomas Hudson
Robb, John Hunter
Robinson, Lucius Franklin
Stevens, Henry

1844

Bell, Richard Dobbs Spaight
Breed, Edward Andrews
Elliot, William Horace
Felder, John Henry
Ferry, Orris Sanford
Fewsmith, William
Fisk, Samuel Augustus
Foote, Thaddeus
Lanier, Alexander Chalmers
Lovell, Joseph
Robb, James Madison
Walker, Joseph Burbeen
Washburn, William Barrett
Wetherell, John Walcott
Wilson, Archelaus

1845

Brickell, James Noaille
Conner, Lemuel Parker
Conner, William Gustine
Cushman, Isaac LaFayette
Esty, Constantine Canaris
Gould, James Gardner
Harding, John Wheeler
Hill, George Canning
Hyde, Alvan Pinney
Kennedy, Thomas
Metcalfe, Orrick
Nickerson, Sereno Dwight
Rankin, Robert
Taylor, Richard
Wales, Leonard Eugene

1846

Backus, Joseph Willes
Brisbrin, John Ball
Eakin, William Spencer
Harrison, Henry Baldwin
Hawley, David
Kellogg, Stephen Wright
Linton, Stephen Duncan
Mulford, David Humphrey
Nelson, Rensselaer Russell
Nevins, William Russell
Phinney, Elihu
Savage, Josiah
Steele, Henry Thornton
Stiles, Joseph
Trask, Charles Hooper

1847

Allison, Samuel Perkins
Baldwin, Roger Sherman
Bayne, Thomas Levingston
Coon, John
Fitch, James
Haight, Ducald Cameron
Hayden, William Hallock
McLallen, Philemon F.
Mills, Alfred
Moore, William Eves
Munn, John
Olmstead, John Hull
Sanford, Charles Frederick
Smith, John Donnell
Wilson, John

1848

Abbe, Frederick Randolph
Aitchison, William
Blake, Henry Taylor
Colton, Henry Martin
Condit, Charles
Emerson, Samuel
Foster, Dwight
Hitchcock, Henry
Kinne, William
Mesick, Richard Smith
Pinckard, Thomas Cicero
Strickler, Samuel Alexander
White, George
Willcox, Giles Buckingham
Young, Benham Daniel

1849

Brandegee, Augustus
Came, Charles Green
Campbell, James
Clarke, William Barker
Dwight, Timothy
Finch, Francis Miles
Fisk, Franklin Woodbury
Hough, Edward Clement
Hurlbut, Joseph
Kirby, Jacob Brown
Metcalfe, Henry Laurens
Miles, James Browning
Morris, Edward Dafydd
Richardson, Walker
Rockwell, John

1850

Bentley, Edward Warren
Bliss, Robert
Bliss, William Root
Camp, Clinton
Chase, Henry
Colton, Willis Strong
Condit, Albert Pierson
Converse, George Sherman
Dechert, Henry Martyn
Foote, Joseph Forward
Ludden, William
Manross, Newton Spaulding
Roberts, Ellis Henry
Storrs, Cordial
Woodford, Oswald Langdon

1851

Alexander, William Felix
Beman, Henry DeWitt
Brinsmade, Horatio Walsh
Crampton, Rufus Cowles
Dana, William Buck
Evans, Evan Wilhelm
Haldeman, Richard Jacobs
Hebard, Albert
Little, Robbins
Manice, William DeForest
Slade, John Milton
Vose, James Gardiner
Wells, Henry Dorrance
White, Henry Dyer
Whitney, Emerson Cogswell

1852

Bigelow, Albert
Blakeslee, Henry Clay
Bliss, Charles Miller
Cooper, Jacob
Crapo, William Wallace
Gilman, Daniel Coit
Helmer, Charles Downs
Houghton, Edward
Johnston, William Preston
Marmaduke, Vincent
McCormick, Henry
Ross, William Baldwin
Safford, George Blagden
Sill, George Griswold   Stan-
ley, William

1853

Aiken, William Pope
Babcock, Henry Harper
Baldwin, George William
Capron, Samuel Mills
Coit, Joshua
Davies, Thomas Frederick
Gleason, William Henry
Grout, Alfred
Heard, Albert Farley
Jack, Thomas Mckinney
Johnson, George Asbury
Kent, Albert Emmett
White, Andrew Dickinson
Whiton, James Morris
Willard, Andrew Jackson

1854

Blackman, Samuel Curtis
Cutler, Carroll
Denny, Thomas
Fenn, William Henry
Hooker, John Worthington
Lambert, Edward Wilberforce
Lombard, James Kittredge
Lord, George DeForest
Morris, Luzon Burritt
Potwin. Lemuel Stoughton
Purnell, Charles Thomas
Slade, Francis Henry
Twombly, Alexander S.
White, Charles Atwood
Whitney, Edward Payton

1855

Alexander, William DeWitt
Barnes, William Henry L.
Bumstead, Nathaniel Willis
Child, Linus Mason
Cobb, Henry Nitchie
Granger, John Albert
Johnson, Charles Fredrick
Kittredge, George Alvah
Lampson, George
Mulford, Elisha
Spring, Andrew Jackson
Tyler, Charles Mellen
Wheeler, William
Woodward, Stanley
Yardley, Henry Albert

1855

Arnot, Matthias Hollenback
Barker, George Payson
Brown, John Mason
Campbell, William Harvey W.
Condit, Stephen
Depew, Chauncy Mitchell
Dickinson, Arthur
Eakin, Emmet Alexander
Fischer, Louis Christopher
Magruder, Benjamin Drake
Nettleton, Edward Payson
Packard, Lewis Richard
Paine, Levi Leonard
Robinson, George Chester
Whitney, James Lyman

1857

Blackman, Charles Seymour
Blake, Eli Whitney
Buckland, Joseph Payson
Butler, Francis Eugene
Croxton, John Thomas
Day, John Calvin
Edwards, Alfred Lewis
Green, James Payne
Holmes, John Milton
Jackson, Joseph Cooke
Northup, Cyrus
Pratt, George
Seymour, Storrs Ozias
Tyler, Moses Coit
Wells, Nathan Dana

1858

Blake, Edward Foster
Eichelberger, Martin Smyser
Grant, Edward Dromgoole
Haskell, Robert Chandler
Heermance, Edgar Laing
Hollister, Arthur Nelson
Kimball, John Edwin
Lee, Samuel Henry
MacLellan, George Boardman
Perkins, Thomas Albert
Porter, Edward Clarke
Scott, Eben Greenough
Stevens, Frederic William
Van Name, Addison
Woodward, William Herrick

1859

Bristol, Louis Henry
Brodhead, Henry
Carpenter, Robert John
Clay, Green
Dunham, George Elliott
Hall, William Kittredge
Hannahs, Diodate Cushman
Harrison, Burton Norvel
Robertson, Charles Franklin
Schuyler, Eugene
Smith, Eugene
Stiles, William Augustus
Taylor, Alfred Judd
White, Roger Sherman
Wilcox, Asher Henry

1860

Beckley, John Werle
Boies, Charles Alred
Boltwood, Edward
Daniels, Joseph Leonard
Davis, Lowndes Henry
Davis, Robert Stewart
Fowler, William
Furbish, Edward Brown
Hebard, Daniel
Johnston, William Curtis
Jones, Luther Maynard
Owen, Charles Hunter
Phelps, William Walter
Seeley, John Frank
Smith, William Thayer

1861

Baldwin, Simeon Eren
Brown, Hubert Sanford
Chamberlain, Robert Linton
Dexter, Franklin Bowditch
Fuller, William Henry
Higgins, Anthony
Kernochan, Francis Edward
Mitchell, John Hanson
Newel, Stanford
Park, William Edwards
Peck, Tracy
Root, Alexander Porter
Shearer, Sextus
Sill, Edward Rowland
Williams, Ralph Omsted

1862

Adams, Frederick
Chamberlain, Daniel Henry
Coe, Edward Benton
Day, Melville Cox
Eaton, Sherburne Blake
Johnston, Henry Phelps
Kitchel, Cornelius Ladd
Lampson, William
MacVeagh, Franklin
Ripley, George Coit
Seely, William Wallace
Stebbins, Henry Hamlin
Taylor, John Phelps
Ward, John Abbott
Weeks, Robert Kelley

1863

Allen, Walter
Arms, Charles Jesup
Bingham, Egbert Byron
Bull, Cornelius Wade
Butler, John Haskell
Chamberlain, Leander T.
Dimock, Henry Farnam
Fowler, Horace Webster
Kernochan, Joseph Frederic
Perry, David Brainard
Sheffield, George St. John
Southworth, George C. S.
Sumner, William Graham
Wesson, Charles Holland
Whitney, William Collins

1864

Boltwood, Thomas Kast
Borden, Matthew C. D.
Boyden, Henry Paine
Clark, Albert Barnes
Hewitt, Thomas Browning
MacLean, Charles Fraser
Merriam, George Spring
Miller, Allanson Douglas
Owen, Henry Elijah
Palmer, William Henry
Pratt, William Hall Brace
Pugsley, Isaac Platt
Sterling, John Williams
White, Oliver Sherman
Woodruff, James Eben

1865

Bent, Joseph Appleton
Brooks, John Edward
Brown, Henry Armitt
Bulkey, Tuzar
Bushnell, William Benedick
Caskey, Taliaferro Franklin
Charnley, Charles Meigs
Ewell, John Lewis
Ford, George Tod
Merrill, Payson
Riggs, Benjamin Clapp
Smith, Charles Edgar
Stimson, Henry Albert
Stone, William
Warren, Henry Waterman

1866

Adams, Charles Hemmenway
Brand, James
Coffin, Edmund
Cole, Hamilton
Farnam, William Whitman
Foote, Harry Ward
Hall, John Manning
Hincks, Edward Young
Holt, George Chandler
Judson, Frederick Newton
Lampman, Lewis
Sloane, Henry Thompson
Southgate, Charles McClellan
Wade, Levi Clifford
White, George Edward

1867

Bissell, Arthur Douglas
Dexter, Morton
DuBois, John Jay
Dunning, Albert Elijah
Harding, Wilder Bennett
Hartshorn, Joseph William
Hedge, Thomas
Lamb, Albert Eugene
Libbey, Frank
Merriam, James Fiske
Seymour, Horatio
Spencer, James Magoffin
Taft, Peter Rawson
Wetmore, George Peabody
Woodward, Richard William

1868

Berry, Coburn Dewees
Brewster, Chauncey Bunce
Coffin, James
Colt, LeBaron Bradford
Dixon, William Palmer
Farnam, Charles Henry
Lewis, John
McKinney, William Allison
Sloane, Thomas Chalmers
Thacher, James Kingsley
Tinker, Anson Phelps
Tweedy, Samuel
Tytus, Edward Jefferson
Wood, William Curtis
Wright, Henry Park

1869

Bannard, Henry Clay
Beers, Henry Augustin
Bissell, Wilson Shannon
Brown, Alexander Lardner
Eno, John Chester
Foster, John Pierrepont C.
Freeman, Henry Varnum
Heaton, Edward
Hooker, Thomas
Isham, John Beach
Lear, Henry
Perrin, Bernadotte
Raymond, Henry Warren
Richardson, Rufus Byam
Shirley, Arthur

1870

Andrews, John Wallingford Jr.
Gulliver, William Curtis
Johnston, Ross
Learned, Dwight Whitney
Mason, Henry Burrall
McClure, James Gore King
McCutchen, Samuel St. John
Miller, George Douglas
Perry, John Hoyt
Selden, Edward Griffin
Shattuck, John Waldon
Stearns, Edwin Russell
Strong, Charles Hall
Tilney, Thomas Joseph
Welch, William Henry

1871

Clark, Charles Hopkins
Collin, Frederick
Elliot, Henry Rutherford
Hine, Charles Daniel
Kinney, Herbert Evelyn
Lea, Robert Brinkley
Mansfield, Howard
Mason, Alfred Bishop
Mead, Frederick
Perry, Wilbert Warren
Sperry, Watson Robertson
Strong, George Arthur
Sweet, Edwin Forrest
Thacher, Thomas
Townsend, William Kneeland

1872

Coe, Robert Elmer
Cushing, William Lee
Deming, Charles Clerc
Deming, Clarence
Deming, Henry Champion
Dennis, Frederic Shepard
Hincks, John Howard
Hoppin, Benjamin
Merriam, Alexander Ross
Moore, George Foot
Owen, Edward Thomas
Payson, Henry Silas
Ramsdell, Charles Benjamin
Spaldin, George Atherton
Woolsey, Theodore Salisbury

1873

Alexander, Eben
Allen, Arthur Huntington
Beebe, William
Daniels, Rensselaer Wilkinson
Denslow, Herbert McKenzie
Elder, Samuel James
Flagg, Wilbur Wells
Grubb, Charles Ross
Johnes, Edward Rudolph
Judson, Issac Nichols
Lathe, Herbert William
Ord, Joseph Pacificus
Prentice, Samuel Oscar
Tarbell, Frank Bigelow
Thomas, Charles Henry

1874

Aldis, Owen Franklin
Barnes, Pearce
Bushnell, Samuel Clarke
Farnam, Henry Walcott
Grover, Thomas Williams
James, Henry Ammon
Munroe, George Edmund
Parkin, William
Robbins, Edwards Denmore
Stapler, Henry Beidleman B.
Townsend, James Mulford
Walden, Russell
Wickes, Thomas Parmelee
Witherbee, Frank Spencer
Wood, John Seymour

1875

Avery, Charles Hammond
Brooks, James Wilton
Chester, Carl Thurston
Clarke, Thomas Slidell
Day, Robert Webster
Gulliver, Henry Strong
Hothhkiss, William Henry
Jenks, Almet Francis
Jones, Dwight Arven
Jones, Frank Hatch
Patton, John
Seymour, John Sammis
Smith, Edward Curtis
Southworth, Edward Wells
Tillinghast, Charles

1876

Allen, John DeWitt Hamilton
Andrews, John Wolcott
Bannard, Otto Tremont
Blaine, Walker
Bottum, Elisha Slocum
Cook, Robert Johnston
Dawes, Chester Mitchell
Fowler, Charles Newell
Hadley, Arthur Twining
Howe, Elmer Parker
Hyde, William Waldo
Marvin, Joseph Howard
Russell, Philip Gray
Smith, Rufus Biggs
Worcester, Edwin Dean

1877

Barnum, William Milo
Bigelow, Walter Irving
Brooks, Walter
Chapin, Charles Frederick
Collin, William Welch
Cooke, Eldridge Clinton
Eaton, Samuel Lewis
Gould, Anthony
Hoysradt, Albert
Kimball, Arthur Reed
Percy, Frederick Bosworth
Sears, Joshua Montgomery
Thacher, John Seymour
Tuttle, George Montgomery
Winston, Frederick Seymour

1878

Campbell, Treat
Carter, Charles Francis
Curtis, George Louis
Edwards, George Benjamin
Foster, Roger
James, William Knowles
Jenks, Tudor Storrs
Kelsey, Clarence
Knott, George Tapscott
Pollock, George Edward
Seely, Edward Howard Jr.
Spencer, Charles Langford
Stone, Charles Martin
Taft, William Howard
Whitney, Edward Baldwin

1879

Bowers, Lloyd Wheaton
Burpee, Lucien Francis
Foster, George Forris
Green, Henry Sherwood
Hitchcock, Henry
Hyde, Frank Eldridge
James, Walter Belknap
Livingston, Herman
Perrin, John
Platt, Lewis Alfred
Rodman, Robert Simpson
Swinburne, Louis Judson
Thompson, Oliver David
Tighe, Ambrose
Woodruff, Timothy Lester

1880

Allen, William Palmer
Amundson, John Arnold
Bentley, Edward Manross
Camp, Walter
Green, Edmund Frank
Jennings, Walter
Nichols, Alfred Bull
Ordway, Henry Choate
Parker, Wilbur
Partridge, Sidney Catlin
Peters, William Allison
Scudder, Doremus
Spencer, Edward Curran
Taft, Henry Waters
Witherbee, Walter Crafts

1881

Aiken, Edwin Edgerton
Barney, Danford Newton
Bartlett, Philip Golden
Burrel, Joseph Dunn
Coleman, John Caldwell
Evarts, Sherman
Fuller, Philo Carroll
Ives, Henry
Leighton, James
Osborne, Thomas Burr
Thompson, Norman F.
Van deGraaff, Adrian S.
Vernon, Frederick Richardson
Walden, Howard Talbott
White, Henry Charles

1882

Badger, Walter Irving
Brewster, Benjamin
Campbell, James Alexander
Eno, Wiliam Phelps
French, Asa Palmer
Johnson, Barclay
Knapp, Howard Hoyt
Lyman, Chester Wolcott
McBride, Wilber
Osborne, Arthur Sherwood
Platt, Henry Barstow
Pollock, William
Wells, John Lewis
Whitney, Joseph Ernest
Worcester, Franklin Eldred

1883

Burpee, Charles Winslow
Deming, Lawrence Clerc
Folsom, Henry Titus
Foote, Charles Seward
Frost, Elihu Brintnal
Hillard, Lord Butler
Hull, Louis Kossuth
Kellogg, Fred William
McLaughlin, Edward T.
Moore, Eliakim Hastings
Palmer, Harry Herbert
Parrott, Joseph Robinson
Taft, Horace Dutton
Thacher, Sherman Day
Woodward, John Butler

1884

Blodgett, George Reddington
Booth, Samuel Albert
Booth, Wilbur Franklin
Evarts, Maxwell
Foster, Reginald
Gruener, Gustav
Jenks, Paul Emmott
Jones, Frederick Scheetz
Lambert, Alexander
Lawrance, Thomas Garner
McMillan, William Charles
Painter, Henry McMahon
Tompkins, Ray
Twombly, Henry Bancroft
Wilder, Amos Parker

1885

Arnot, John Hulett
Baldwin, Henry DeForest
Bertron, Samuel Reading
Brandegee, Frank Bosworth
Bridgman, John Cloyse
Brooks, Henry Stanford
Flanders, Henry Richmond
Hidden, Edward
Hobbs, Charles Buxton
Mallon, Guy Ward
McHenry, John
Richards, Eugene Lamb
Robinson, Lucius Franklin
Terry, Wyllys
Worcester, Wilfred James

1886

Anthony, Benjamin Harris
Bremmer, Samuel Kimball
Cowles, Alfred
Crapo, Stanford Tappan
Day, Thomas Mills
Knapp, Wallace Percy
Lewis, Charlton Miner
Peters, Frank George
Phelps, Edward Johnson
Phelps, Sheffield
Pierson, Charles Wheeler
Schwab, John Christopher
Shipman, Arthur Leffingwell
Stewart, Philip Battel
Winston, Dudley

1887

Bennetto, John
Corwin, Robert Nelson
Cowles, William Hutchinson
Coxe, Alexander Brown
Douglass, Willard Robinson
Hare, Clinton Larue
Haven, George Griswold
Jennings, Oliver Gould
Kendall, William Burrage Jr.
Kent, William
Knight, Samuel
Pomeroy, John Norton
Rogers, John
Sheppard, Walter Bradley
Thacher, William Larned

1888

Cooley, Harlan Ward
Fisher, Irving
Gill, George Metcalf
Hurd, Richard Melancthon
Isbell, Orland Sidney
McMillan, James Howard
Morison, David Whipple
Roby, Samuel Sidney Brese
Seward, William Henry
Solley, Fred Palmer
Stagg, Amos Alonzo
Stevenson, Frederic Augustus
Stimson, Henry Lewis
Waite, Morrison R.
Walker, Samuel Johnson

1889

Buchanan, Thomas Walter
Corbin, William Herbert
Donnelley, Thomas Elliott
Fisher, Samuel Herbert
Gill, Charles Otis
Griggs, John Cornelius
McQuaid, William Adolph
Pinchot, Gifford
Reed, Harry Lathrop
Robinson, Henry Seymour
Smith, Herbert Augustine
Stokes, Horace Sheldon
Walker, Horace Flecher
Wells, Herbert Wetmore
Woodruff, George W.

1890

Bayard, Thomas Francis
Corwith, John White
Crosby, John
Day, Arthur Pomeroy
Farnham, John Dorrance
Harrison, Fairfax
Haslam, Lewis Scofield
James, Norman
Kellogg, Charles Poole
Kneeland, Yale
Morse, Sidney Nelson
Sage, Henry Manning
Simmons, Wallace Delafield
Stewart, Percy Hamilton
Tracy, Evarts

1891

Calhoun, Governeur
Cox, John Joughin
Doane, John Wesley Jr.
Estill, Joe Garner
Graves, William Phillips
Isham, Edward Swift
Kenerson, Vertner
McClintock, Norman
Morison, Samuel Benjamin
Poole, William Frederick
Simms, William Erskine
Thomson, Samuel Clifton
Townsend, John Barnes
Tweedy, Henry Hallam
Walcott, Frederic Collin

1892

Bayne, Hugh Aiken
Boltwood, Edward
Cheney, Howell
Cheney, Knight Dexter Jr.
Crosby, Benjamin Lewis Jr.
Day, Clive
Graves, Henry Solon
Husted, James William
Ingersoll, James Wernham D.
Jay, Pierre
Kitchel, William Lloyd
McClung, Thomas Lee
Morison, Stanford Newel
Price, Frank Julian
Ryle, Ernest

1893

Begg, William Reynolds
Cooke, James Barclay
Dwight, Winthrop Edwards
Gallaudet, Edson Fessenden
Hay, Logan
Ives, Sherwood Bissell
Jones, Alfred Henry
Lambert, Adrian VanSinderen
Martin, George Greene
Parker, William White Wilson
Parsons, Francis
Robinson, John Trumbull
Roby, Joseph
Rogers, Derby
Wallis, Alexander Hamilton

1894

Case, George Bowen
Cochran, Thomas
Davies, Thomas Frederick
Hall, John Loomer
Hare, Meredith
Holter, Edwin Olaf
Howland, John
James, Robert Campbell
McMillan, Philip Hamilton
Paine, Ralph Delahaye
Stewart, Walter Eugene Jr.
Stillman, Leland Stanford
Walcott, William Stuart
Whitney, Harry Payne
Word, Charles Francis

1895

Beard, Anson McCook
Buckner, Mortimer Norton
Butterworth, Frank Seiler
Cable, Benjamin Stickney
Carter, Walter Frederick
Clark, Alexander Ray
Cooke, Walter Evans
Davis, Benjamin
Denison, Lindsay
Harrison, Francis Burton
Hinkey, Frank Augustus
McKee, Lanier
Phelps, Zira Bennett
Shepley, Arthur Behn
Sloane, William

1896

Beard, William Mossgrove
Brown, Alexander
Cheney, Ward
Cross, William Redmond
DeSibour, Jules Henri
Griggs, Maitland Fuller
McKee, McKee Dunn
Neale, James Brown
Smith, Winthrop Davenport
Stokes, Anson Phelps
Thorne, Samuel
Thorne, Samuel Brinckeroff
Treadway, Ralph Bishop
Trudeau, Edward L. Jr.
Weyerhaeuser, Frederick E.

1897

Bailey, Philip Horton
Brooke, George Clymer
Coffin, Henry Sloane
Fincke, Clarence Mann
Garrison, Elisha Ely
Gerard, Sumner
Gillette, Curtenius
Kerr, Albert Boardman
Kitchel, Cornelius Porter
Pinchot, Amos Richards Eno
Sage, Dean
Smyth, Nathan Ayer
Sumner, Graham
Wheelwright, Joseph Storer
Williams, Norman Alton

1898

Cheney, Clifford Dudley
Fearey, Morton Lazell
Gallaudet, Herbert Draper
Hale, Eugene Jr.
Hinsdale, Frank Gilbert
Kernochan, Frederic
Lord, Franklin Atkins
Montgomery, Grenville D.
Parker, Grenville
Rogers, David Francis
Simmons, Frank Hunter
Wadsworth, James Wolcott Jr.
Whitney, Payne
Wickes, Forsyth
Wright, Henry Burt

1899

Adams, Mason Tyler
Ames, Sullivan Dobb
Bowles, Henry Thornton
Brooke, Frederick Hiester
Brown, Jamot
Callahan, Hugh Andrew
Day, Dwight Huntington
Griswold, William Edward S.
Maffitt, Thomas Skinner
Magee, James McDevitt
Preston, Ord
Sweet, Carroll Fuller
Vanderbilt, Alfred Gwynne
Welles, Charles Hopkins Jr.
Whitehouse, William F.

1900

Adams, Frederick Baldwin
Allen, Frederick Winthrop
Camp, Stuart Brown
Cheney, Frank Dexter
Coffin, William Sloane
Cross, John Walter
Douglas, Malcolm
Greenway, James Cowan
Hopkins, John Morgan
Leavitt, Ashley
Lyon, George Armstrong
Paddock, Brace Whitman
Rockefeller, Percy Avery
Sullivan, Corlis Esmonde
Taft, Hulbert

1901

Allen, Arthur Dwight
Carlisle, James Mandeville
Cheney, Philip
Cheney, Thomas Langdon
Christian, Henry Hall
Coy, Sherman Lockwood
Edwards, Richard Henry
Eels, John Shepard
Hixon, Robert
Hoysradt, J Warren
Keppelman, John Arthur
Morris, Ray
Richardson, Allan Harvey
Welch, George Arnold
Wright, Alfred Parks

1902

Carpenter, George Boone
Cressler, Alfred Miller
Cushing, Charles Cyprian S.
Day, William Edwards
Ferguson, Alfred Ludlow
Guernsey, Raymond Gano
Potter, Roderick
Rumsey, Bronson Case
Sincerbeaux, Frank Huestis
Stebbins, Edwin Allen
Stone, Harold
Swan, Joseph Rockwell
Taylor, Alan McLean
Trowbridge, Mason
White, Percy Gardiner

1903

Chadwick, George Brewster
Clark, Harold Terry
Corning, Erastus
Dreisbach, John Martin
Hamlin, Chauncey Jerome
Hewitt, Brower
Holt, Henry Chandler
Lamb, Albert Richard
Moore, Frank Wood
Sutphin, Stuart Bruen
Thompson, Donald
Wallace, Henry Mitchell
Waring, Antonio Johnston
White, John Richards
Wilhelmi, Frederick William

1904

Adams, Charles Edward
Adams, George Webster
Cheney, Russell
Crane, Winthrop Murray
Cross, Walter Snell
Dodge, Francis Talmage
Jennings, Percy Hall
Kittle, John Caspar
Metcalf, Harold Grant
Miller, James Ely
Pierce, Frederick Erastus
Reed, Lansing Parmalee
Soper, Willard Burr
Thacher, Thomas Day
Wiggin, Fredrick Holme

1905
Bradford, Arthur Howe
Ellsworth, John Stoughton
Fish, Stuyvesant
Hogan, James Joseph
Hollister, Buell
Hughes, Berrien
Lathrop, John Hiram
Richardson, Gardner
Rogers, Edmund Pendleton
Sargent, Murray
Sloane, John
Tilney, Robert Fingland II
Turner, Harold McLeod
Van Reypen, William K. Jr.
Whitehouse, Edwin Sheldon

1906
Bruce, Donald
Dousman, Louis deVierville
Ely, Grosvenor
Flinn, Alexander Rex
Hoyt, Lydig
Magee, John Gillespie
McClure, James Gore K. Jr.,
McGee, Donald Ashbrook
Moorhead, William Singer
O'Brien, Frank
Perrin, Lee James
Rockwell, Foster Harry
Smith, Bruce Donald
Turner, Spencer
Wilson, Hugh Robert

1907
Barnes, William Deluce
Blair, William McCormick
Camp, Arthur Goodwin
Daniels, Forest Leonard
Danielson, Richard Ely
Dixon, Theodore Polhemus
Dodge, Philip Lyndon
Glaenzer, Georges Brette
Knox, Hugh Smith
Little, Mitchell Stuart
Morse, Samuel Finley Brown
Truesdale, Calvin
Tuttle, George Coolidge
Wells, Harold Sherman
Woolsey, Heathcote Muirson

1908
Biglow, Lucius Horatio
Dahl, George
Davis, Walter Goodwin
Dines, Tyson
Foster, Joseph Taylor
Griswold, Dwight Torrey
Perrin, Lester William
Seymour, Charles
Shepard, Roger Bulkley
Stanley, Harold
Thornton, James Carlton
Townsend, George Henry
Townsend, James Mulford Jr
Watkins, Charles Law
Williams, James Willard

1909
Bundy, Harvey Hollister
Burch, Robert Boyd
Campbell, Charles Soutter
Clark, Avery Artison
Dominick, Gayer Gardner
Howard, James Merriam
Howe, Henry Almy
Jefferson, Edward Francis
Klots, Allen Trafford
Lippitt, Henry
Perrin, John Bates
Rand, Stuart Craig
Sanderson, Benjamin Blethen
Seabury, Mortimer Ashmfad
Stokes, Harold Phelps

1910
Bayne-Jones, Stanhope
Coy, Edward Harris
DeSilver, Albert
Franchot, Charles Pascal
French, Robert Dudley
Harrison, George Leslie
Heron, John
King, Lyndon Marrs
Knight, Augustus
Logan, Walter Seth
Lohmann, Carl Albert
Murphy, Frederick James
Philbin, Stephen H II
Taft, Robert Alphonso
Wodell, Ruthven Adriance

1911
Badger, Paul Bradford
Corey, Alan Lyle
Daly, Frederick Joseph
Davis, Clinton Wildes
Day, Sherwood Sunderland
Dempsey, John Bourne
Gammell, Arthur Amory
Hyde, Frederick Walton
Lombardi, Cornelius Ennis
McDonnell, John Vincent
Randolph, Francis Fitz
Rowland, John Tilghman
Soule, Leslie
Van Sinderen, Henry B.
Wheeler, Lawrence Raymond

1912
Boyd, Francis T
Gardner, Robert Abbe
Hartley, Cavour
Howe, Arthur
Hyde, Donald Robertson
McClure, Archibald
Merritt, Henry Newton
Mullins, Frederic Parsons
Murphy, Gerald Clery
Paul, Charles Henry
Smith, James Gregory
Street, Henry Abbott
Strout, Edwin Augustus Jr.
Tener, Alexander Campbell
Twombly, Edward Bancroft

1913
Allen, Calvin Durand
Allen, Clarence Emir Jr.
Baker, Richard Wheeler
Colgate, Henry Auchincloss
Cortelyou, George Bruce
Cowles, Alfred
Harman, Archer
Harriman, William Averell
Lovett, August Sidney
McAndrew, Alexander
Philbin, Jesse Holladay
Sawyer, Homer Eugene Jr.
Schwab, Laurence vonPost
Shelden, Allan
Waters, William Otis

1914
Avery, Benjamin F.
Cornish, Percy Gillette Jr.
Daniels, Thomas Leonard
Gile, Clement Moses
Hobson, Henry Wise
Jenks, Almet Francis
Jones, George Gill
Ketcham, Henry Holman
King, Stoddard
Lippincott, William Jackson
Osborn, Richard
Patterson, George Washington
Rogers, Herman Livingston
Shepard, Lorrin Andrews
Warren, William Candee Jr.

1915
Burtt, Edwin Arthur
Carter, Lyon
Cornell, Thomas Hilary
Davenport, Stephen Rintoul
Denegre, Thomas Bayne
MacDonald, Ranald Hugh II
MacLeish, Archibald
Middlebrook, Louis Shelton
Paris, Irving
Pumpelly, Harold Armstrong
Reilly, John Sylvester
Shedden, William Martindale
Slocum, Edwin Lyon
Stackpole, Edward James
Swift, Walker Ely

1916
Darling, Arthur Burr
Gaillard, Samuel Gourdin Jr.
Hadley, Morris
Johnstone, Henry Webb
Knapp, Farwell
Oler, Wesley Mardon
Porter, Gilbert Edwin III
Putnam, Phelps
Roberts, Charles Holmes Jr.
Shepard, Donald Carrington
Stewart, Donald Ogden
Tener, Kinley John
Tighe, Laurence Gotzian
von Holt, Herman Vademar
Walker, Charles Rumford

1917
Bellinger, Alfred Rammond
Bush, Prescott Sheldon
Cooper, Henry Sage Fenimore
Cunningham, Oliver Bulg
Duryee, Samuel Sloan
Harriman, Edward Roland N.
Isham, Henry Porter
James, Ellery Sedgewick
LeGore, Harry William
Mallon, Henry Neil
Olsen, Albert William
Overton, John Williams
Shepard, Frank Parsons Jr.
Simpson, Kenneth Farrand
Woolley, Knight

1918
Ames, Allen Wallace
Baldridge, Howard Malcolm
Clay, Cassius Marcellus
Davison, Fredrick Trubee
Deans, Robert Barr
Farrar, John Chipman
Garfield, Newell
Gates, Artemus Lamb
Gould, James
Lovett, Robert Abercrombie
Snell, Raymond Franklin
Stewart, Charles Jacob
Taft, Charles Phelps
Vorys, John Martin
Woolley, John Eliot

1919
Allen, Parker Breese
Baldwin, Sherman
Campbell, Alan Barnette
Carter, Frederic Dewhurst
Depew, Ganson Goodyear
Gaillard, Edward McCrady
Hadley, Hamilton
Haffner, Charles Christian Jr.
Mallon, John Howard
McCormick, Alexander A. Jr.
McKee, Elmore McNeill
Mead, Winter
Otis, James Sanford
Smith, Traver
Walker, George Nesmith

1920
Adams, Lewis G.
Davison, Harry Pomeroy
Hadden, Briton
Heffelfinger, Frank Peavey
Hincks, John Morris
Hobson, Francis Thayer
Ingalls, David Sinton
Luce, Henry Robinson
McHenry, James
Patterson, Morehead
Safford, Theodore Lee
Sargent, Joseph Weir
Schermerhorn, Alfred Cosler
Van Slyck, DeForest
Winter, Daniel Robbins

1921
Acosta, John Sidney
Bradley, Charles Harvey
Brewster, Walter Rice
Bundy, Frederick McGeorge
Cowles, William Sheffield
Heminway, Bartow Lewis
Hord, Stephen Young
Jenckes, Marcien
Litt, Willard David
Lunt, Storer Boardman
Neville, James Eugene
Parsons, Langdon
Shevlin, Edward Leonard
Stewart, John
Winter, Edwin Wheeler II

1922
Aldrich, Malcolm Pratt
Bush, James Smith
Cheney, Ward
Crosby, Albert Hastings
Frost, Albert Carl, Jr.
Hilles, Frederick Whiley
Larner, Robert Johnson
Lord, William Galey
Page, Robert Guthrie
Root, Wells
Solley, Robert Folger
Strong, Henry Barnard
Thomas, John Allen Miner
Townsend, Frederic deP. Jr.
Woodward, Stanley

1923
Becket, George Campbell
Bulkey, Jonathan Ogden
Cooper, John Sherman
Davenport, Russell Wheeler
Day, Huntington Townsend
Foster, Maxwell Evarts
Hyde, Louis Kepler Jr.
Jones, Edwin A
Jordan, Ralph Edward
Luckey, Charles Pinckney
Matthessen, Francis Otto
Norton, George W. Jr.
Pelly, Bernard Berenger
Tighe, Richard Lodge
Wheeler, Alfred Newton

1924
Allen, Henry Elisha
Appel, George Frederick Baer
Blair, Edwin Foster
Diller, John Cabot
Ewing, Sherman
Haines, Thomas Frederick D.
Heffelfinger, George Wright P.
Hilles, Charles Dewey Jr.
Houghton, Walter Edwards
Lusk, William Thompson
Mallory, William Neely
McCallum, Revell
Melton, William Davis Jr.
Spofford, Charles Merville
Thomson, Clifton Samuel

1925
Ardrey, Rushton Leigh
Ashburn, Frank Davis
Bench, Edward Cajetan
Bissell, William Truesdale
Blair, James Grant
Gage, Charles Stafford
Ives, Gerard Merrick
Jones, Walter Clyde
Lovejoy, Winslow Meston
Lufkin, Elgood Moulton
Luman, Richard John
Norton, William Bunnell
Scott, Henry Clarkson
Stevens, Marvin Allen
Stevenson, Donald Day

1926
Allen, Daniel
Bronson, James Davis
Coke, Henry Cornice Jr.
Crosby, Henry Stetson
Cutler, Benjamin Crawford
Davenport, John
Ferguson, Alfred L. Jr.
Hoysradt, John McArthur
Kingsbury, Howard Thayer
Lord, Oswald Bates
Michel, Anthony Lee
Poore, Charles Graydon
Root, Reginald Dean
Russell, Frank Ford
Willard, Charles Hastings

1927
Bunnell, Phil W.
Look, Allen MacMartin
McIntosh, Harris
Noble, Lawrence Mason
Patterson, Thomas Cleveland
Post, Russell Lee
Ritchie, Wallace Parks
Robbins, William Wells
Robinson, Frederick Flower
Stokes, Anson Phelps Jr.
Wadsworth, James Jeremiah
Walker, George Herbert Jr.
Wardwell, Edward Rogers
Warren, John Davock
Watson, Charles 3rd

1928
Bartholomew, Dana Treat
Berger, Jr., George Bart
Bingham, Charles Tiffany
Fishwick, Dwight Brown
Griggs, Herbert Stanton Jr.
Haight, George Winthrop
Ives, Chauncey Bradley
Lapham, Raymond White
Mallory, Barton Lee Jr.
Prentice, John Rockefeller
Robertson, Arthur C.
Ross, "Lanny" Lancelot P.
Scott, Stewart Patterson
Stewart, Peter Hellwege
Walker, Stoughton

1929
Ashforth, Albert Blackhurst
Costikyan, Granger Kent
Crile, George Jr.
Decker, Edmund L. Jr.
Dodge, Washington
Eddy, Maxon Hunter
Garvey, John Joseph
Gillespie, Kenrick Samson
Grove, Manasses Jacob
Manville, Hiram Edward Jr.
Merrill, Henry Riddle
Paine, Ralph Delahaye Jr.
Smith, Lloyd Hilton
Wack, Damon deBlois
Wells, George

1930
Allison, Robert Seaman Jr.
Ellis, Harland Montgomery
Ellis, Raymond Walleser
Erskine, Albert DeW. Jr.
Garnsey, Walter Wood
Greene, Waldo Wittenmyer
Gwin, Samuel Lawrence
Hall, Robert Andrew
Janeway, Charles Anderson
Ladd, Louis Williams Jr.
Longstreth, George Brown
Look, Frank Byron
Musser, John Miller
Palmer, Arthur Edward
Prideaux, Tom

1931
Austen, David Edward
Donnelley, Gaylord
Heinz, Henry John II
Lapham, Lewis Abbot
Loeser, Frederic William
Lydgate, William A.
Messimer, Robert Laughlin Jr.
Peltz, William Learned
Rathborne, Joseph Cornelius
Stewart, James Ross
Sutherland, Richard Orlin
Swoope, Walter Moore
Tucker, Luther B.D.
Vincent, Francis Thomas
Walker, John Mercer

1932
Adams, Frederic Baldwin Jr.
Barres, Herster D.
Bates, Emmert Warren
Fitch, George Hopper
Fulton, Robert Brank
Gillespie, Samuel Hazard Jr.
Hodges, William VanD. Jr.
Laundon, Mortimer H. Jr.
Lindenberg, John Townsend
McCrary, John Reagan Jr.
Mills, James Paul
Ogden, Alfred
O'Neill, Eugene Gladstone, Jr
Savage, Boutelle Jr.
Williams, Samuel Goode

1933
Caldwell, Samuel Smith Jr.
Cooke, Francis Judd
Davis, Richard Marden
Fletcher, Alexander Charles
Garnsey, William Smith
Hall, Frederick Bagby Jr.
Jones, Theodore Stephen
Levering, Walter Barnum
Lindley, Frances Vinton
McGauley, John Michael
Newton, James Quigg Jr.
Parker, Robert Boyd
Parsons, Henry McIlvaine
Stebbins, Hart Lyman
Wilbur, John Smith

1934
Bradford, Amory Howe
Cunningham, Hugh Terry
Gordon, George Arthur
Hallett, John Folsom
Hambleton, Thomas Edward
Harper, Harry Halsted Jr.
Holmes, John Grier
Jackson, John Herrick
Kilcullen, John MacHale
Kimball, Walter Sugden
Mills, Edward Ensign
Morse, John Bolt
Nichols, Edward
Ranney, George Alfred
Stetson, Eugene William Jr.

1935
Bowles, John Eliot
Collier, Samuel (Sam) Carnes
Curtin, Francis Clare
Fuller, Stanley Evert
Haas, Frederick Peter
Johnson, Joseph(Joe) Hale
Kilborne, William Skinner
Pillsbury, John Sargent Jr.
Rodd, Thomas
Seymour, Charles Jr.
Shepard, Roger Bulkley Jr.
Spitzer, Lyman B. Jr.
Stillman, George Schley
Terry, Henry Porter Baldwin
Tufts, Bowen (Sonny) C.

1936
Barr, Richard James Jr.
Bingham, Jonathan Brewster
Cooke, Robert Barbour
Davis, Horace Webber II
Gill, Brendan
Hall, Jesse Angell
Hersey, John Richard
Knapp, John Merrill
Moore, Richard Anthony
Pillsbury, Edmund P.
Rankin, Bernard Courtney
Shepard, Blake
Train, Robert
Walker, Louis
Whitehead, Mather Kimbal

1937
Blake, Dexter B.
Brooke, Frederic Hiester Jr.
Burke, Charles Clinton Jr.
Cross, Richard James
Draper, Arthur Joy
Field, John Warner
Kelley, Lawernce Morgan
McLemore, John Briggs Jr.
Miles, Richard Curtis
Orrick, William Horsley Jr.
Robinson, John Trumbull
Runnalls, John Felch Bertram
Stewart, Potter.
Stone, Louis Talcott Jr.
Turner, Harold McLeod

1938
Davenport, Bradfute Warwick
Dempsey, James Howard Jr.
Dilworth, Joseph Richardson
Dunham, Lawrence B. Jr.
Ecklund, John Edwin
Fox, Joseph Carrere
Frank, Clinton E.
Gordon, Edward McGuire
Hessberg, Albert II
Schermerhorn, Amos Egmont
Stevens, Joseph Benson Jr.
Thompson, John R.
Weed, George Haines
Whitman, Francis Slingluff Jr.
Wilbur, Richard Emery

1939
Belin, Gaspard d'Andelot
Blanchard Jerred Gurley
Bundy, William Putman
Chittenden, George Hastings
Clucas, Lowell Melcher
Dyess, Arthur Delma Jr.
Gile, Clement Dexter
Hoxton, Archibald R. Jr.
Kellogg, William Welch
Miller, Andrew Otterson
Miller, Charles Lewis Jr.
Mitchell, Harry Hartwood
Shepard, Jr., Lloyd M.
Wilhelmi, Frederick W. Jr.
Williams, Burch

1940
Bundy, McGeorge
Erickson, Thomas Franklin
Glover, Charles Carroll III
Grayson, James Gordon
Holden, Reuben Andrus
Howe, Harold II
Orrick, Andrew Downey
Rodd, David Beckwith
Stack, Jr., Joseph William
Stevens, Albert B.
Stillman, Peter Gordon B.
Stucky, William McDowell
Swenson, Edward Francis Jr.
Thorne, Peter Brinckerhoff
Watson, Jr., William Berkley

1941
Cross, Walter Redmond Jr.
Devor, Donald S. Jr.
Ellis, Franklin Henry Jr.
Hall, Edward Tuck
Jackson, William Eldred
Kiphuth, Delaney
Madden, John Beckwith
Pickett, Lawrence Kimball
Price, Charles Baird Jr.
Solbert, Peter O.A.
Stevenson, Charles Porter
Thomas, Walton Dowdell
Tighe, Laurence Gotzian Jr.
White, Warren Benton
Zorthian, Barry

1942
Aycrigg, William Anderson II
Bartholemy, Alan Edmund
Bell, William Tompkins
Chouteau, Rene Auguste
Ford, William
Grayson, Cary Travers, Jr.
Halsey, Ralph Wetmore Jr.
Harrison, Fred Harold
Jessup, John Baker
Kemp, Frank Alexander
Kirchwey, George Washington
Smith, Howard Freeman Jr.
Sprole, Frank Arnoit
Walker, John Stanley
White, William Gardiner

1943
Acheson, David Campion
Caulkins, George Peck
Daniels, John Hancok
Doolittle, Duncan Hunter
Drain, Richard Dale
Healy, Harold Harris Jr.
Hoagland, Donald Wright
Klots, Allen Trafford Jr.
Liley, Frank Walder Jr.
MacLean, John Helm
Miller, Dudley Livingston
Moseley, Spencer Dumaresq
Stewart, Zeph
Tabor, John Kaye
Vogt, Tom D.

1944
Brown, Samuel Taylor Glover
Buckley, James Lane
Elebash, Shehand Daniel
Ellis, Alexander Jr.
Ferguson, James Lord
Goodenough, John Bannister
Grayson, William Cabell
Holden, John Morgan
Hoopes, Townsend Walter
Kelley, William Cody II
Lindsay, David Alexander
Little, Stuart West
Walker, Jeffrey Pond
Whitmore, James Allen Jr.
Witter, Dean Jr.

1945
Allen, Archibald John Jr.
Blake, Gilman Dorr Jr.
Connick, Louis Jr.
Dale, Edwin Lyon Jr.
Davison, Endicott Peabody
Early, Hobart Evans
Elwell, Francis Bolton Jr.
Harman, Archer Jr.
Lynch, Russell Vincent
McElroy, Benjamin Thomas
McGaughey, Guy Ennis Jr.
Moorhead, William Singer Jr.
Seaman, Irving Jr.
Spaulding, Josiah Augustus
Sumner, William Sayre

1945W
Brown, Walter Henderson
Carey, John
Finney, J.John Warren
Holmes, George Burgwin
Hurlbut, Gordon Buckland Jr.
Mallon, Thomas Ridgway
O'Brien, Phillip Jr.
Twichell, Charles Pratt
Vose, Elliot Evans
Warren, George Upson

1947
Alling, Charles Booth Jr.
Andrews, Edward W.Jr.
Boulos (Bouliaratis), W. M.
Bronson, David Bennet
Chafee, John Hubbard
Finley, John George Gilpin
Goedecke, William Skinner
Leavenworth, Donald Loyal
Moore, James I.
O'Brien, Frank Jr.
Palmer, Charles Edgar
Read, Richard Rollins
Robinson, Howard C.Jr.
Tucker, Carl Jr.
Whitehouse, Charles Sheldon

1948
Ashley, Thomas William L.
Biglow, Lucius Horatio Jr.
Bush, George Herbert Walker
Caulkins, John Ervin
Clark, William Judkins
Connelly, William James Jr.
Cook, George III
Grimes, David Charles
Jenkins, Richard Elwood
Mack, Richard Gesrtle
Moseley, Thomas Wilder
Pfau, George Harold Jr.
Walker, Samuel Sloan Jr.
Weaver, Howard Sayer
Wilkie, Valleau Jr.

1949
Baribault, Richard Pfeifer
Bassett, Barton Bradley II
Coffin, William S. Jr.
Davison, Daniel Pomeroy
Goodyear, Robert M.
Hollister, John Baker Jr.
Lavelli, Anthony Jr.
Leiper, Joseph McCarrell II
Lippincott, David McCord
Lord, Charles Edwin II
Lufkin, Sr., Peter Wende
Raymond, George T. Perkins
Sherrill, Franklin Goldwaithe
Van Dine, Vance
Wickwire, Winthrop Ross

1950
Breen, John Gerald
Buckley, William Frank Jr.
Draper, William Henry III
Frank, Jr., Victor Harry
Galbraith, Evan Griffith
Guinzburg, Thomas Henry
Henningsen, Victor W. Jr.
Kemp, Philip Sperry
Lambert, Paul Christopher
Lovett, Sidney
Luckey, Charles Pinckney
MacLeish, William Hitchcock
McLean, Robert III
Pionzio, Dino John
Shepard, Donald C. Jr.

1951
Anderson, Thomas Hill
Eden, John W.
Ellis, Garrison McClintock N.
Ellis, George Corson Jr.
Love, Ralph Frank
Lufkin, Chauncey Forbush
Mathews, Craig
Mayer, Charles Theodore
McNamara, Thomas Philip
Price, Raymond Kissam Jr.
Reid, Edward Snover III
Ross, Thomas Bernard
Russell, Richard Warren
Ryan, Joseph Mather
Shepard, Charles Robinson S.

1952
Aberg, Donlan Vincent Jr.
Buckley, Fergus Reid
Claude, Abram Jr.
Connick, Andrew Jackson
Cruikshank, Paul F. Jr.
Eisler, Colin Tobias
Finney, Graham Stanley
Haight, Charles Seymour Jr.
Hincks, John Winslow
Kittredge, Frank Dutton
Roberts, George Brooke Jr.
Senay, Edward Charles
Spears, Robert Samuel
Steadman, John Montague
Vorys, Martin West

1953

Bulkey, Jonathan Duncan
Bush, Jonathan James
Donaldson, William Henry
Durham Edwin A. II
Emerson, Christy Payne
Lufkin, Dan Wende
Marshall, John Birnie
McLane, James Price
Menton, John Dennis
Mitinger, Joseph Berry
Noble, Lawerence Mason Jr.
Novkov, David Arthur
Walker, George Herbert III
Weber, John William
Woodsum, Harold Edward Jr.

1954

Benninghoff, Harry Bryner
Evans, Tilgham Boyd
Fortunato, S. Joseph
Giesen, Arthur Rossa, Jr.
Gifford, Richard Cammann
Hiers, Richard Hyde
Kilrea, Walter Charles
Meyer, Russell William Jr.
Morton, Thruston Ballard Jr.
Polich, Richard Frank
Price, Ross Edward
Reponen, Robert Gordon
Ryan, Allan A III
Schnaitter, Spencer Jason
Thornton, Edmund Braxton

1955

Bryan, Lloyd Thomas Jr.,
DeForest, Stephen Elliott
Fehr, Gerald F.
Gow, Richard Haigh
Green, Charles Grady
Guidotti, Hugh George Jr.
Hansen, Roger Allen
Hudson, Franklin Donald
Johanson, Stanley Morris
Mathias, Philip Hoffman II
McCullough, David Gaub
Searles, Paul David
Shugart, Thorne Martin
Steadman, Richard Cooke
Walker, Ray Carter

1956

Banks, Howard Daniel
Boasberg III, James Emanuel
D'Avanzo, Louis A.
Dempsey, Andrew Squire
Durfee, Charles Gibson Jr.
Esselstyn, Caldwell B.Jr.
Gaines, Milton John
Ingalls, David Sinton Jr.
Jamieson, Thomas C. Jr.
Malloy, Terrence Reed
McGregor, Jack Edwin
Menton, James Paul
Orr, Andrew Alexander
Speed, James Breckinridge
Traphagen, Peter Abraham

1957

Ackerman, Stephen Harry
Bowman, Ralph David
Carlsen, Ray Allen
Clark, Russell Inslee Jr.
Cushman, Charles W.
Dunn, George J.
Fritzche, Peter B.
Loucks, Vernon Reece Jr.,
Loughran, Anthony Hookey
Lumpkin, Richard Anthony
Owseichik, John Philip
Palmer, Lindley Guy II
Ritchie, Wallace Parks Jr.
Somerville, John Wheeler
Williams, William Bruce

1958

Allen, Charles Edward
Blue, Linden Stanley
Cassel, John A.
Chency, Ronald Lawton
Cushman, Robert Edgar Jr.
Embersits, John Frank
Howe, Gary Woodson
Morey, Robert Willis Jr.
Pendexter, John Fowler
Phelan, Howard Taylor
Post, Russell Lee Jr.
Preston, John Louis
Shackelford, Robert Campbell
Van Antwerp, William M. Jr
Wheeler, Thomas Beardsley

1959

Adams, Stephen
Bodman, William Camp
Connors, James Joseph III
Cooke, John Parick
Ercklentz, Alexander Tonio
Esselstyn, Erik Canfield
Hemphill, James Tierney
Holbrook, John Jr.
Kingsley, Charles Capen
Lightfoot, Richard Bissett
Lord, Winston
Mayor, Michael Brook
Sheffield, James Rockwell
Thorson, Peter Andreas
Tyler, Cheever

1960

Ball, David George
Beane, Frank Eastman Jr.
Capron, Paul III
Dominick, David DeWitt
Ernst, Frederick Vincent
Garnsey, William Herrick
Giegengack, Robert Francis Jr.
Holbrook, David Doubleday
Lindgren, Richard Hugo
Lusk, Peter Anthony
McCarthy, Charles Edward
Meek, John Burgess
Northrop, Robert Smitter
Scott, Eugene Lytton
Smith, Bruce Donald III

1961

Bissell, George Thomas
Bockrath, Richard Charles Jr.
Bowles, William Carter Jr.
Clark, Thomas Whitton
Cogswell, John Marshall
DeNeufville, John Phillip
Hamlin, Charles B.
Lindsay, Dale Alton Jr.
MacLean, Kenneth Jr.
Pyle, Michael Johnson
Seeley, George Wheeler
Singleton, Thomas Hall
Stewart, James Corb
Waddel, Geoffrey Hamilton
Walsh, John Joseph Jr.

1962

Back, Samuel Hutchins
Brandt, John Henry
Brewster, James Henry IV
Brooks, Tristam Anthony
Burr, Charles Bentley II
Childs, Henry Clay
Chimenti, Norman Victor
Hamilton, William
Holland, Henry Thompson
LeFevre, Ronald Eaton
Ligon, Thomas B.
Peck, Arthur John Jr.
Spitz, Robert Wayne
Terry, Wyllys III
Zucker, Bernard Benjamin

1963

Ahlbrandt, Roger S. Jr.
Becket, Peter Logan
Borne, Senator David Lyle
Clay, Jesse Loring
Frank Charles Augustus III
Gill, Michael Gates
Gwin, Samuel Lawrence Jr.
Hewitt, Henry Hollis
Jones, Theodore Stephen
Marsh, William Lee
Moser, Richard Eugene
Nordhaus, William Dawbney
O'Connell, Timothy James
Rose, Jonathan Chapman
Rulon-Miller, Patrick

1964

Best, Geoffry Donald Charles
Cirie, John Arthur
Clay, Alexander Stephens
Francis, Samuel Hopkins
Gillette, Howard Frank Jr.
Kaminsky, Robert Isadore
Lynch, Dennis Patrick
McBride, Jonathan Evans
Prindle, Thomas Harrison
Pulaski, Charles Alexander Jr.
Rowe, Thomas D. Jr.
Straw, Ralph Lynwood
Van Loan, Eugene
Wilbur, John Smith Jr.
Wolfe, Stephen II

— 293 —

1965

Ali, Mehdi Raza
Benoit, Charles Edward Jr.
Clark, Gerald Holland
Clark, Stephen Edward
Clay, Timothy J.
Coombs, Orde Musgrave
Corey, Alan Lyle III
Desjardins, Peter Earl
Fetne, Philip Jay
Lagercrantz, Bengt Magnus
Pinney, John Mercer
Pond, Jeffrey Craig
Quarles, James Perrin III
Shattuck, HF John III
Zallinger, Peter Franz

1966

Bockstoce, John R.
Bradford, Timothy McFall
Brown, George Clifford
Cross, Alan Whitmore
Dalby, Michael Thomas
Howard, James Ernest
Kerry, John Forbes
Laidley, Forrest David
Pershing, Richard Warren
Rumsey, David McIver
Singer, Ronald Leonard
Smith, Frederick Wallace
Stanberry, William Burks Jr.
Thorne, David Hoadley
Vargish, Thomas

1967

Afeoju, Bernard Ikecukwu
Ashe, Victor Henderson
Bush, Derek George
Foster, David John
Garnsey, Walter W., Jr.
Lilley, Robert McGregor
Miller, James Whipple
Mitchell, H. Coleman Jr.
Neighe, Geoffrey Mark
Preston, James Marshall
Richards, Davi Alan
Saxon, James M
Snell, Bradford Curie
Swil, Roy Anthony
Thompson, Stepehn Eberly Jr.

1968

Austin, Roy Lesley
Birge, Robert Richards
Brown, Christopher Walworth
Bush, George Walker
Cohen, Kenneth Saul
Cowdry, Rex William
Etra, Donald.
Gallico, G.Gregory III
Guthri, Robert Karle III
Kolar, Bruton Ward (Britt)
McCallumx, Robert Davis Jr.
Saleh, Muhammad Ahmed
Schmidt, Thomas Carl
Schollander, Donald Arthur
Thorne, Brinkley Stimpson

1969

Arras, Robert Edward Jr.
Bouscaren, Michael Frederic
Buck, Charles Henry III
Cosgrove, Thomas Francis Jr.
Demares, Frank Edward II
Dowling, Brian J.
Fuller, Henry W.
Livingston Ii, Richard H.B.
Madden, Bernard Patrick
Miller, Wentworth Earl
O'Leary, John Joseph Jr.
Schwarzman, Stephen Allen.
Selander, Duane Arthur
Thompson, William McI. Jr.
Woodlock, Douglas Preston

1970

Brown, William Scott
Case, Philip Benham Jr.
Downing, Earl S. III
Eyre, Lawrence L.
Friedland, Johnathan David
Greenberg, Stephen David
Hodes, Douglas Michael
Jackson, Terrence John
Miller, Thomas Clairborne
Morgan, Robert McNair
Ohene-Frempong, Kwaku
Peters, Daniel James
Scattergood, Thomas Bevan
Thompson, Jonathan Penfield
Trower, C. Christopher

1971

Babst, James Anthony
Bryan, James Taylor
Ekfelt, Richard (Dick) Henry
Feinerman, James Vincent
Fortgang, Jeffrey
Galvin, Michael Gerard
Halpin, Thomas Michael
Hernandez, Carols Arturo
Inman, Robert Davies
Johnson, Wilbur John Jr.
Kosturko, William Theodore
Levin, Charles Herbert
Morgan, James Wallace
Noyes, Edward MacArthur
Taft, Thomas Prindle

1972

Cangelosi, Russell Joseph
Clark, Douglas Wells
Csar, Michael F.
Evans, Peter Seelye
Fisher, Scott B.
Lewis, Mark Sanders
Lutz, Karl Evan
MacDonald, Richard J. II
McLaren, Michael Glenn
Moyer, Douglas Richard
Ritterbush, Stephen Grover Jr.
Sauber, Richard Alan
Walden, Robert Stewart
Wilson, Zebuon Vance
Ziegler, Stan Warren

1973*

Barasch, Alan Sidney
Bellis, Tedric Lawrence
Finney, C. Roger
Green, Benjamin P.
Highfill, Philip Henry III
Huey, Mark Christopher
Karageorge, James Louis
Liles, Coit Redfearn
Lonsdorf, David B.
MacDonald, Stephen Joseph
Mattlin, Fred Walter
McPhee, Stephen Joseph
Moore, David Clement
Scott, William Iain
Sulzer, James Sothern

1974*

Ayeroff, Frederick Charles
Barge, Richard Mason
Bellis, Jon Michael
Bisaro, Larry R.
Cohen, Robert Lewis
Connors, David Michael
Diamond, Peter C.
Doyle, Thomas James Jr.
Eisenberg, Bruce Alan
Gonzalez, Timoteo F.
Kelly, Brian Christopher
Lewis, George Emanuel
Murchison, Brian Cameron
Spear, Wesley John
Thorne, Charles H. McKinstry

1975*

Ashenfelter, Alan Thompson
Bender, Kenneth Arthur
Buckley, Christopher Taylor
Burke III, James Eugene
English, William Deshay Jr.
Gaines, Edwin Frank
Green, Rudolph
Kanehl, Phillip Edwin
MacKenzie, Kenneth Malcolm
Reigeluth, Douglas Scott
Saffen, David
Struzzi, Thomas Allen
Wald, Stephen George
Zorthian, Gregory Jannig

1976*

Blattner, Robert William
Brubaker, John Kim
Capozzalo, Douglas Daniel
Casscells, Christopher Dyson
Childs, Starling Winston
Davies, Philip Turner
Fort, Donald Kenneth
Gates, Edward Raymond
Gibson, Richard Channing Jr.
Hart, Dennis Charles
Leverett, Miles Watson
Mehta, Arjay Singh
Morgenstern, Marc Jaime
Oler, Clark Kimberly Jr.
Williams, Darryl L.

1977

Blakely, Marvin
Brubaker, James Robert
Cooper, Carnell
Fredericks, Joel Richard
Goldberg, Richard Julius
Grayson, William Cabell, Jr.
Kee, Christopher Andrew
Lalley, Patrick William
Lawler, Quentin John
Newman, Thomas M.
Perry, David Bulkey
Rimar, Stephen III
Schlesinger, Daniel Adam
Scott, Larry Glenn
Tom Chan Bruce III

1978

Albritton, Paul Berem
Baran, Mark R.
Bassi, Keith Alan
Clark, J. Bruce
Gile, Lawrence Maclester
Holmes, Peter Samuel
Hook, Noble
Karp, Benjamin C
Marinelli, David Leonard
Owens, Samuel I.
Piel, Geoffrey D.
Rizzo, Robert John
Roy, John Marcus
Sullivan, Charles S.
Turner, Elvin D.

1979

Brown, Robert Nelson
Edozien, Anthony O.
Fore, John Arthur
Holmbee, Jeffrey Arthur
Lorenson, David Harold
McNally, Edward E.
Moses, Jack Thomas
Nondorf, Kurt D.
O'Brien, Donald Patrick
Peters, Eric Brooks
Skrovan, Stephen Thomas
Stevenson, Charles P.
Westerfield, Richard H.
Wilson, Daniel Richard
Yent, James B. Jr.

1980

Austin, Samuel Monroe
Chibundu, Maxwell O.
Davenport, George Leovy
DeVore, Mark Samuel
Dilworth, George Toby
Fleming, Andrew T.
Hatem, John J.
Kagan, Robert William
Lawrence, Gary Martin
Mulhern, Daniel Kevin
Peters, Elliot Remsen
Stevens, Eric Eugene
Teig, Joseph Benjamin
Tumpane, Timothy Michael
Zigerelli, Lawrence John

1981*

Bullock, Stanton B.
Campbell, Kimberly C.
Carlsson, Mats Erik
Choa, Christopher James
Conway, Joseph Leo Jr.
Grandine, Thomas Allan
Novosel, David Gerard
O'Keefe, Regis James
Peters, Kenneth Graham
Peterson, Paul Clifford
Russell, Richard George
Staven, Karl Eric
Stratton, Daniel James
Tingey, Douglas Stuart
Troy, Alexander

1982*

Bass, James Edward
Breslau, Jonathan
Burkus, Gregory James
Campbell, Gavin Elliott
Devlin, Michael William
Leone, Frederick Anthony
McAfee, William Andrew
Meyers, Bryan Fitch
Murchison, Robert W.
Rachlin, David Isaiah
Reid, Jasper
Salzman, Mark Joseph
Sanhago, Eddie
Towers, Jonathan David
Wright, William Henry II
Yang, James Ting-Yeh

1983*

Abrams, Peter Mark
Brooks, Peter Moody
Cerveris, Michael Ernest
Franklin, Richard David
Gale, Frederick Scott
Kafoglis, Christian Nicholas
Kaushal, Shalesh
Montesano, Michael John III
Nichols, William Allen
Noel, Christopher
Pinela, Carlos
Sharp, Jonathan Douglas
Sheffield, John Van Loon
Wagner, Victor Edmond

1984*

Andrie, Paul James
Coggins, Daniel Seton
Crawley, Brian Scott
Davison, Henry Pomeroy
Graves, Earl Gilbert Jr.
Henston, Douglas Robert
Herskovits, David Nathaniel
Jung, Michael David
Kahle, Jeffrey Lewis
Lambert, Edward Scott
Litt, David Geoffrey
Skibell, Steven Alan
Urquijo, Conzalo
Weinstein, Adam
Wiseman, Stephen II

1985

Boasberg, James Emanuel
Carlin, William John Carr JR
Chandrasekhar, Ashok Jai
Frankel, Scott David
Grossman, Jay Alan
Kwok, Wei-Tai
Lindy, Peter Barnes
Misner, Timothy Charles
Mnu Chin Steven Terner
Petela, James Gerard
Powers, Richard Hart
Smock, Morgan Robert
Taft, Horace Dutton
Thomson, Gregory Allan
Walsh, Kevin Sanchez

1986

Boasberg, Thomas Alexander
Budill, Edward McRae
Chittenden, John Sisson
Crotty, Sean Patrick
Dodge, William Sickels
Gottheim, Joshua Chess
Havas, Steffan Thayer
Hilliard, Jeffrey
Kline, David Franklin
Meyer, Tory Austin
Quamina, Alvan Vincent George
Reeves, William Huntington
Schillinger, Edward Alexander
Strong, Thomas Joseph
Walton, Reginald Keith

1987

Cheeks, George Arthur
Dudley, Andrew Jenkins
Ewing, Dino Bartlett
Guettel, Adam Arthur
Jeffries, Christopher Warden
Keck, David Alderson
Loveyjoy, John Cooper
Millard, Hugh
Moscoso, Ricardo
Nguyen, Linh Cuu
Shapiro, Michael David
Sylvain, John Stanislaus Henry, II
Wheeler, Kenneth Edward
Wishnie, Michael Joel
Yoder, Paul Justin

1988

--
--
--
--
--
--
--
--
--
--
--
--
--
--
--

1989

Agha, Sohail
Alicea, Noel
Ashby, Arlan Marcus Caine
Cervepis, Todd Christopher
Cornwell, Michael James
Fisher, Whitney Charles
Giamatti, Paul Edwards Valentine
Haas, James Andrew
Korn, Daniel
Lawerence, Glover Harold
O'Brien, Edward Orestes
Puchtler, Joel Scobie
Ryan, Michael David
Walsh, Michael Francis
Williams, Derrick Maurice

1990

Abrams, Lawrence Dewyatt
Aibel, Matthew Benjamin
Allara, Willis Chapman
Arndt, Willis Chapman, Jr.
Cohen, Andrew Jay
Figueroa, Richard
Gajdusek, Karl Lawrence
Hajanal, Zoltan Lloyd
Liu, Eric P.
Milbank, Dana Timothy
Nondorf, James Gregory Robert
Pike, Stephen Langdon
Reed, Mark Armstead
Sellars, Reginald Bryant
Wertheim, John Vincent

1991

Alston, Jonathan Adriel
Battle, Marell Eston
Campbell, Cecil Dean Clarke
Delevett, Peter Christian, II
Estep. Bryon Stearns
Goolsbee, Austan Dean
Johnson, Terrell Gordon
Jones, Benjamin Silliman
Keaveney, Kevin Michael
Passoja, Erik Allen
Schwimmer, David Adam
Stracks, John Steven
Vasquez, Wilfredo
Webster, Douglas Clifford
Worth, John Harold

1992

Abdul, Makunda
Bernstein, Daniel Jeremy
Davis, Marco Antonio Enrique
Castaneda
Gitchell, Joseph Graham
Gray, David Edman
Kirchman, Dana
Kouri, Christopher Henry
O'Buachalla, Ciaran Padraig
Romain, Alex
Sharkey, Catherine Moira
So, Lilly Yang
Stanley, Elizabeth Ahylyn
Strain, Christian Raymond
x
x

1993

Boren, Carrie Christine
Colavito, Peter Nicholas
Gonzales, Oscar Reynaldo
Lehman, Ann Louise
Ngo, Karen Ka-Kei
Park, Chan
Peters, Gregory Kent
Pihl, Tina
Rothman, Adam
Ruff, Tayna Renee
Sheronas, David Anthony
Skidmore, Robert Riley
Taylor, Camilla Bronwen
Vishio, Eva Patrice
Whyte, Paul Andrew

1994

Breyer, Nell Beryl
Clark, Philip
Gilhool, Nicholas Kane
Grennan, Kate
Hess, Mignon Page
Lee, Simon Craddock
Leonhardt, David René
Lieberman, Aaron Oscar Lewis
Martinson, Haldan
Perry, Imani Nia Chiara
Rocha, Alina Merceds
Saunders, John Kenneth
Singley, M'Balia Kafi
Warnick, Angela Lee
Waterman, Shana Christie

1995

Dacosta, Michelle Marcia
Emerson, Geoffrey Guy
Grunstein, Yoav
Hadayia, Jennifer Marie
Joo, Sonya Yunee
Martin, Donald Washington
Martinez, Enrique
Mellish, Daniel Joseph
Nelson, Emily
Phan, Anh Ngoc
Poole, Yusef
Rivera, Aimee
Rosenbaum, Judith
Shiffman, Daniel Thomas
Wagner, Janna Marie

1996

Crane, Monica Kim
Flores, Israel
Guckenberger, Virginia Walker
Hahn, Albert Sanghyup
Jackson, Kwame Addae
Krishnamurthy, Preethi
Malvestutto, Carlos Diego
Mazurkiewicz, Tony
Norton, Nadjwa Effat Laila
Oda, Jonathan Francis Tadashi
Okpokwasili, Okwuchukwu Addania
Oppenheimer, Mark Edward
Pipersburgh, Denise Joan
Taylor, Clinton Watson
Weintraub, Rebecca Lynn

1997

Arputhasamy, Paula
Das, Sarba
Estrada, Francisco Javier
Farhadian, Tali Farimah
Johnston, Michael Christopher Cox
Klein, Jonathan Adam
Obioha, Nkechinyere Lovena
Park, Hyun
Reeder, Gary Lacy, II
Selzer, Robert Jackson
Shakman, Matthew Joseph
Sims, Patrick James
Sweet, David McIntyre
Whaley, Darcy Anne
Yoon, Jane

1998

Bain, Regina
Choo, Michael Youngjun
Feigelson, Joshua Meir
Fromm, Blanca Monica Nele
Gastic, Blue (Billie)
Gilbert, Laura Elaine
Herskovits, Adrianna Zara
Hunterton, Gaberiel Sargent
Hoo, Robert George
Knable, Miles Andrew
Kronman, Matthew Pattersom
Min, Hae-Won
Pan, Christopher
Wilson, Isaiah, II
Williams, Lorelei

1999

Abbot, Frances Reyburn (Frankie)
Auh, Eugene
Benton, Scott Richard
Eisenstadt, Leora F.
Falcon, Angel Luis, Jr.
Fromm, Juliette Erica
Gonzalez-Altamirano, Julio
Lee, Earl Andrew
McBride, Webster Dean
Medard, Wilodene Anastasia-Marie
Murphy, Maiya Jane
Petit, Charles J.
Raborar, Farrah Ann
Rashid, Tauheedah
Scott, Shannon

2000

Anderson, Dargie
Berrelez, Manuel
Blake, Benjamin
Borghese, Luca
Charles, Anana
Denit, Kelly
Heikkila, Jennifer
Hirway, Hrishikesh
Hongo, Andrew
Johnson, Ayanna
Kirowski, John
Lester, Sara
Mizrahi, Celine
Renan, Daphna
Walker, Christopher

2001*

Amaez, Daniel
Barret, Annie Rachel
Boone, Louvonia
Cavaco, Isaiah
Duncan, Mark MacKenzie
Gahan, Kimberly Ann
Harris, Melanie
Maserati, Sarah Anne
Mazza, Peter
Nam, Steve Taek
Popper, Lauren Jane
Proper, Scott Bradley
Reyes, Patrick
Sandy, Akobe
Slade David

2002*

Austin, Scott Alan
Bair, Caitlin
Banerjee, Bidisha
Bazzle, John Bradley
Gaughen, Patrick Robert
Goldsmith, William Dixon
Heilwig, Paige Lynn
Hudson, Jared McCabe
Im, Jaisohn
Jiminez, Carlos
Montgomery, Kenita Trenae
Montoya, Maceo
Penna, Timothy Rick
Premejee, Sharmeen Malik
Ruiz, Sara Elizabeth

2003*

Archibong, Ime
Cobbett, Ashley
Feins, Eric
Kelly, E. B.
Lange, Jason
Norris, Graham
Pearce, James
Schraufnagel, Billy
x
x
x
x
x
x
x

2004*

Almy, Chad
Ashraf, Sumeyya
Burke, James
Melniker, Sophie
So, Perry
Vitelli, Paul
x
x
x
x
x
x
x
x

2005*

Carr, Rob
Croffy, Ally
Fairbanks, Eve
Favors, Jeohn
Grimm, Dan
Morales, Derek
Ng, Derek
Schemmer, Katharine
Shamas, Raja
Shanor, Dicky
Smith, Kirby
Sokolow, Eleanor
Tang, Aaron
x
x

2006*

Austin, Paige
Babha, Satya
Dalby, Owen
Dyches, Brandon
Edsail, Caroline
Fei, Jessica
Frericks, Anson
Hopkins, A. J.
Mehta, Nazneen
Liebenluft, Jacob
Phan, Don
Raza, Gul
Sarnelli, Crissaris
Shamas, Diala
Thomas, Andre

BUSH, 1967, DEREK GEORGE—(Student)—Born Oct. 15, 1943, Buenos Aires, Argentina, S.A.; M.B.A. expected in '71, Harvard Sch. of Bus. Adminis,; res., Rocky Run Farms, McLean, Va.; m. June 15, '68, Emily Blair Chewning.

BUSH, 1948, GEORGE HERBERT WALKER—Born June 12, 1924, Milton, Mass.; res., Apt. 8, 5000 Longmont Dr., Houston, Texas 77002; U.S. Congressman, '66-'70; Lieut.(j.g.), USNR Aug. '42-Sept. '45; DFC, 3, Air Medals; m. Jan. 6, '45, Barbara Pierce; s. George W., ('68), John Ellis, Neil Mallon, Marvin Pierce; d. Dorothy W.

BUSH, 1968, GEORGE WALKER—(Armed Services)—Born July 6, 1946, New Haven, Conn.; Lieut., Pilot, USAF, June '68-June 70'; res., Apt. 8, 5000 Longmont Dr., Houston, Texas 77027.

BUSH, 1922, JAMES SMITH—(Finance)—Born April 11, 1901, Milwaukee, Wis.; Pres., Inter Mundis, Ltd. (domestic and internatl. finance), 745 5th Ave., New York, N.Y. 10022; res., 450 E. 63rd St., New York 10021; Curator, Univ. of Missouri, '50-'56; Pres., Yale Club of St. Louis, '50-'52; Managing Dir., Export-Import Bank of Washington, '59-'63; Lieut. Col., USAF, '42-'45; Bronze Star; m. I, Jan. 19, '29, Caroline Patterson; II, Dec. 21, '53, Lois Kieffer; s. Samuel Prescott II; d. Shelley (Jansing), Caroline (Cole), Mary Livingston, Ethel Walker Smith.

BUSH, 1953, JONATHAN JAMES—(Investments)—Born May 6, 1931, Greenwich, Conn.; Pres., Broker, J. Bush & Co., 76 Beaver St., New York, N.Y. 10005; res., 130 East End Ave., New York 10028; Gen. Ptnr., G. H. Walker & Co., June '60-July '70; Lieut., Army, '53-'55; m. Dec. 2, '67, Josephine Colwell Bradley; s. J.J.B., Jr.

BUSH, 1917, PRESCOTT S., M.A., LL.D.—(Finance retired)— Born May 15, 1895, Columbus, Ohio.; res., Pheasant Lane, Greenwich, Conn. 06830; Greenwich Rep. Town Meeting, '32-'52 (Moderator, '35-'52); Yale Corporation, '44-'58; U.S. Senator (R.-Conn.), '52-'63; formerly Ptnr., Brown Brothers Harriman & Co., N.Y.; m. Aug. 6, '21, Dorothy Walker; s. P.S.B., Jr. ('44), George, ('48), Jonathan, ('53), William T., ('60); d. Nancy (Ellis).

Bush surnames from Skull & Bones 1971 Membership Catalogue

Index

INDEX

Since 1954, the world's most powerful people have met in secret once a year ... until now!

The True Story of

Daniel Estulin

3RD U.S. PRINTING – OVER 1,500,000 COPIES SOLD WORLDWIDE

The True Story of the Bilderberg Group

BY DANIEL ESTULIN   NORTH AMERICAN UNION EDITION

More than a center of influence, the Bilderberg Group is a shadow world government, hatching plans of domination at annual meetings ... and under a cone of media silence.

THE TRUE STORY OF THE BILDERBERG GROUP goes inside the secret meetings and sheds light on why a group of politicians, businessmen, bankers and other mighty individuals formed the world's most powerful society. As Benjamin Disraeli, one of England's greatest Prime Ministers, noted, "The world is governed by very different personages from what is imagined by those who are not behind the scenes."

Included are unpublished and never-before-seen photographs and other documentation of meetings, as this riveting account exposes the past, present and future plans of the Bilderberg elite.

Softcover: **$24.95** (ISBN: 9780979988622) • 432 pages • Size: 6 x 9

Dr. Mary's Monkey

How the Unsolved Murder of a Doctor, a Secret Laboratory in New Orleans and Cancer-Causing Monkey Viruses are Linked to Lee Harvey Oswald, the JFK Assassination and Emerging Global Epidemics
BY EDWARD T. HASLAM, FOREWORD BY JIM MARRS

Evidence of top-secret medical experiments and cover-ups of clinical blunders

The 1964 murder of a nationally known cancer researcher sets the stage for this gripping exposé of medical professionals enmeshed in covert government operations over the course of three decades. Following a trail of police records, FBI files, cancer statistics, and medical journals, this revealing book presents evidence of a web of medical secret-keeping that began with the handling of evidence in the JFK assassination and continued apace, sweeping doctors into cover-ups of cancer outbreaks, contaminated polio vaccine, the genesis of the AIDS virus, and biological weapon research using infected monkeys.

Softcover: **$19.95** (ISBN: 0977795306) • 320 pages • Size: 5 1/2 x 8 1/2

Dr. Mary's Monkey

How the unsolved murder of a doctor, a secret laboratory in New Orleans and cancer-causing monkey viruses are linked to Lee Harvey Oswald, the JFK assassination and emerging global epidemics

EDWARD T. HASLAM   FOREWORD BY Jim MARRS

The Oil Card
Global Economic Warfare in the 21st Century
BY JAMES NORMAN

Challenging the conventional wisdom surrounding high oil prices, this compelling argument sheds an entirely new light on free-market industry fundamentals.

By deciphering past, present, and future geopolitical events, it makes the case that oil pricing and availability have a long history of being employed as economic weapons by the United States. Despite ample world supplies and reserves, high prices are now being used to try to rein in China—a reverse of the low-price strategy used in the 1980s to deprive the Soviets of hard currency. Far from conspiracy theory, the debate notes how the U.S. has previously used the oil majors, the Saudis, and market intervention to move markets—and shows how this is happening again.

Softcover **$14.95** (ISBN 0977795390) • 288 PAGES • Size: 5.5 x 8.5

The Oil Card
GLOBAL ECONOMIC WARFARE
IN THE 21ST CENTURY

James R. Norman

The 9/11 Mystery Plane
And the Vanishing of America
BY MARK GAFFNEY
FOREWORD BY
DR. DAVID RAY GRIFFIN

Unlike other accounts of the historic attacks on 9/11, this discussion surveys the role of the world's most advanced military command and control plane, the E-4B, in the day's events and proposes that the horrific incidents were the work of a covert operation staged within elements of the U.S. military and the intelligence community. Presenting hard evidence, the account places the world's most advanced electronics platform circling over the White House at approximately the time of the Pentagon attack. The argument offers an analysis of the new evidence within the context of the events and shows that it is irreconcilable with the official 9/11 narrative.

Mark H. Gaffney is an environmentalist, a peace activist, a researcher, and the author of *Dimona, the Third Temple?*; and *Gnostic Secrets of the Naassenes*. He lives in Chiloquin, Oregon. Dr. David Ray Griffin is a professor emeritus at the Claremont School of Theology, and the author of *The 9/11 Commission Report: Omissions and Distortions*, and *The New Pearl Harbor*. He lives in Santa Barbara, California.
Softcoverr • $19.95 • SBN 9780979988608 • 336 Pages

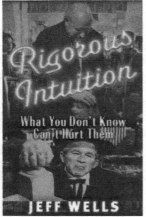

Rigorous Intuition
What You Don'y Know, Can't Hurt Them
BY JEFF WELLS

"In Jeff's hands, tinfoil hats become crowns and helmets of the purest gold. I strongly suggest that you all pay attention to what he has to say." —Arthur Gilroy, Booman Tribune

A welcome source of analysis and commentary for those prepared to go deeper—and darker—than even most alternative media permit, this collection from one of the most popular conspiracy theory arguments on the internet will assist readers in clarifying their own arguments and recognizing disinformation. Tackling many of the most difficult subjects that define our time—including 9/11, the JonBenet Ramsey case, and "High Weirdness"—these studies, containing the best of the Rigorous Intuition blog as well as original content, make connections that both describe the current, alarming predicament and suggest a strategy for taking back the world. Following the maxim "What you don't know can't hurt them," this assortment of essays and tools, including the updated and expanded "Coincidence Theorists' Guide to 9/11," guides the intellectually curious down further avenues of study and scrutiny and helps readers feel empowered rather than vulnerable.

Jeff Wells is the author of the novel *Anxious Gravity*. He lives in Toronto, Ontario.
Softcover • $19.95 • 978-0-9777953-2-1 • 505 Pages

PERFECTIBILISTS
The 18th Century Bavarian Illuminati
BY TERRY MELANSON

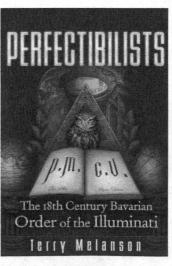

The shadowy Illuminati grace many pages of fiction as the sinister all-powerful group pulling the strings behind the scenes, but very little has been printed in English about the actual Enlightenment-era secret society, its activities, its members, and its legacy ... until now.

First choosing the name Perfectibilists, their enigmatic leader Adam Weishaupt soon thought that sounded too bizarre and changed it to the Order of the Illuminati.

Presenting an authoritative perspective, this definitive study chronicles the rise and fall of the fabled Illuminati, revealing their methods of infiltrating governments and education systems, and their blueprint for a successful cabal, which echoes directly forward through groups like the Order of Skull & Bones to our own era.

Featuring biographies of more than 400 confirmed members and copiously illustrated, this book brings light to a 200-year-old mystery.
Softcover: **$19.95** (ISBN: 9780977795381) • 530 pages • Size: 6 x 9